THE STORY OF SCOTTISH DESIGN

THE STORY OF SCOTTISH DESIGN

EDITED BY PHILIP LONG AND JOANNA NORMAN

WITH 201 ILLUSTRATIONS

Contents

Foreword

The design history of Scotland is a remarkable one, and one that deserves to be more widely known. Design creativity has for a long time been vital to the country's enterprising spirit and has helped construct Scotland's identity. This book relates that story.

Fundamental to the V&A is its role in promoting and encouraging the development and understanding of British design, and indeed it was founded in part for that purpose. V&A Dundee provides a new and welcome focus for the design of Scotland, where it will be shown within a national and international context. This richly illustrated book has been published to accompany permanent galleries in this new museum. *The Story of Scottish Design* features over 60 essays by a range of experts and specialists, commissioned to provide an unprecedented overview of design connected with Scotland, whether created in the country or, as is often the case, thousands of miles away. Design from the fifteenth century to the present is explored, not in isolation but within the context of the country's historical and political changes, social circumstances, and industrial, scientific, intellectual and artistic progress. Many of the objects featured are from the V&A's superlative collections – some especially conserved and newly photographed for display in V&A Dundee – shown alongside material from our partners in this project (other collections, designers and companies), which we gratefully acknowledge.

What emerges from the pages of this book is an extraordinarily rich heritage, characterized by creativity, craft and entrepreneurship. Every reader is likely to find something surprising, whether the role that Scots played in the development of the city of St Petersburg under Catherine the Great, or in the foundation of innovative textile companies such as Speedo, or in the international impact of the Callum brothers in today's automotive design. Many disciplines are featured, representative of the myriad applications to which design thinking contributes. That means of course there are omissions, and so we hope this book results in a passionate response both to what has, and what has not, been included, encouraging new investigation into this rich vein in our history. Especially, we hope it provides inspiration for future creativity and gives confidence in our ability to produce outstanding design.

PHILIP LONG
Director, V&A Dundee

V&A Dundee, 2018
Kengo Kuma & Associates

Introduction JOANNA NORMAN

1 Tartans retailed by James Locke at the Great Exhibition, London, 1851

See p. 59
V&A (FROM LEFT TO RIGHT): T.317–1967, T.325–1967, T.323–1967

The story of Scottish design is one of local specialism and global connections, innovation, entrepreneurship, and adaptation to change. Over the centuries Scotland's history has been characterized by its relationships with its larger neighbour to the south – England – with Europe and with the wider world. As these relationships have fluctuated, so have Scotland's designers responded, adapted and innovated.

Although this book largely deals with the last 600 years, it represents a much longer design history. Some of the earliest traces of what we might now call design in Western Europe survive in what is now Scotland, such as the extraordinary Neolithic remains at Skara Brae (2) on Orkney: remarkably well-preserved dwellings from about 5,000 years ago that contain 'fitted' stone furniture such as box-beds and 'dressers'. Dating from about 1,000 years later, and made in the

Highlands, are pottery beakers with simple incised decoration and elaborately carved stone balls: enigmatic objects of uncertain purpose. All of these examples of design testify to the long history of not simply creating what is necessary, but of making it distinctive and decorative as well.

A location such as Orkney also encapsulates how travel, trade and migration have been crucial to Scotland's history and how they are reflected in its design. Together with Shetland, Orkney bears the traces of its complex past as part of the Pictish kingdom and, from the ninth century, as an annex to Norway. It only became part of Scotland in 1472, when it was handed over to the Scottish crown as surety against payment of the dowry of Margaret of Denmark to King James III. Just as Orkney's material culture reveals these influences, so does that of the Western Isles. On Iona, alongside Norse traces are those testifying to the island's

2 Neolithic dwellings with stone furniture at Skara Brae
Orkney, C.3100–2500 BC

important role in bringing Christianity to Scotland, through the sixth-century mission of the Irish monk St Columba. These are visible above all in the abbey and Celtic crosses (3) that grew up around his shrine.

The interplay of diverse cultural influences on Scotland's design history is an important theme in the period covered by this book. Until the seventeenth century continental influences arose from the country's strong diplomatic links with France through the Auld Alliance and trade links with parts of northern Europe, particularly the Low Countries (see pp. 18–23). These are most visible in the Romanesque or Gothic style of monastic foundations such as Melrose Abbey (founded 1136); the Renaissance architecture of the remodelled Falkland Palace (1501–41) and the style of carving of the so-called Stirling Heads (c.1540), the magnificent oak medallions commissioned by James V to decorate the King's

3 Iona Abbey, by Joseph Skelton
*c.*1820–30

Etching
Given by Miss Blanche F.R. Lecluse in memory of her father, Mr Alphonse Auguste Edmond Lecluse
V&A: E.165–1955

presence chamber at Stirling Castle; the use of continental print sources as designs for embroidery such as that produced by Mary, Queen of Scots, and her court (4); and the style, techniques and craftsmanship of sixteenth-century silverware and jewellery.

However, it is Scotland's shifting relationship with England over the centuries that has proved particularly significant for its design. The decline of French influences and a look instead towards England began in the seventeenth century, with the Union of the Crowns in 1603, and continued after the Acts of Union in 1707. Well before this, of course, English influence – or reaction to it – could be found in design in Scotland. Tower houses, constructed in the Borders from the fourteenth century, were designed as fortified, defensive strongholds providing protection from aggressive English incursions. The first book printed in Scotland, the Aberdeen Breviary of 1510, commissioned by William Elphinstone, Bishop of Aberdeen and founder of the city's university, was produced at the instigation of James IV. He desired a Scottish religious rite that could be used instead of the English one known as the Sarum Rite.

The importance of the Union of the Crowns in 1603 and Acts of Union in 1707 in defining much of Scotland's subsequent history – and design history – cannot be overestimated. The year 1603 brought a Scottish king, James VI, to the English throne, as James I, but also an end to a separate Scottish royal court. The removal of the king and his court to London inevitably led to the movement south of many architects, artists, designers and craftsmen seeking the highest levels of patronage. It was hardly surprising that George Heriot, goldsmith to James VI and I and the principal supplier of jewellery to James's queen, Anne of Denmark, should have travelled to London with the monarch and remained there for the rest of his life. Nor was it unexpected that, a century later, the young Colen Campbell should have sought to try his hand at architecture in London. The city was by then both the courtly and commercial centre of the kingdom, and as such offered architects the most significant pool of potential clients keen to assert their status through the building of town and country residences in the latest fashionable style (see pp. 32–33).

The loss of Scottish independence through the Acts of Union was devastating. It immediately generated a rise in Scottish support for the Jacobite cause, which came to be seen as a means of re-establishing an independent Scotland with a restored Stuart monarchy (see pp. 30–31). The loss of artistic talent from Scotland to the south that had begun in 1603 was exacerbated after 1707. However, the Union did open up certain

4 Textile panel of a dog, 'Jupiter', probably made by Mary, Queen of Scots, with Elizabeth Talbot, Countess of Shrewsbury
England, 1570–85
Embroidered linen canvas with silk threads
Presented by Art Fund
V&A: T.33P–1955

opportunities, networks and markets for Scottish designers, craftsmen and industries, which they enthusiastically embraced, and which characterized the course of Scottish design in the eighteenth and nineteenth centuries. Historically, Scotland's economy was relatively small and suffered from competition with England's much greater economic power. In the 1690s this disparity was worsened by the failed attempt (known as the Darien scheme) to establish a Scottish colony in the Gulf of Darién, which would have helped Scotland become a major international trading power. With Scotland's economy in a parlous state by 1707 as a result, the Acts of Union offered significant economic benefits, such as free trade with England. Fashions from London reached Scotland more quickly because of free trade and the weavers of Paisley took advantage of the freer movement of goods to sell their woven textiles into English markets (see pp. 50–51). Official efforts also encouraged particular design industries, motivated by a concern for Scotland to achieve economic parity with England. The Board of Trustees for Fisheries, Manufactures and Improvements in Scotland, established in 1727, helped to promote and encourage Scotland's linen industry, most significantly (5). It awarded grants to linen manufacturers to enable them to compete with German linen producers rather than directly with England's woollen industry. Another significant impact of the Union was the growing dominance of the professions in Edinburgh in the eighteenth century – which emerged owing to the lack of a royal and aristocratic court in the city. They facilitated the development of the

Scottish Enlightenment, made manifest through the architectural order of the city's Georgian New Town (see pp. 34–37).

It was perhaps through the expansion of the British Empire that Scots benefited most from the Union. Trade, migration and external cultural influences had a strong impact on the development of Scotland's design enterprises, but this was also a two-way exchange. Scots had long sought out new opportunities by travel and emigration, whether as clerics, merchants, mercenaries or, in the case of eighteenth-century Russia, masons (see pp. 46–47). The Empire, however, offered many more prospects for Scottish individuals and industries to prosper, leading to the spread of Scottish design ideas and products around the world. The Turkey Red dyeing industry was one such example, established in the Vale of Leven in 1804 by the Frenchman Pierre Jacques Papillon, with endorsement from the Board of Trustees. The producers of Turkey Red fabrics consciously targeted particular markets, most notably India, with a range of designs intended to appeal to clients in those places. Similarly, the Glasgow ceramics firm J. & M.P. Bell cultivated South-East Asian client bases with its transfer-printed designs, whose names and motifs were taken specifically from these intended markets (see pp. 68–73).

In these enterprises networks of agents and relationships with other industries proved extremely important. J. & M.P. Bell, for example, established a number of agents in ports such as Rangoon (now Yangon) to help export its ceramics. Dundee's intercontinental jute trade developed thanks both to the presence of existing weaving expertise in the city and to the

5 Napkin, inscribed 'C'EST LES ARMES D'ECOSSE' (It is the arms of Scotland), 'Nemo Me Impune Lacesset' (No one assails me with impunity) and 'May Lawrie 1762'
Possibly Dunfermline, 1762
Woven linen damask
V&A: T.112–1932

interconnections between shipbuilding, imperial trade and the whaling industry (as whale oil was used to soften jute fibre in order to work it; see pp. 60–63). Design industries also expanded and adapted to suit global markets, especially that of ironwork. The Carron Ironworks, founded in the eighteenth century in Falkirk, was joined in the nineteenth century by others such as Walter Macfarlane & Co., also known as the Saracen Foundry, established in Glasgow in 1850. Macfarlane designed and produced cast-iron elements and prefabricated structures, ranging from banisters, railings and balcony fronts to bandstands and fountains, that were exported around the world and can still be found internationally from Australia to Brazil (6). Expertise in ironworking also laid the foundations for Scotland's success in heavy industry and shipbuilding. On the Clyde, ships were designed and built for a wide range of functions and environments, from Egyptian bucket dredgers to Burmese paddle steamers (see pp. 64–67).

By the late nineteenth century such industrial and trade success had brought significant wealth and prosperity to Scotland, as well as urbanization on an extraordinarily large scale. With these changes came significant concerns: about the lack of housing for the rapidly increasing urban populations; about the impacts of industrialization on society; and about the quality of design in manufacture. Such issues were not unique to Scotland: concern about the quality of design in industry was a major motivating factor behind the creation of the South Kensington Museum (now the V&A) following the 1851 Great Exhibition in London. Attempts to improve

standards led to the founding of the Industrial Museum of Scotland (now part of the National Museum of Scotland) in 1854, with collections intended to serve as examples of 'good' design. From the mid-nineteenth century more art and design schools were founded in Scottish cities, including the Glasgow Government School of Design in 1845 (which later became

6 Theatro José de Alencar, with cast iron by Walter Macfarlane & Co.
Fortaleza, Ceará, Brazil, 1910

7 High-backed chair, designed by
Charles Rennie Mackintosh

Glasgow, 1897–1900
Oak, upholstered seat
Given by The Glasgow School of Art
V&A: CIRC.130–1958

The Glasgow School of Art); Duncan of
Jordanstone College of Art and Design in
Dundee (which evolved from the Dundee
Technical Institute); and Edinburgh College
of Art, established in 1907 but originating in
the Trustees' Drawing Academy established in 1760 by the Board of Trustees.
International exhibitions, such as those
held in Edinburgh in 1886 and 1890, and in
Glasgow in 1888 and 1901, offered a means
of improving taste and design quality, not
just by temporarily displaying the products
of Scotland's design industries; the
profits of the 1888 Glasgow exhibition, for
example, were used to build Kelvingrove
Art Gallery and Museum. For the Glasgow
1901 international exhibition, and later in
Dundee and Aberdeen, collections of 'Celtic'
plaster casts were formed; that in Aberdeen
was a conscious effort to improve design
standards in the local granite industry.

If education was one route to improving
design quality, designers offered other
solutions in response to the concerns
generated by mass industrialization. The
issue of housing, highlighted in the 1860s
by Thomas Annan's photography of the
slums, was tackled in Glasgow through
the building of tenements that improved
residents' access to fresh air and light (see
pp. 86–87). In the east Patrick Geddes
argued against urban planning in grids and
instead for a more organic approach (see
pp. 88–89). Meanwhile, Arts and Crafts artists and designers challenged the perceived
negative impacts of industry on society;
they offered an alternative approach based
on a close interest in and understanding
of making and materials, as well as a
reconsideration of the past in terms of
stylistic inspiration as well as handcrafting
techniques (see pp. 94–97).

The flourishing of Scotland's art
and design in the years around 1900 is
testament to this vibrant, if conflicted,
environment. By then the country had
become an industrial powerhouse
whose products were in use around the
world and proudly displayed in the grand
(if ephemeral) surroundings of international exhibitions. Consumers of the Arts
and Crafts aesthetic proved to be an
enthusiastic market for the handmade
style of the Orkney chair, while in Vienna
and Turin, Charles Rennie Mackintosh
(7) and his compatriots were making a
name for their bold and daring variant
of Art Nouveau, thereafter known as the
'Glasgow Style' (see pp. 104–11; 116–17).

The design industries in Scotland
experienced difficult times for much of
the twentieth century, with the effects of
two world wars, the demise of the Empire
and the decline of traditional industries.
However, there were stand-out successes.
Shipbuilding on the Clyde produced
vessels such as the *Queen Mary*, built by
John Brown & Co. shipyard from 1930 to
1934. This world-renowned ocean liner
was splendidly fitted out in Art Deco style
by local design firms, such as James
Templeton & Co. (8) and the Morris
Furniture Company. The Empire Exhibition
of 1938 in Glasgow, intended to stimulate
Scotland's economy during the Great
Depression, attracted 13 million visitors
to its Modernist buildings, overseen by
Thomas Tait. He was supported by some
of the country's most talented young
designers, including Basil Spence and
Jack Coia, both of whom after the Second
World War went on to lead practices
responsible for important and innovative
architectural schemes in Scotland and, in

Spence's case, much further afield (see pp. 134–41). From the 1950s onwards designers such as Eduardo Paolozzi, James Stirling, Bernat Klein and Bill Gibb forged individual and highly distinctive paths, while industries continued to adapt to new styles and markets (see pp. 132–33; 150–57). Textile manufacturers such as Donald Brothers and Edinburgh Weavers, for example, collaborated with fine artists and designers to produce modern textiles for the modern home (see pp. 126–31). These won a number of Design Council awards, as did pieces made by Caithness Glass, established in 1961 to provide employment for the local area. The firm's designer, Domhnall O'Broin, led the production of series of glass vessels that were influenced by Scandinavian forms and the colours of the Scottish landscape. Such endeavours did not result in automatic financial success, however, with many firms unable to survive the competition generated by an increasingly globalized economy.

In the early twenty-first century the design industries for which Scotland was renowned, particularly textiles, continue to bear the imprint of the decline of traditional manufacturing and the impact of globalization (Dundee's jute industry being a prime example). But also in evidence is an adaptability to change that has enabled certain fields of design to develop in new ways. The Borders may no longer be the centre for textiles at the scale that it once was, but the firms that still exist maintain their prestige and international reputation through high-quality design and craftsmanship (see pp. 120–21). Education and training, provided by such institutions as Heriot-Watt University's

long-standing School of Textiles and Design in Galashiels, will ensure this status continues.

In other areas of textile design and manufacture, adaptation has led to hyperspecialization, with the production of technical fabrics for uses as diverse as high-performance sportswear,

8 First-class lounge on the *Queen Mary*, with carpet by James Templeton & Co. *c.*1934

medicine or the automotive industry (see pp.168–69; 184–85). In other disciplines new technologies and trends, such as design for videogames, have become a stable and thriving part of Scotland's contemporary design scene. Again, the country's universities and colleges have played a vital role: in 1997 Abertay University offered the world's first course in digital games design. Rockstar Games, which includes Edinburgh-based Rockstar North, is one of the most successful games developers in the world (see pp. 164–65; 200–3).

Today design is appreciated ever more widely as a vital contributor to a country's economy, and Scotland is embracing this. With interdisciplinary approaches across education, industry and public services, the utilization of design, and therefore the definitions and understanding of it, grows ever larger. Creative 'design-thinking'

approaches, for example, are used increasingly by businesses and public-sector organizations, such as healthcare services, as tools for clarifying, processing and solving problems (see pp. 186–87). Thus the range of professions designers are involved in is broadening, while digital technology is making it more feasible for designers and makers to develop their careers within and across Scotland, indicating an encouraging future.

The country's widely respected colleges of art and design continue to nurture talents who make an international impact, whether from a base in Scotland or by seeking opportunity further afield – a recurring characteristic of Scottish design. The country's dynamic past and its contemporary situation continue to influ-ence international and Scottish designers alike, such as the Catalan architect Enric Miralles' Scottish Parliament (completed 2004) in Edinburgh or Gareth Hoskins' Visitor Centre (9) at Culloden Battlefield (2008). From the cabinetmaking success of Aberdeenshire-born Thomas Affleck in Philadelphia in the late eighteenth century (see pp. 44–45) to the fashion and automotive design of Holly Fulton and Ian Callum (see pp. 172–75; 198–99) respectively in the twenty-first century, Scotland's rich design history can inspire future generations of designers and, indeed, everyone. With its opening, V&A Dundee aims not only to represent this history but also to contribute to the future success of the country's design industries and creativity.

9 Culloden Battlefield Visitor Centre, designed by Gareth Hoskins, Hoskins Architects
Culloden, 2008

Scotland and France: Design and the Auld Alliance

At the end of the thirteenth century the English monk and chronicler Walter of Coventry wrote that 'the more recent kings of Scots profess themselves to be rather Frenchmen, both in race and in manners, language and culture'. Walter's comment clearly reflects the high degree of familiarity with French language and customs that was held by the medieval Scottish court.

It was not only the court that shared this familiarity with France, but Scottish churchmen, scholars, soldiers and merchants as well. Before the fifteenth century, with no university yet established in Scotland and with Anglo-Scottish conflicts such as the Scottish Wars of Independence (1296–1328) making access to English universities difficult, students travelled from Scotland to continental Europe to study. A Scots College was established as part of the University of Paris in 1333 to house Scottish students, some 17 or 18 Scots served as rector of the same university, and it was from Paris that a group of scholars came to St Andrews in 1410 to establish Scotland's first university. These academic links reinforced those already held through Scottish religious foundations, many of which housed monastic orders originally founded in France. In the military sphere, Scots were highly valued in France as mercenaries and, at an elite level, as the Garde Écossaise, the personal bodyguards to the French monarch from 1418. Not only did they become part of the French royal household, but they were also often rewarded with gifts of land for their service, encouraging them to settle in France.

Formalizing these relationships from the late thirteenth century onwards was the Auld Alliance, the diplomatic treaty first signed by the rulers of Scotland and France in 1295 and renewed by every subsequent monarch except Louis XI of France until 1560. Motivated by a common desire to curtail aggressive and expansionist efforts by the English, the treaty promised military aid by each nation to the other against English offensives and celebrated a bond that legend dated back to the eighth century between Achaius, 65th King of Scotland, and the King of the Franks (and later Holy Roman Emperor) Charlemagne. Aside from military benefits, the alliance granted Scottish merchants the right to import the finest French wines and facilitated the movement between the two countries of both people and things: from France came luxury goods such as silver, fashionable clothing and books, artistic and architectural ideas, and highly skilled craftsmen, from

↑ **Psalter**

Scotland, 1500–30 · Manuscript on parchment, with painted miniatures and decorations
V&A: NATIONAL ART LIBRARY, MSL/1902/1693 (REID 52)

Probably produced for the Cistercian abbey of Kinloss in Morayshire, this psalter shows the clear links between north-eastern Scotland and the Low Countries in the early 16th century. Its illuminations include a miniature of King David playing a harp, based on a well-known Flemish composition. Like the Playfair Hours, this psalter's litany includes Scottish saints as well as those of the Cistercian order founded in France and established in Scotland by King David I (r.1124–53).

→ **Book of Hours, known as the 'Playfair Hours'**

Rouen, 1480–90 · Manuscript on parchment, with painted miniatures and decorations
V&A: NATIONAL ART LIBRARY, MSL/1918/475

The 'Playfair Hours', named after its early 20th-century Scottish owner Rev. Dr Playfair, was produced in Rouen, an important trading port and prolific centre for the production of illuminated manuscripts. Its month-by-month calendar includes illustrations of the Labours of the Months and a list of religious feast days. The list is notable for the inclusion of several Scottish saints, such as St Monan (whose feast day is 1 March), indicating that it must have been made for a Scottish owner, probably resident in France.

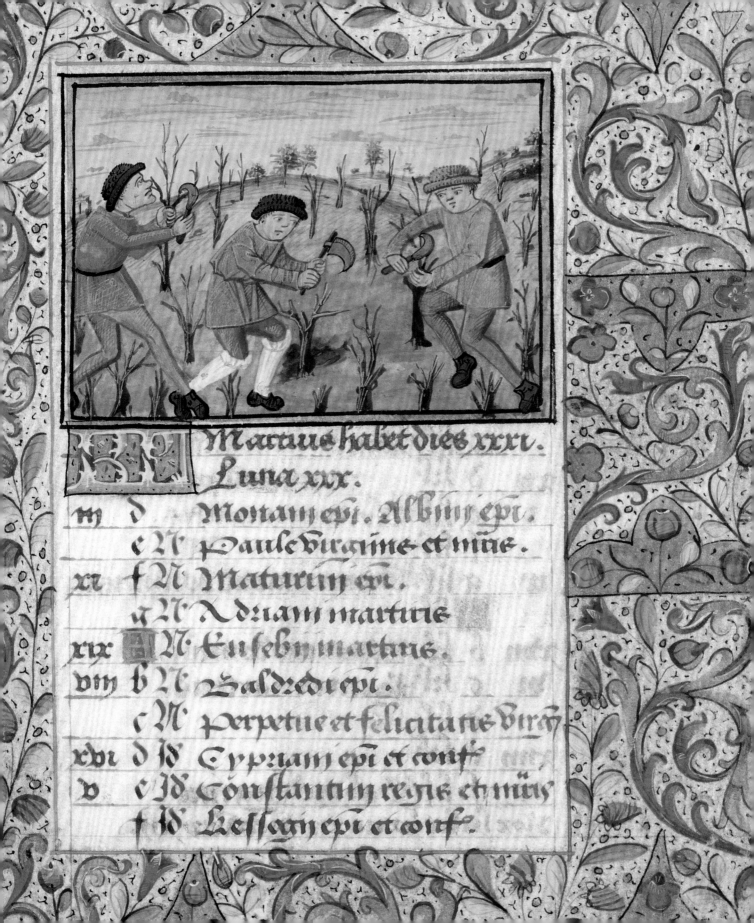

Martius habet dies xxxi.
Luna xxx.

m	d		Montani epi. Albini epi.
	e	Kl	Paule virginis et mrie.
xi	f	Kl	Maturini epi.
	g	Kl	Adriani martiris
xix	A	Kl	Eusebii martiris.
viii	b	Kl	Baldredi epi.
	c	Kl	Perpetue et felicitatis virgm̄
xvi	d	Id	Cypriani epi et conf.
v	e	Id	Constantini regis et mris
	f	Id	Lessem epi et conf.

masons to armourers to silversmiths, producing an intertwined design language in Scotland.

By the mid-sixteenth century these long-standing Franco-Scottish relations were fully cemented through King James v's marriages to two French princesses – Madeleine of Valois and, after her death, Mary of Guise – both of which brought substantial wealth into Scotland. With the marriage of James's daughter Mary, Queen of Scots, to François I, King of France, in 1558, uniting the crowns of Scotland and France for the first time, the Auld Alliance can be said to have reached its greatest strength. However, this proved to be short-lived: in 1560 the effects of the Protestant Reformation in Scotland, and of Europe-wide conflicts between the Habsburg and Valois dynasties, resulted in the signing of the Treaty of Edinburgh, the first diplomatic alliance between Scotland and England, opening up the country to a dif-ferent set of influences and connections. Nonetheless, centuries of shared culture did not disappear overnight. Education, art and design, and – in the parts of Scotland that remained Catholic – religion ensured that while the formal military alliance might have ended, close cultural ties would long continue. JOANNA NORMAN

↑ **Valance**

Scotland, France or England, 1570–99
Linen canvas, embroidered with wools and silks
Bequeathed by Miss Maud Lilian Ochs
V&A: T.136–1991

Originally part of a set of bed hangings, this valance depicts a pair of lovers in a garden, accompanied by musicians and allegorical figures of Prudence and Fidelity. Although probably embroidered in France, hangings like this are found in several Scottish collections. This provenance, the courtly setting and the figures' fashionable dress testify to the courtly culture shared between Scotland, France and England at the end of the 16th century.

→ **Falkland Palace, plate from**
***Theatrum Scotiae,* by John Slezer**

Published in London, printed by John
Leake for Abell Swalle, 1693
Engraving
NATIONAL LIBRARY OF SCOTLAND:
EMS.B.5.1

Engraved by John Slezer in his graphic
survey of Scotland's landscapes, towns
and buildings, Falkland Palace was
transformed between 1501 and 1541
under Kings James IV and V from a former
hunting lodge and castle into an elegant
Renaissance palace. At least two French
masons contributed to its remodelling,
one of the most important architectural
projects to introduce French Renaissance
style into Scotland.

East Coast Trade and its Influence on Design

In the sixteenth and seventeenth centuries a strong relationship existed between the east coast of Scotland and the coastal regions of northern Europe, particularly the Low Countries, Germany, the Baltic and Scandinavia. At a time when large numbers of Scots were serving as soldiers in the armies of European rulers such as Gustavus Adolphus, King of Sweden, many of their compatriots instead developed trading relationships that would lead to influences on art and design, from silverware to architecture.

From the fifteenth century a Scottish staple port existed – first at Bruges, then Middelburg and Veere and finally Rotterdam – through which all Scottish imports to the Low Countries had to pass, and in which Scottish merchants' interests were strongly represented. Simultaneously, Scottish merchants and factors (agents) resident in ports such as Copenhagen, Elsinore, Stockholm and Danzig (Gdańsk) facilitated Scottish trade in the Baltic and Scandinavia. From these regions came iron, tar and timber, the last vital for the building of Scottish palaces, houses and ships, and the flax and hemp required for Scotland's weaving industries. From the Low Countries came goods ranging from finer linen cloth to other building materials such as pantiles. In exchange, Scotland's exports included woollen cloth and stockings, fish, hides and, at times, mined elements such as lead, sent to Delft factories to create the tin glaze used on delftware ceramics.

This trade could prove highly profitable for Scots. The textile merchant Alexander Chalmers (Czamer), originally of Aberdeenshire, served four times as Mayor of Warsaw between 1691 and 1703; the Danzig merchant Robert Gordon left his fortune in 1731 to found a hospital for poor boys in his native Aberdeen; and William Forbes, whose success as a Baltic merchant led him to be known as 'Danzig Willie', was the builder of Craigievar Castle, completed in 1626. At the same time, these links influenced Scotland's design, whether through architectural style, the form of church vessels or the work of craftsmen such as the Dutch carvers who worked at Kinross and Holyrood. But traces of this Scottish presence can also be found across northern Europe, from the 'Old Scotland' (Stary Szkoty) and 'New Scotland' (Nowe Szkoty) districts of Gdańsk to the Rosenkrantz tower in Bergen, built by Scottish masons in the 1560s, and the substantial 'Scottish houses' that still stand in Veere. JOANNA NORMAN

← Section of painted ceiling from Craig Castle

Scotland, mid-16th century
Wood painted with tempera
NATIONAL MUSEUMS SCOTLAND:
A.1929.571B

Decorative painted ceilings can be found in Scottish houses and churches from the 16th and 17th centuries. They were often constructed of boards and beams, the timber probably imported from Scandinavia or the Baltic. The decoration followed the construction with narrow bands of ornament, as in this fragment from Craig Castle in Montrose. Decoration was often based on contemporary European printed sources, indicating the transmission of design ideas through this medium.

→ **Pair of communion beakers for Nigg Church, marked by George Walker**

Aberdeen, 1700–5
Silver
Purchased in 1974 with assistance from the National Fund for Acquisitions
ABERDEEN ART GALLERY & MUSEUMS COLLECTIONS: ABDAG001037

This form of straight-sided communion beaker is found in Scotland only in the north-east, and can be traced directly to Dutch influence. A pair of similarly shaped beakers from Ellon Kirk in Aberdeenshire (now in the National Museum of Scotland) comprises one beaker made in Amsterdam and given to that kirk in 1634, and a companion piece made in Aberdeen to match it. This form was used for both sacred and secular drinking vessels in the Netherlands.

→ **Houses with crow-stepped gables and pantiled roofs**

Shoregate, Crail, 17th and 18th centuries

The trade links between Scotland's east coast and the Low Countries are seen in shared architectural features, most notably the crow-stepped gabled and red clay pantiled roofs. Pantiles are known to have been imported into Scotland in large quantities from the 17th century, while stepped gables are found in Scottish architecture from the 16th century onwards. These characteristics are seen especially in the East Neuk of Fife, where links to the Low Countries were particularly strong.

Craftsmanship, Training and Trade Incorporations

From the Middle Ages until 1846 the work of artisans – such as weavers, tailors and goldsmiths – in Scotland was structured and governed by trade incorporations. Like guilds elsewhere, these bodies provided trade protection for their members, and set and maintained the standards of quality of their production. Operating in and from individual burghs, trade incorporations also offered craftsmen a means of participating in the civic life of their town.

The number and nature of incorporations in each burgh differed: Aberdeen had seven, Dundee nine, Glasgow fourteen and Edinburgh fifteen. In some cases, one incorporation encompassed several trades: the wrights were sometimes joined with the coopers or masons, while the Hammermen could include gold- and silversmiths, armourers, pewterers, clock- and watchmakers and all those whose craft was based on the skilled use of a hammer.

Any craftsman wishing to work within a burgh was obliged to belong to the relevant incorporation, enabling it to keep tight control over its trades. This control included setting numbers of apprentices, the duration and terms of apprenticeships and the essay, or master-piece, that each craftsman had to produce to become a master of his trade. Protection of the trade also extended to supporting aged and infirm members and their families; it was provided by the incorporations to serve as a counterpart to burghs' powerful merchants' guilds.

In addition, incorporations protected consumers. The apprenticeship system provided practical training that ensured a certain standard of quality of a trade's production. In the case of goldsmiths, Edinburgh's incorporation served a dual function, as it was also responsible for ensuring the quality of gold and silver through the assaying (testing) process.

Like merchants' guilds, trade incorporations served as an element of burgh government and played an important role in civic life. Heraldic panels, ceremonial chairs and banners document this role, as they were produced for individual incorporations to be carried in procession or displayed in churches or meeting halls.

Although some of Scotland's incorporations still survive, their power waned from the eighteenth century with the advent of industrialization and ended officially with the Burgh Trading Act of 1846. Prior to that, however, they played an important role as the main providers of training in materials-based design and techniques until the establishment of more formalized art and design education.

JOANNA NORMAN

↑ **Patch box and cover with wirework and filigree scrolls, by William Clerk**

Glasgow, c.1695
Silver
GLASGOW MUSEUMS AND LIBRARIES COLLECTIONS: E.1981.95.A

This patch box would have held the artificial beauty spots worn by fashionable ladies in the late 17th and early 18th centuries. It may originally have formed part of a toilet service, together with other items such as a mirror, candlesticks, brushes and bowls, and boxes for cosmetic powders and pastes or for jewels. Marked by the Glasgow silversmith William Clerk, it is a unique Scottish example of such a box made in the finest filigree wirework.

→ **Hammermen trades panel**

Edinburgh, 1660
Paint on wood
MUSEUMS GALLERIES EDINBURGH, CITY OF EDINBURGH COUNCIL

The role of trade incorporations as civic bodies was often expressed through banners, panels, badges and ceremonial chairs. Decorated with the incorporation's insignia, these might be carried in procession in public celebrations, or displayed in ceremonial environments such as the meeting hall of all the incorporations of a burgh. This panel was made for the Incorporation of Hammermen of South Leith, the hammer of the trade prominently displayed at its centre.

1660

OUR ART Our all Mechanics
Bears Renown OUR ARMS the
HAMMER and the ROYAL CROWN.

↑ Bullet-form teapot, by George Cooper

Aberdeen, *c.*1735
Silver and ivory
Purchased in 1996 with the assistance of the
National Fund for Acquisitions
ABERDEEN ART GALLERY & MUSEUMS
COLLECTIONS: ABDAGO08911

Founded in 1519, Aberdeen's Incorporation
of Hammermen included silversmiths, who
supplied a predominantly local clientele with
fashionable silver wares. In the 18th century
Scotland saw a growing market for tea wares
to serve the new social custom of tea drinking,
which silversmiths were ready to supply. The
Aberdeen silversmith George Cooper's mark
appears on a number of teapots, including
some in this bullet shape, a particularly
Scottish form.

**→ George Heriot's Hospital,
Edinburgh, plate from *Theatrum
Scotiae*, by John Slezer**

Printed and sold in London by J. Smith, 1719
Engraving
Mistakenly inscribed 'Being the Seat of His
Grace the Duke of Athol near Aberdeen'
NATIONAL LIBRARY OF SCOTLAND:
EMS.B.5.1

Born in 1563 and admitted to the
Incorporation of Goldsmiths in Edinburgh
in 1588, George Heriot became jeweller
to King James VI (and later James I of
England) in 1601. Heriot amassed a vast
fortune, leaving a considerable sum to
found a hospital for 'puir, faitherless bairns'
('poor fatherless children') in his home
city. Built just outside the city walls, the
magnificent George Heriot's Hospital (now
George Heriot's School) is testament to the
status and wealth that it was possible to
achieve as a royal goldsmith.

Being the

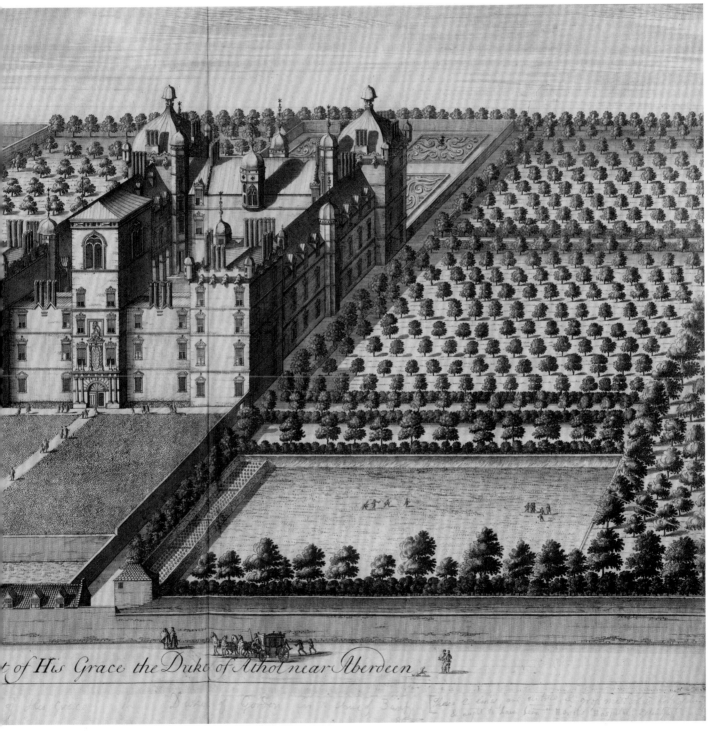

...t of His Grace the Duke of Athol near Aberdeen.

Scottish Pistols

From the seventeenth century gunsmiths in Scotland produced pistols that were unique to the country. Made entirely of steel, elaborately engraved and with distinctively shaped butts, they acquired the name 'Highland pistols' because many of the towns where they were made – Tain, Inverness, Brechin, Perth, Doune – skirted the southern and eastern edges of the Highlands. Their market was international and their reputation legendary: it was reputedly a Scottish pistol that fired the first shot in the American War of Independence in 1775.

Scottish guns with wooden stocks survive from the seventeenth century but more robust, all-steel examples are first associated with the shop of Thomas Caddell in Doune. Five generations of Thomas Caddells and the gunsmithing families – Campbell, Christie, Murdoch – that they trained as apprentices expanded and dominated the trade until the nineteenth century. They sold pistols to local aristocrats, to Highland regiments and to foreign royalty: Peter the Great of Russia and Louis XIV of France both owned examples.

Scottish pistols were sold in pairs, sometimes with their mechanisms on opposite sides so that they could be used in each hand. A long belt hook enabled them to be worn against the body or tucked inside a plaid, protected against the weather. Their butts are also characteristic. Early examples are shaped like fishtails, lemons and hearts. The most common form, the ram's horn or scroll butt, is associated with pistols from Doune. These were weapons of self-possession as much as self-defence. Added silver plaques displayed coats of arms and, by the 1740s, lock, stock and barrel were engraved with Celtic ornament or stylized foliage. By the Act of Proscription (1746), any 'side pistol, gun, or other warlike weapon' was prohibited along with traditional Highland dress, in an attempt to stamp out loyalty to the Stuarts. However, some pistols proclaimed political allegiance through symbols hidden in their decoration.

By the late eighteenth century the heyday of these guns had passed. 'Scottish pistols' carried by the 42nd Highlanders were actually made in Birmingham by a gunsmith called Isaac Bissell. Fifty years later the *Costume of the Clans* (1844), the romantic portrayal of traditional Scottish culture, lampooned the pistols still in production as 'coarse pop guns, resembling more the tin toys of a bazaar than the weapons of an army'. 'Costume pistols', much smaller than the traditional Scottish pistols, became a term of derision for a gun whose primary function had become an accessory for Highland dress. ANGUS PATTERSON

→ Pistol, signed 'IO:MURDOCH' for John Murdoch

Doune, 1775–1800
Steel engraved and inlaid with silver, with flintlock mechanism
V&A: M.2801–1931

Sir John Sinclair's *Statistical Account of Scotland* (1798) lauded John Murdoch's 'ingenuity in the craft' which 'furnished pistols to the first nobility of Europe'. It was a Murdoch pistol, fired by Major John Pitcairn at the Battle of Lexington in 1775, that reputedly began the American War of Independence. Murdoch was the last of the traditional gunsmiths in Doune, his market undercut by cheaper guns from England. 'When Mr Murdoch gives over the business,' claimed Sinclair, 'the trade in all probability will become extinct.'

→ Pistol, signed 'I.McKENZIE', probably for James McKenzie

Brechin, c.1701–20
Steel engraved and inlaid with silver, with flintlock mechanism
Major Victor Alan Farquharson Bequest
V&A: M.648–1927

Pistols with heart-shaped butts were common at the turn of the 18th century and are unique to Scotland. Although this example is fitted with silver bands, diamonds and half-moons, it is relatively plain in keeping with pistols of the period. The lock is signed 'I.McKENZIE', probably for James McKenzie, the best known of the gunsmiths of Brechin. The stone lintel from his shop doorway, carved with a musket and two heart-butted pistols, survives in the collection of Angus Council.

→ Pistol, signed 'Alexʳ.Campbell.' for Alexander Campbell

Doune, 1740–60
Steel engraved and inlaid with silver, with flintlock mechanism
V&A: 1425–1874

This pistol has a ram's horn or scroll butt, a feature of guns made in Doune. Alexander Campbell is known to have supplied similar guns to Highland officers loyal to the Stuarts. This gun dates from a period of extreme suppression of Highland identity. Subtly incorporated into the engraving on the trigger, the pricker button and the cock on the gunlock are roses and a five-pointed star, symbols of loyalty to the Jacobites.

→ Pistol, signed 'I.Paterson Doune' for James Paterson

Doune, 1775–1800
Steel engraved and inlaid with silver, with flintlock mechanism
Given from the collection of the late Col Stovell
V&A: M.179–1928

The repeal of the Act of Proscription in 1782 revived interest in traditional Highland dress. This pistol, engraved with patterns derived from Celtic ornament, dates from this period. Wear and tear on the frizzen – the steel plate that is struck by the flint – suggests this gun has seen action. Its lobed butt, a rare form closer in style to English guns, and its self-conscious decoration, however, indicate that its primary role was probably as a costume accessory.

Jacobitism: Allegiance through Design

'**From and after the first day of August, one thousand seven hundred and forty seven, no man or boy, within that part of Great Briton called Scotland, other than shall be employed as officers and soldiers in his Majesty's forces, shall on any pretence whatsoever, wear or put on the clothes commonly called Highland Clothes (that is to say) the plaid, philibeg, or little kilt, trowse, shoulder belts, or any part whatsoever of what peculiarly belongs to the highland garb.'**
(**Act of Proscription, 1746**)

From 1689 Jacobitism was part of Scottish, British and European politics. Belief in the rightful monarchy of the deposed King James VII of Scotland and II of England and his successors was encouraged by recognition from European rulers and the papacy. In Scotland, Jacobitism, combined with economic depression around the Acts of Union (1707), led many to view a return of the Stuart monarchy as the most effective way to regain independence. Also specific to Scotland was the possibility to mount armed resistance, the clan system providing a means of rallying troops. The Jacobite rising of 1715, led by John Erskine, 6th Earl of Mar, was a largely Scottish affair (with French support), while that of 1745 had a strong Scottish base, with victory at Prestonpans and the establishment of the court of Prince Charles Edward Stuart ('Bonnie Prince Charlie') at Holyroodhouse seeming briefly to bring the Jacobite cause close to success.

Jacobite sympathies were expressed through design in a plethora of personal objects such as fans, rings, snuffboxes and garters. Some of these disguised the allegiance they represented, while others were used in select company such as in Jacobite clubs, which ritually drank toasts to 'the king over the water' in glasses engraved with motifs and mottoes supporting the exiled Stuarts.

The failure of the Jacobite risings led to harsh retribution, including execution, deportation and the forfeiture of lands. Military campaigns of mapping and of road, bridge and fortification building aimed to prevent future Scottish uprisings, though helped to open up the country. The Act of Proscription may have banned Highlanders from possessing and carrying weapons, and from wearing Highland dress unless in the service of the king. However, it was difficult to enforce and, with the escape of Bonnie Prince Charlie after his defeat at the Battle of Culloden in 1746, contributed (even after its repeal in 1782) to a perpetuation of Jacobitism's mystique, romanticism and material culture into the nineteenth century. JOANNA NORMAN

↑ '**Amen' glass**

Engraved with the full four verses of the Jacobite anthem, a dedication 'To His Royal Highness the Duke of Albany and York. And to The Increase of the Royal Familie' and 'JR 8' for James VIII of Scotland
Probably made in Newcastle-upon-Tyne, engraved in Scotland, 1740–50
Glass with diamond-point engraving
Purchased with contribution from the Hugh Phillips bequest
V&A: C.117–1984

Over 30 so-called 'Amen' glasses survive, engraved with mottoes and anthems in support of the exiled James Francis Edward Stuart, son of James VII of Scotland. The glasses were probably engraved in Scotland: some are dedicated to notable Scottish Jacobites, while the '8' under the royal cypher refers to James as the rightful James VIII of Scotland. Such glasses were used to toast the health of the Stuart king at Jacobite clubs: these were particularly numerous in England but 13 existed in Scotland.

→ Folding fan depicting Prince Charles Edward Stuart with Mars and Minerva, after Robert Strange

Probably Great Britain, *c.*1745
Engraved leaf painted with gouache, with carved and pierced ivory sticks
Given by HM Queen Mary
V&A: T.204–1959

This fan has been painted over: only the central scene, depicting Prince Charles Edward Stuart with the classical gods Mars and Minerva, is original. Several fans survive with the complete scene, showing the Prince being crowned by Fame and the Hanoverian family fleeing from Jupiter's thunderbolts. Fans such as this were supposedly given by the Prince to ladies at a ball held at the Palace of Holyroodhouse in September 1745 to celebrate his victory at the Battle of Prestonpans.

→ Jacobite garter, inscribed 'OUR PRINCE IS BRAVE OUR CAUSE IS JUST'

Probably Manchester, *c.*1745
Woven silk
Bequeathed by Miss Evelyn Cooke
V&A: T.121–1931

In December 1746 the *Manchester Magazine* referred to the weaving of 'watch strings and garters' with mottoes such as this. Together with the chequered pattern, alluding to plaid, the motto identifies the wearer of the garter with Jacobite support. Worn above the knee under long skirts, garters were hidden from view, providing an excellent opportunity to express allegiance in secret. In 1748 the *Gentleman's Magazine* described such garters as 'daubed with plaid and crammed with treason'.

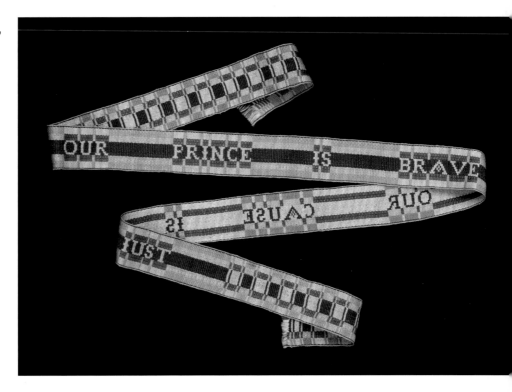

Architecture, Innovation and Dissemination

The publication of the first volume of *Vitruvius Britannicus* in 1715 marks an important moment in the history of architecture. A new type of publication, for the first time in Britain it foregrounded the modern architect and his works. It transformed British architectural taste with its rejection of Baroque excess and promotion of the Neo-Palladian style. Finally, it launched the career of its hitherto little-known Scottish author Colen Campbell (1676–1729), establishing him as the leading architect working in that style.

Although it is Campbell's name that remains associated with *Vitruvius Britannicus*, the book was conceived by print publishers to pre-empt the rival publication of the first complete English-language edition of the work of the Italian architect Andrea Palladio. In three volumes, presenting a combination of existing buildings and speculative designs (many of which were Campbell's own), *Vitruvius Britannicus* pioneered the classical simplicity of the Neo-Palladian style, proclaimed the supremacy of the seventeenth-century English architect Inigo Jones as its greatest proponent, and promoted Campbell himself as the heir to Jones. A lengthy list of prestigious subscribers and the publisher's networks ensured its dissemination, with Campbell acquiring important patronage as a result.

The novelty and significance of such a publication can be seen in its imitation, soon afterwards, by William Adam (1689–1748) in his *Vitruvius Scoticus*, intended to survey Scotland's architecture and to promote Adam as the country's leading architect. However, *Vitruvius Scoticus* was fraught with difficulties: although Adam gathered numerous plates representing the best of Scotland's classical architecture from the 1670s onwards, the work was left unfinished at his death and was published only a century later by his grandson, by which time the architectural style it promoted was thoroughly outdated.

Nonetheless, the potential of such publications – and their even broader reach through the copying of designs into builders' manuals – was not lost on the Adam family. When William's sons John, Robert and James (see pp. 38–41) found themselves in financial crisis, they immediately set about creating their *Works in Architecture* (published in several sections between 1773 and 1778), a publication that served to re-establish their reputation and disseminate their form of Neoclassicism throughout Europe and beyond. JOANNA NORMAN

→ **Hopetoun House, designed by Sir William Bruce, plate from vol. 2 of *Vitruvius Britannicus; or, The British architect, containing the plans, elevations, and sections of the regular buildings, both publick and private in Great Britain, with variety of new designs ... , by Colen Campbell**

Published in London, 1717
Printed book with engraved illustrations
V&A: NATIONAL ART LIBRARY, L.4059–1961

Among the buildings represented in *Vitruvius Britannicus* was Hopetoun House, originally built by Sir William Bruce in 1699–1702. The plate represents the first of two 18th-century remodellings of the house, reflecting the increasingly elevated status of its then owner, Charles Hope. The illustration of houses such as Hopetoun, his dedication of the plate to their owners, and the inclusion of his own designs, executed and speculative, were intended to disseminate Campbell's ideas and increase his possibilities for patronage.

→ **Hamilton Palace, as remodelled by James Smith, plate from *Vitruvius Scoticus; being a collection of plans, elevations and sections ... principally from the designs of the late W.A. Edinburgh*, by William Adam**

Published by A. Black in Edinburgh, 1810
Printed book with engraved illustrations
V&A: NATIONAL ART LIBRARY, 38041800159980

When Adam was compiling his plates, the two most important modern Scottish buildings to represent were Holyroodhouse, recently remodelled to designs by Sir William Bruce in 1671–79, and Hamilton House, remodelled by James Smith in 1691–1701 to reflect the Hamiltons' restoration to favour after the house had been seized from them during the Interregnum (1649–60). Smith's design demonstrates his knowledge of French and Italian architecture, revealed in his classical cladding of the north and south façades, the latter with a monumental portico at its centre.

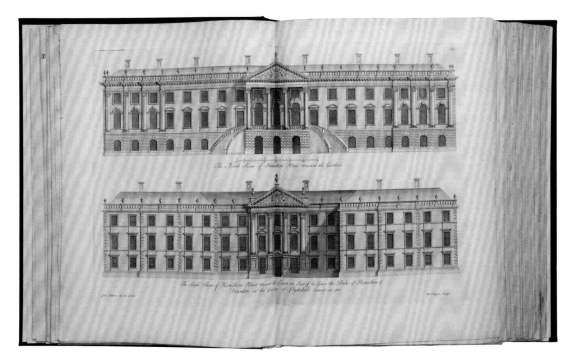

Enlightenment Edinburgh

'Among the several causes to which the prosperity of a nation may be ascribed, the situation, conveniency, and beauty of its capital, are surely not the least considerable. A capital where these circumstances happen fortunately to concur, should naturally become the centre of trade and commerce, of learning and the arts, of politeness, and of refinement of every kind.' (Sir Gilbert Elliot of Minto, *Proposals for Carrying on Certain Public Works in the City of Edinburgh*, 1752)

The second half of the eighteenth century, and the early years of the nineteenth, witnessed a climate of scholarly and philosophical enquiry generally known as the Scottish Enlightenment. Its epicentre was Edinburgh, a city seeking to renew itself within a united Britain, having lost its former importance as the capital of an independent Scotland. Combined with significant population growth, these circumstances fostered an intellectually and architecturally vibrant period that encompassed the planning of the New Town, the creation of learned societies and the design of new scientific instruments, the building of public educational institutions and the publication of new forms of knowledge.

Edinburgh's population rose from about 50,000 in 1750 (including Leith port) to about 90,000 at the start of the nineteenth century. Particular to it, however, was the relative proportion of 'nobles and gentry' (5.4 per cent in 1773–74) to 'professional men' (28.8 per cent in the same period). This was largely a result of the Union: the absence of a royal court from 1603 and of a separate parliament from 1707 led the Scottish aristocracy to adopt London as its primary base, though connections between the cities and to European centres remained strong. In their absence, professionals became the dominant group in Edinburgh, including lawyers,

→ **Plan of the new streets and squares intended for the city of Edinburgh, by James Craig**

Edinburgh, 1768
Engraving
NATIONAL LIBRARY OF SCOTLAND: EMS.S.647

The competition to 'give in Plans of a New Town' was launched by Edinburgh Town Council in March 1766, motivated by chronic overcrowding and unsanitary conditions in the Old Town. Craig's simple, rectilinear plan made excellent use of the sloping site, his well-proportioned outer streets (Princes Street to the south and Queen Street to the north) built on one side only to give their inhabitants good views and air and a feeling of space.

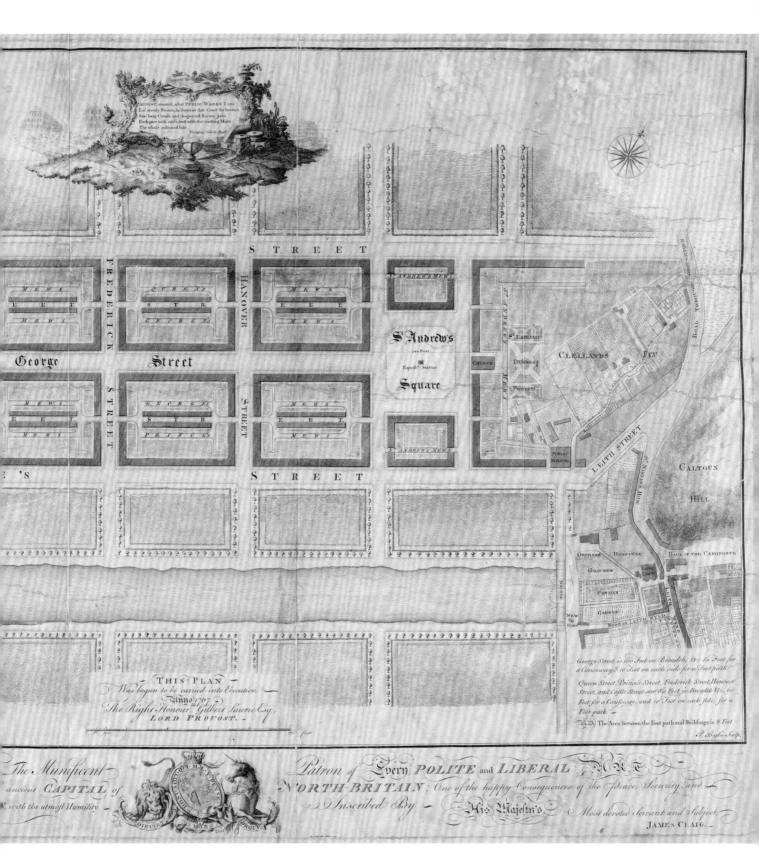

AUGUST, around, what PUBLIC WORKS I see!
Lo' stately Streets, lo Squares that Court the breeze,
See long Canals and deepened Rivers join
Each part with each and with the circling Main
The whole enlivend Isle.

Thomson's Liberty Part V

STREET

FREDERICK   HANOVER

QUEENS
STREET
GEORGE's

MEWS
MEWS

St ANDREWS MEWS

St. ANDREW's

George   Street

MEWS
STREET
PRINCES

GEORGES
STR

MEWS
STREET
NEW

St. Andrew's
500 Feet
Equestr. Statue

Square

St. ANDREW's MEWS

CHURCH

St. LAWRENCE
DUNDAS's
PROPERTY

CLELLANDS FEU

ROAD THROUGH ——

LEITH STREET

CALTOUN
HILL

STREET   STREET   STREET

BRIDGE
HORSE WYND

ORPHANS HOSPITAL
GROUNDS
PHYSICK
GARDEN
NEW
PORT
Road to LEITH WYND
LEITH WYND

BACK OF THE CANONGATE

THIS PLAN
Was begun to be carried into Execution
Anno 1767
The Right Honour.* Gilbert Laurie Esq.*
LORD PROVOST.

George Street is 100 Feet in Breadth, viz. 80 Feet for
a Causeway & 10 Feet on each side for a Foot path.

Queen Street, Prince's Street, Frederick Street, Hanover
Street, and Castle Street are 60 Feet in Breadth Viz. 60
Feet for a Causeway, and 10 Feet on each side, for a
Foot path.

N.B. The Area between the Foot path and Buildings is 8 Feet

P. Begbie Sculp.

The Munificent ——
ancient CAPITAL of
with the utmost Humility ——

Patron of Every POLITE and LIBERAL
NORTH-BRITAIN; One of the happy Consequences of the Peace, Security, and
Inscribed By ——   His Majesty's ——   Most devoted Servant and Subject,
JAMES CRAIG.

DIEU ET MON DROIT

↘ Telescopic kaleidoscope, designed by David Brewster and retailed by I. Ruthven

Edinburgh, c.1820
Brass and silver with enamelled body, with leather and brass box
NATIONAL MUSEUMS SCOTLAND: T.1985.20

Its name taken from the Greek words for 'beautiful', 'form' and 'to see', Brewster's kaleidoscope became an immediate sensation in Britain and Europe upon its invention in Edinburgh in 1816. Its simple construction encouraged vast numbers of cheap copies before Brewster managed to patent it. Brewster saw his optical instrument – a direct result of his experiments with the reflection of light using mirrors – as serving 'all the ornamental arts' and as 'a popular instrument for the purposes of rational amusement'.

doctors, churchmen, university administrators and professors. New learned societies were created, including the Society of Antiquaries of Scotland and the Royal Society of Edinburgh. An active printing and publishing industry that had recently issued the first Scottish newspapers (the *Edinburgh Evening Courant* in 1718 and the *Caledonian Mercury* in 1720) also facilitated the production of literary and scientific journals and treatises.

The dominance of the professions enabled Edinburgh to present itself as the cultural, intellectual and educational capital of the United Kingdom. This presentation was articulated architecturally through the building of the New Town from 1766, with its ordered grid pattern of wide, elegant streets, and in the construction of public buildings such as Robert Adam's Register House (1774–92) and the university courtyard now known as Old College (begun by Adam in 1789, finished long after his death). This was taken further by the following generation, in such Greek Revival buildings as William Playfair's Royal Institution (1822–26, extended in the 1830s; now the Royal Scottish

Academy) and Surgeons' Hall (1830–32), and Thomas Hamilton's Royal High School (1826–29) and Royal College of Physicians of Edinburgh (1844–46), all of which asserted Edinburgh's status as cultural centre and heir to the classical civilization of ancient Greece.

It was not just in public but also in private that professionals brought about changes in culture and design. The large numbers of middle-ranking households occupying the New Town's tenements furnished them to represent their own status as part of an intellectual, genteel and increasingly prosperous milieu, their homes serving to host private gatherings for entertainment, refreshment and discussion. As a result, these homes had to contain the appropriate goods: a dining table with a set of matching chairs, preferably in an expensive imported tropical wood; fine linen for the table; and a range of tableware – glasses and punchbowls for drinking, tea and coffee sets, new forms of cutlery and dining vessels, all representative of new fashions in behaviour and style. JOANNA NORMAN

→ **Title page to vol. 1 of the third edition of *Encyclopaedia Britannica: or, A dictionary of arts and sciences ...*, 18 vols**

Published by Andrew Bell and Colin Macfarquhar, Edinburgh, 1797
Engraving
NATIONAL LIBRARY OF SCOTLAND: EB.5

The engraver Andrew Bell and the printer Colin Macfarquhar collaborated to produce the phenomenally successful *Encyclopaedia Britannica*. Published in instalments and in quarto editions from 1768, it was the first alphabetically organized compendium of knowledge of the arts and sciences in Scotland. The third edition established it as the premier British encyclopedia, dedicated to King George III, with a lengthy list of illustrious subscribers and articles by numerous expert contributors including key figures of the Scottish Enlightenment.

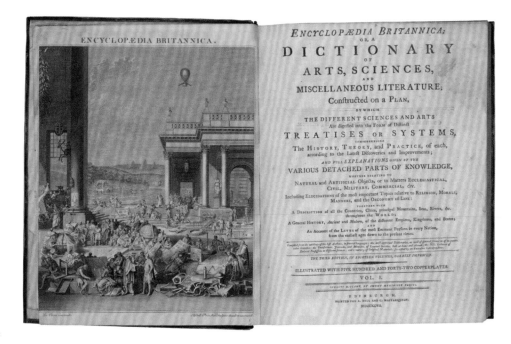

↓ **Jug, made by West Pans factory**

West Pans, 1764–70
Soft-paste porcelain painted with enamels
Given by Lady Charlotte Schreiber
V&A: 414:99–1885

New social rituals became established throughout Europe in the 18th century, from the drinking of tea and coffee to different forms of dining, all requiring new specialized vessels. In 1764 William Littler (previously of Longton Hall, one of the Staffordshire potteries) founded a porcelain manufactory at West Pans, near Musselburgh. One of Scotland's first and principal porcelain factories, West Pans produced a wide range of tablewares to serve these fashionable activities.

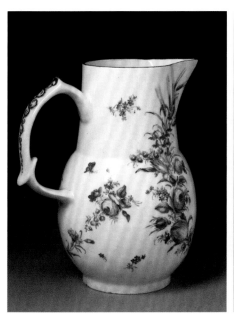

Robert Adam and the Creation of a Style

'We have not trod in the path of others, nor derived aid from their labours. In the works which we have had the honour to execute, we have not only met with the approbation of our employers, but even with the imitation of other artists, to such a degree, as in some measure to have brought about, in this country, a kind of revolution in the whole system of this useful and elegant art.'
(Preface to *The Works in Architecture of Robert and James Adam*, vol. 1, 1773)

For much of the second half of the eighteenth century Robert Adam (1728–92) was one of the most important architects in Britain. Through his development of a particular, individual style of Neoclassicism, cultivation of important and influential patrons, concerted use of print publishing, and phenomenal ambition, he – together with his brothers John (1721–92), James (1732–94) and William (1738–1822) – created a highly successful 'Adam style' that they applied to urban residences, country houses and public institutions.

William Adam (1689–1748), their father, was the foremost Scottish architect of his day, awarded contracts by the Board of Ordnance from 1733 to build fortifications such as Fort George, near Inverness, intended to control potential Jacobite threats. At William's death in 1748 his sons inherited these contracts as well as unfinished private commissions, such as the building of a new house for the Earl of Dumfries in Ayrshire. While John remained in Scotland, running these projects from an Edinburgh office, Robert undertook the Grand Tour of continental Europe from 1754, studying ancient ruins and modern buildings and taking drawing lessons with Charles-Louis Clérisseau and Giovanni Battista Piranesi. The vast and varied corpus of drawings that he made (as did James, on a similar tour) provided him, upon his return and establishment in London in 1758, with a wide-ranging classical sourcebook. This also demonstrated his knowledge of the classical world to potential patrons, further boosted by his publication in 1764 of *The Ruins of the Palace of Emperor Diocletian at Spalatro* with engraved views by Clérisseau.

Although Robert decried his native country as 'a narrow place' where 'scarce will ever happen the opportunity of putting one noble thought in execution', Scotland provided a steady stream of work upon which he and the family firm relied. The construction of Edinburgh's New Town provided opportunities for designing urban schemes and public buildings such as Charlotte Square (1791) and Register House (begun in 1774). In London patronage by leading Scots, especially the Earl of Bute, led to Robert's joint appointment, with his arch-rival William Chambers, as Architect to the King's Works in 1761, an appointment that passed to James in 1768 when Robert became MP for Kinross-shire. A financial crisis, however, was brought on by excessive borrowing against the speculative Adelphi development (1768–74) that they designed and built in London between the Strand and the Thames. Thereafter it was principally Scottish commissions, combined with the success of their publication of *The Works in Architecture*, that ensured the continuation of the firm, albeit with further financial crises leading ultimately to bankruptcy in 1801 for the last surviving brother, William.

Despite the architects' claim in *The Works in Architecture* not to have 'trod in the path of others', the Adam style is characterized by a masterful synthesis of disparate influences, forms and ornamental motifs, as highlighted in Robert's interiors designed for the 1st Duke and Duchess of Northumberland: at Syon House, Middlesex, he created a Neoclassical villa (1760–69); at Alnwick, Northumberland, a Gothic castle (late 1760s–c.1780); and at Northumberland House, a fashionable London residence (1770–75). Above all, the Adam style is fully expressed in interior decoration. Now held in the V&A, the Glass Drawing Room from Northumberland House exemplifies this: in a bold use of colour recalling ancient Roman interiors; in elegant, linear ornament inspired by a range of classical sources rather than strict archaeological accuracy; and in the concept of total design that unified ceilings, carpets, walls, furnishings and all decorative elements. It represents a highly individual, immediately recognizable and innovative approach whose influence would prove long-lasting. JOANNA NORMAN

↑ 1:12 Scale Model of the Glass Drawing Room from Northumberland House, designed by Robert Adam, 1773–74

Made by Lucy Askew with The Network Modelmakers and Historic Classic Houses for the British Galleries at the V&A
London, 2001
Wood, plastic and metal
V&A: E.3837–2004 (MODEL)
V&A: W.3–1955 (ROOM)

Robert Adam designed the Glass Drawing Room in 1773–74 as the spectacular centrepiece to the 1st Duke and Duchess of Northumberland's London house. He set large, expensive plate-glass mirrors into wall panels and pilasters inset with red and green glass, backed with coloured pigment and metal elements and surmounted with gilded scrolling decoration, to give a glittering effect when lit by candlelight, evoking the richness and colour of ancient Roman interiors. This glass lining formed part of an overall unified design that also encompassed the ceiling, carpet and furnishings. Removed when Northumberland House was demolished in 1874, the surviving elements of the Glass Drawing Room have been part of the V&A's collections since 1955.

→ **Section of Register House, plate VII from vol. 1 of *The Works in Architecture of Robert and James Adam***

Printed for the authors in London, 1773–78
Engraving
V&A: NATIONAL ART LIBRARY, 38041800989097

In 1772 Robert and James Adam were appointed architects for a new building to house Scotland's public records, Robert leading the design from London with support from John in Edinburgh. The design employed brick vaults and stone floors to protect the archives from damp and fire. The top-lit rotunda was inspired by the Pantheon in Rome, while plaster decoration by the Edinburgh-based Thomas Clayton Jr combined Scottish thistles with classical Greek and Roman ornament. The building of Register House, situated on Princes Street on the edge of Edinburgh's New Town, began in 1774. However, rising costs and technical challenges led to a hiatus between 1779 and 1785, and it finally opened to the public in 1788.

The Carron Iron Company

↓ Balcony front from 5 Robert Street, London, designed by Robert and James Adam and probably made by the Carron Iron Company

The availability of natural resources, adoption of new technologies to manufacture a wide range of products, collaborations with architects and designers, and access to markets: these combined factors contributed to the eighteenth-century success of the Carron Iron Company. It marks the beginnings of Scottish excellence in the production of and working with iron, from Thomas Telford's bridges to the prefabricated structures produced by Glasgow firms such as Macfarlane's for export all over the world.

Established in 1759, the Carron Iron Company was the first in Scotland to adopt the new technique of smelting with coke rather than charcoal. Located in Falkirk, the ironworks benefited from its surroundings, which were rich in coal and ironstone deposits and had plentiful supplies of running water. Carron also profited from the opening up of markets through the Acts of Union (1707) and from its proximity to both east and west coasts. The links from these coasts to overseas markets gave it a clear economic advantage over English competitors.

Initially specializing in cannon and ordnance, Carron established its reputation with the 1778 design of the carronade, a short-barrelled naval cannon that achieved huge success during the Napoleonic Wars (1803–15). However, the company's wide range of products also included utilitarian and decorative goods, from tools, pans and anvils to stoves, firegrates and balcony fronts. For its decorative pieces the Carron Iron Company collaborated with renowned designers, pattern makers and carvers including the Adam brothers, John Adam serving as a partner in the company from 1763. This collaboration was of clear mutual benefit, not just economically: iron casting was the perfect way to produce multiple identical linear elements, such as balcony fronts, railings and gates, to adorn the Neoclassical architecture promoted by the Adams and disseminated through pattern books. In turn, such highly visible use promoted the work of the Carron Iron Company: by 1814 it was the largest ironworks in Europe, its products could be seen in houses across Scotland and its exports had reached markets from Iberia to Scandinavia. JOANNA NORMAN

Designed in London, probably made in Falkirk
*c.*1773–75
Cast iron
Gift of the Adelphi Development Company
V&A: M.428–1936

5 Robert Street was part of the Adelphi, built by the Adam brothers between 1768 and 1774 as a speculative development between the Strand and the River Thames in London. The Carron Iron Company's cast-iron balcony fronts, featuring linear Neoclassical motifs such as anthemia and Vitruvian scrolls, provided simple, elegant decoration for the long, unified façades of buildings such as the Adelphi or parts of the New Town in Edinburgh.

Scots and North America: Emigration and Entrepreneurship

Scotland's history is characterized by waves of emigration of its people, caused variously by displacement, or economic difficulty, or through the seeking of opportunity elsewhere. As the colonization of North America progressed in the eighteenth century, particularly by the British along the Atlantic coast, Scots were attracted there. They included the cabinetmaker Thomas Affleck (1740–95) and Alexander Wilson (1766–1813), who had trained as a weaver. Through their work each contributed to the history and culture of the New World.

Affleck was born in Aberdeen, and is thought to have learned his craft in Edinburgh in the mid-eighteenth century. After a short period in London, he emigrated to Philadelphia in 1763. Not long after establishing a shop there, he was fortunate in securing a commission for a suite of furniture from John Penn, a grandson of Pennsylvania's founder, William Penn. Such patronage, and the elaborate carved style of Affleck's cabinetmaking, which reflected the elegance of Thomas Chippendale and so the latest in British fashion, attracted further commissions from the most notable and the wealthiest in Philadelphia society.

In 1776 Affleck became caught up in political events, protesting against the American War of Independence with Great Britain. He was banished to Virginia, but a few months later was allowed to return to Philadelphia, where he continued his work, including, it has been suggested, production of the chairs for Congress Hall, the seat of the United States Congress from 1790 to 1800.

In the 1770s Affleck's fellow Scot, the Paisley-born Alexander Wilson, also fell foul of authority, having written a poem severely satirizing a local mill owner for poor working conditions. Following imprisonment, Wilson emigrated to Pennsylvania. Unable to find work as a weaver, he developed his interest in ornithology and painting. With the same conviction he had shown as a writer and commentator, he set about travelling and producing illustrations of the complete bird life of North America, published in the nine-volume *American Ornithology* (1808–14). His illustrations studiously record and expressively capture the life, form, plumage and sometimes brilliant colour of the native species, and they influenced and inspired the work of many naturalists who followed in the nineteenth century. PHILIP LONG

↑ **Plate XIV from vol. 2 of *The American Ornithology or the Natural History of the Birds of the United States …*, by Alexander Wilson**

Published by Bradford & Inskeep in Philadelphia, 1810
Coloured engraving
PAISLEY PUBLIC REFERENCE LIBRARY, RENFREWSHIRE COUNCIL: REF A852

Known as the 'Father of American Ornithology', Wilson was the first person to attempt to illustrate and document all the birds of North America. He represented 268 species, including 26 previously undescribed; five species are named after him. Wilson's first-hand study of birds' posture, behaviour and habitat resulted in such scientifically accurate illustrations that they could be used to identify birds for the first time.

→ **Chest-on-chest, attributed to Thomas Affleck**

Philadelphia, USA, 1770–85
Mahogany, mahogany veneer, red gum, white cedar, yellow poplar, brass
Purchased with the Elizabeth S. Shippen Fund, 1926
THE PHILADELPHIA MUSEUM OF ART: 1926-19-1

Thomas Affleck is acknowledged as one of Philadelphia's finest craftsmen of the latter 18th century. He benefited from the patronage of fellow Scots and Quakers, who commissioned him to execute pieces of fashionable seat and case furniture such as the chest-on-chest. Affleck is known to have collaborated with the Philadelphia carver James Reynolds on some such elegant architectural pieces, enlivened with carved naturalistic ornament, in the style made popular and fashionable by the London publication of Thomas Chippendale's *The Gentleman and Cabinet Maker's Director* (1754).

Scots in Russia

'For her Majesty the Empress of all the Russias: Wanted!'
So began an advertisement placed in the *Edinburgh Evening Courant* on 21 January 1784 by the architect and designer Charles Cameron (1745–1812), seeking craftsmen to work with him in Russia for Catherine the Great. Seventy-three Scots, including bricklayers, plasterers, blacksmiths and twenty-seven stonemasons, soon departed from Leith to enter the service of the Russian Empress. Two of them, in particular, had a lasting impact on Russia's built and landscaped environment.

The arrival of Scots in Russia was not a new phenomenon: Scottish academics, doctors, merchants and, particularly, soldiers are recorded in Russia from the fourteenth century. However, the late eighteenth and early nineteenth centuries marked a particularly momentous period in Scottish–Russian relationships. Catherine the Great was a renowned Anglophile, avidly collecting British goods and patronizing Charles Cameron, of Scottish heritage, who designed and built an antique-style baths complex at her summer residence of Tsarskoe Selo. It was Cameron's need for expertise in building with stone (lacking in Russia) that led to his 1784 advertisement and to the arrival in Russia of William Hastie (1754/5–1832) and Adam Menelaws (c. 1748/9–1831).

A stonemason when he arrived in Russia aged 29, William Hastie rapidly made his name there. His reputation was secured from 1806, when he designed and built the first of several cast-iron bridges in St Petersburg. Their success elevated him to the status of chief architect for the town of Tsarskoe Selo in 1808 and, from 1811, to that of master planner. From Kiev to Krasnojarsk, Hastie redesigned provincial towns with regular, rectilinear plans, monumental perspectives and standardized house types, his designs circulating as models for use across the Russian Empire.

Hastie's compatriot, Adam Menelaws, arrived in Russia with more experience of building in Scotland, and so was immediately sent to work on a prestigious cathedral project in Mogilev. Similarly successful, Menelaws designed a number of residences, gardens and parks for clients including the noble Razumovsky family and the imperial court, establishing a new Russian taste for Romantic architecture. If Hastie was responsible for establishing a new way of building bridges in Russia, Menelaws left his mark on its gardens and garden buildings, from the Egyptian gates of Tsarskoe Selo to a rustic 'Kottedzh' (cottage) at Peterhof for Tsar Nicholas I. JOANNA NORMAN

dans

↓ The New Iron Bridge on the Nevsky Prospekt in St Petersburg, after Benjamin Patersen

Russia, 1806 · Coloured etching
V&A: E.1099–1900

Hastie designed the first cast-iron bridge in St Petersburg in 1806. Cast in prefabricated sections that were then bolted together, and supported on each bank by stone pillars, the bridge was so elegant and lightweight that it was adopted as a model for all other bridges over the River Moika. The iron was cast at the Petrozavodsk foundry, established by Charles Gascoigne, the former director of the Carron Iron Company in Falkirk.

Le nouveau Pont de fer
perspective de Newsky à S.t Petersbourg.

Thomas Telford

By about 1800 Scotland had made a distinctive design contribution to the Industrial Revolution. Scottish foundries had revolutionized production methods in iron and were collaborating with architects to improve the design quality of goods. Mills in the west of the country were developing an international reputation for the quality of their textiles, particularly in silk and linen. But perhaps the most enduring developments of that period were those in transport infrastructure, helping to accelerate industrial progress, trade and employment. The dominant figure in this was the civil engineer Thomas Telford (1757–1834), whose vast number of projects and innovative design solutions led to him being dubbed 'the Colossus of Roads'.

The son of a shepherd, Telford was born on a hill farm in rural Dumfriesshire, and was educated in the Scottish parish school system. Apprenticed as a mason, he had an early ambition to become an architect, and he also wrote poetry. In the 1780s he moved south and, after working at Portsmouth docks, he began to design and manage building projects. Aged 30, Telford was appointed Surveyor of Public Works in Shropshire, where he completed 40 bridges. These included his first bridge in iron across the River Severn at Buildwas, the design of which improved significantly on Abraham Darby's famous Iron Bridge. Several years later, still in his 30s, Telford designed and engineered the Ellesmere Canal, which included the spectacular Pontcysyllte Aqueduct across the River Dee in Wales. The aqueduct comprises 19 arches, each with a 13.7-metre (45 feet) span.

In Scotland, Telford undertook a massive survey of the Highlands, commissioned by the government in 1801 with the intention of improving communications. Over the next 20 years he oversaw the construction of some 900 miles of roads and 120 bridges, as well as harbours and jetties (particularly in fishing centres), bringing much-needed work across the country. The centrepiece was the Caledonian Canal, connecting the lochs of the Great Glen and creating a navigable passage across Scotland, from west-coast Fort William to Inverness in the north-east. PHILIP LONG

↑ *The Wonders of the Menai in its Suspension and Tubular Bridges,* engraved by J. Fagan

Published in Bangor, Wales, by S. Hughes, 1850
Colour lithograph
Given by Mr A.R. Harvey
V&A: E.566–1936

Among Telford's greatest innovations was the Menai Suspension Bridge, completed in 1826 and designed to take traffic from mainland Wales to the island of Anglesey, and on to Holyhead, a principal port serving Dublin. Telford recommended a suspension bridge for the dangerous crossing, designing a bridge with a span of 176 metres (577 feet) that was high enough to allow tall ships to pass underneath. The bridge remains in use, and in 2005 it became a UNESCO World Heritage Site.

The Paisley Weaving Industry

The dramatic rise in the eighteenth century of Paisley, from a small rural town in Renfrewshire to one of Europe's leading textile manufacturing centres, is one of the most remarkable stories in the history of Scottish design and production. From 1760 to 1870 the various fabrics designed and produced in Paisley were in vogue throughout Europe and beyond. At the same time the local spinning company J. & P. Coats went on to become the largest manufacturer of sewing thread in the world.

Local textile skills were developed from the seventeenth century by a small community of handloom weavers, producing linen cloth to be sold to Glasgow merchants at a weekly market in the town. Easier access to English markets after the Acts of Union in 1707 stimulated growth, and the Paisley weavers earned a high reputation for the production of fine linen fabrics, including plain, striped, spotted and figured lawns, and also gauze.

The successful introduction of silk gauze weaving in 1759 induced several manufacturers to move to Paisley from Spitalfields, London. Elegant and richly ornamented Paisley gauzes were considered haute couture in Europe and were also exported to Russia and America. At this time weavers both designed and made the fabrics, the constant need to produce novel fashionable effects stimulating an unprecedented degree of creativity and technical innovation.

With the introduction of industrial cotton spinning in the 1780s, weavers turned to the manufacture of muslin, producing an amazing variety of light, elegant figured designs to suit new fashions, and in 1805 the weaving of shawls was introduced. Originally known as the 'imitation Indian' shawl (in fact imitating those from Kashmir), this became the town's main product throughout the nineteenth century, during which time its design developed and acquired its own unique characteristics. It was so successful that it became known as the Paisley shawl, its distinctive teardrop pattern referred to as the Paisley pattern.

The complexity of these shawls demanded a division of labour and a high level of specialization at each stage of manufacture. Weavers were no longer involved in design but were confined to solely operating the loom. Just as the shawl had come into fashion in the late eighteenth century, however, it went out of fashion in the 1870s, marking a terminal decline in the long tradition of handloom weaving in Paisley. DAN COUGHLAN

↑ **Pattern book with figured silk gauze samples, made by Brown & Sharp**

Paisley, c.1770
Silk and cotton on paper, in a half-leather binding with paper sides
PAISLEY MUSEUM, RENFREWSHIRE COUNCIL

It was standard practice for manufacturers to compile books containing samples of each fabric they produced, to be used for reference by buyers when ordering. A letter inside this book shows that another copy was held at the London premises of Brown & Sharp. Containing samples produced on various types of loom, it highlights the level of the weavers' design and technological capabilities in late 18th-century Paisley.

→ **Paisley shawl**

Paisley, c.1845–47
Wool
V&A: T.213–1922

This shawl is typical of those woven in Paisley in the 1840s. The sophisticated design effect is achieved by a complex arrangement of ornate pines, scrolls and stylized floral motifs in a harmonious scheme of eight colours. Woven in one piece, on a draw loom or a jacquard loom, it is a fine example of the technical virtuosity of 19th-century handloom weaving.

Ayrshire Needlework

In the second half of the eighteenth century the west of Scotland became a centre for the production of high-quality linen fabric. By the 1780s cotton yarn was being produced cheaply and was widely adopted by former linen weavers, who soon began to produce fine cotton muslin in quantity. French fashions prevailed with a preference for plain, soft muslin rather than rich silks, leading to a desire for decoration that retained the simplicity of undyed material. Whitework embroidery provided the solution.

New economic opportunities were being sought and developments in textile manufacture were seen to offer ways forward, if the appropriate skills could be sourced. Financial support from the Board of Trustees allowed the Swiss embroiderer Luigi Ruffini to set up an industrial school in Edinburgh in 1784. Another Swiss craftsman, Mr Halbick, was engaged by the Cessnock estate in Ayrshire to employ and train local children. The technique primarily used at this stage was tambouring, in which a fine pointed hook was employed to pull worked thread through fabric stretched on a frame, forming a continuous looped stitch. By the end of the eighteenth century this craft formed the basis of a burgeoning cottage industry employing a female workforce.

Trade was controlled by merchants whose agents distributed fabric to workers and later gathered in the decorated muslin. One such agent was a Mrs Jamieson of Ayr. Further changes in fashion meant the preference for simplicity in female dress gave way to romantic reinterpretations of an earlier era. Cuffs, collars and caps rendered in lacelike fabrics were in vogue, requiring the embroiderer's skills. In 1814 Mrs Jamieson encountered an example of French needlework recently brought back from the continent. The sophisticated embellishments included needlepoint inserts – a form of lace crafted by the needle alone. This formed the basis of the white-on-white embroidery known as Ayrshire needlework.

During the first half of the nineteenth century Ayrshire needlework flourished. Babies' day dresses, bonnets and robes survive as exemplary products of this period. Glasgow merchants exported them to London and Dublin but also to America, France, Germany and Russia. However, changes in fashion, along with the introduction of new manufacturing technologies during the final decades of the nineteenth century, led to the eventual decline of this highly distinctive craft industry.

LINDA FAIRLIE AND BRUCE MORGAN

→ **Christening robe decorated with Ayrshire needlework**
Ayrshire, *c.*1840s
Muslin
Given by Mrs M. Eadie
V&A: T.30–1963

'Jess's rarest possession was, perhaps, the christening robe that even people at a distance came to borrow. Her mother could count up a hundred persons who had been baptised in it.' (J.M. Barrie, *A Window in Thrums*, 1889)

Ayrshire needlework is often associated with christening robes, which have survived as family heirlooms. It is distinguished by intricate needlepoint lace infills, frequently arranged within small, wheel-shaped, floral perforations. The craft was often referred to as 'floo'erin'. While the broad outlines of the decoration were predetermined by a stamped pattern, the infills allowed the embroiderer creative freedom on a microscopic scale – each infill having the uniqueness we might associate with a snowflake.

Highland and Traveller Crafts

Traditional crafts of the Highlands not only reflect the ingenuity of the peoples in that area but also their appreciation for the natural, often ephemeral, resources around them: wood, heather, horn, leather and grasses. Much of the Highlanders' vernacular material culture is represented in natural, organic and vulnerable objects. In many cases it could be said that the climate and the indigenous materials of the Highlands dictated the development of particular skills over others and certain vernacular traditions.

The making of horn spoons was a craft skill closely guarded by the Travellers. After being softened by heating, by either fire or boiling, the cow horn was pressed between the two parts of a wooden mould to create a crudely shaped spoon. Horn spoons were indispensable in Highland homes and were widely used until the mid-19th century.

Silversmithing was a craft practised by the Travellers from the 16th to the 17th centuries. By the 18th century many Travellers were settling down and these skilled craftsmen were producing very fine silverware in burghs such as Inverness, Elgin and Wick. Each burgh had its own mark for silver and the craftsmen turned out quaichs, brooches and spoons. This traditional heart-shaped brooch was made from the bowl of a spoon, indicating the practice of recycling and adapting materials.

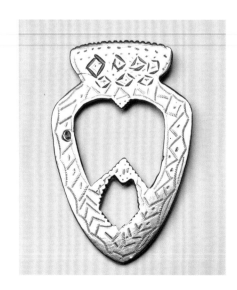

In spite of the variety of tasks that Highland people performed themselves, there has long been, except in the poorest and remotest communities, a certain number of specialized craftsmen employed to produce goods. As in other areas, these craftsmen came to have a social status in Highland communities. Important craft skills from the sixteenth century onwards included tanning and leatherworking, textile weaving, woodworking, horn crafts, blacksmithing, thatching, wheelwrighting and stone masonry.

Many of these craft skills were provided to the settled inhabitants of the Highlands by the Travelling people. Travellers have been part of the Highland culture for many centuries and can be traced back to Iron Age cairds (Gaelic: *cearden*), itinerant ironworkers from the Celtic peoples. Later Travellers included Romany peoples in the late medieval period, and dispossessed clansmen in the late seventeenth to nineteenth centuries. As well as supplying additional labour to farms at busy times, Travellers had many craft skills – including silversmithing, hornworking, basketry, pearl fishing, the making of pine tar and tinsmithing – which made them important and valued members of the community.

The importance of Travellers in Highland society continued well into the nineteenth century, when many of their traditional roles were superseded owing to the growth of local shops and the greater use of mass-produced goods. RACHEL CHISHOLM

↓ Staved vessel

Isle of Mull, *c.*1840
Wood, sycamore and alder, bound with split rattan
HIGHLAND FOLK MUSEUM: SJ 3

One very distinctive part of the furnishings of Highland households were staved vessels, made from local woods, designed to hold various liquids. Ranging from small drinking cups to larger containers, these vessels were skilfully created by 'feathering' the staves together. In this method, the edges of each stave were finely cut to interlock the next, making for a watertight seam. Staves were bound together with bands of wicker, rattan or metal.

Highlandism: The Romanticization of Scotland

'At ¼ to 6 we reached Taymouth, situated in a valley sur-
rounded by very wooded hills, – most beautiful … The house
is a sort of granite Castle & the "coup d'oeil" was splendid
when we drove up, with a number of Highlanders drawn up
in front of the house … There was a great crowd, & the whole
scene, with the firing of guns, to add to its impressiveness,
was the finest sight imaginable, & seemed like the reception
in olden Feudal times, of the Sovereign by a Chieftain.'
(Queen Victoria's Journal, 7 September 1842)

From the late eighteenth century a romantic image of Scotland
emerged that still holds sway today. Fascination with the doomed
Jacobite cause and the Highland clan system, and a Europe-wide
taste for the 'picturesque', led Scotland to be seen as a potent
symbol of remote, untameable nature and age-old traditions.
Much of this was due to literature, namely the publication from
1760 of James Macpherson's *Ossian*, the supposed poems of an
ancient Celtic bard, and in the first half of the nineteenth century
the novels and verse of Sir Walter Scott. Both *Ossian* and Scott
depicted a Scotland of dramatic landscapes inhabited by tragic
heroes. Disseminated internationally, translated widely and
inspiring a swathe of artistic representations, they had a strong
influence on the perception of Scotland as an awe-inspiring,
sublime environment – a perception that drew little distinction
between the Highlands and the rest of the country.

The appeal of the picturesque also revealed itself in architecture, with architects such as William Burn and David Bryce
looking back to medieval tower houses, adding crenellations, turrets and crow-stepped gables to country houses in what became
known as the Scottish Baronial style. Such houses formed the

→ **Perspective view of Blair Castle, by David Bryce**

Edinburgh, 1869
Watercolour
HISTORIC ENVIRONMENT SCOTLAND: PTD127/2

Six hundred years after its original construction, Blair Castle was
transformed in 1869 from its 18th-century Georgian appearance as
'Atholl House' into a medieval-looking castle in the Scottish Baronial
style. David Bryce's design for the 7th Duke of Atholl, shown in this
watercolour perspective painted for the Royal Scottish Academy, added
crenellations, crow-stepped gables and bartizans (round corner turrets)
to the exterior to create an impression of antiquity.

perfect complement to the picturesque landscapes in which they were situated, their exteriors conveying a sense of unchanging permanence that was often replicated inside through antiquarian displays of Scottish weapons.

The equation of the Highlands with Scotland as a whole also asserted itself in the burgeoning interest in tartan as a national style of dress. Stage-managed by Scott, the visit of George IV to Edinburgh in 1822 (the first by a reigning monarch since the seventeenth century) was notable partly for the King's appearance in full Highland dress. Together with illustrated publications such as *The Clans of the Scottish Highlands* (1845–47), this royal approval helped to expand an already growing fashionable market for tartan, boosted by its supposedly ancient use as an expression of clan identity. Such resonance proved compelling for many, including Queen Victoria, who regularly wore and actively promoted tartan. Victoria and Albert's first visit to Scotland in 1842, said to have been instigated by her reading of Scott's novels, inaugurated a long love affair with the country. She related this through her journal entries that emphasize the picturesque effect created through the combination of landscape, architecture and local people in Highland dress.

Amid the rapidly industrializing world of the nineteenth century, the Highlands seemed to represent a rare example of a remote, empty, unchanging environment, even if the railways were in the process of making it more accessible and the emptiness was largely the result of the displacement of people through emigration and the Highland Clearances. At the same time, the cult of this landscape, combined with the adoption of tartan as a national dress and the creation of Scottish Baronial architecture, seem to have represented an attempt to collect and reinterpret the past in order to forge a new sense and expression of Scottish national identity: one that equated the Highlands with the whole of Scotland, and that was thus thoroughly distinct from that of Scotland's southern neighbour, England. JOANNA NORMAN

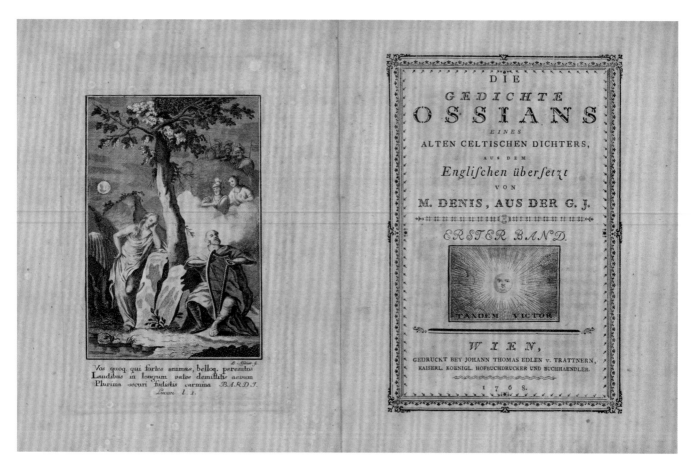

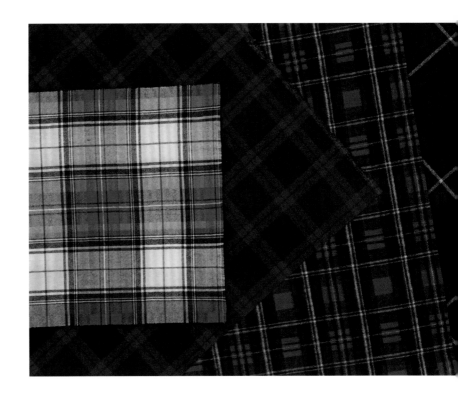

↙ Frontispiece from *Die Gedichte Ossians eines alten celtischen Dichters*, by James Macpherson, translated into German by M. Denis

Published in Vienna, 1768
Engraving
NATIONAL LIBRARY OF SCOTLAND: NG.1168.G.21

Although the authenticity of Macpherson's *Ossian* poems was contested, their popularity across Europe was immense. The heroic characters and sublime Highland landscapes described by the supposed Celtic bard (shown in this frontispiece) tapped into a taste for the romantic: the French emperor Napoleon was an avid reader and numerous translations rapidly appeared. Denis's German version was the first complete translation into another language, and had a significant impact on the development of European romantic literature, art and music.

↗ Tartans retailed by James Locke at the Great Exhibition, London (from left to right: Royal Stewart, Black Watch, Prince Charles, Gordon)

United Kingdom, 1851
Wool twill
Presented by Messrs Locke, formerly of Regent Street, London
V&A (FROM LEFT TO RIGHT): T.317–1967, T.325–1967, T.323–1967, T.319–1967

These tartan swatches were retailed by James Locke of Regent Street at the Great Exhibition of 1851. About that date publications such as *The Clans of the Scottish Highlands* promoted the ancient use of specific patterns, or 'setts', to demonstrate clan identity, although there is no evidence of this before the 18th century. Woven in wool and silk, tartan was used for fashionable dress and furnishing fabrics, influenced by the example of Queen Victoria and Empress Eugénie of France.

→ Targe (shield)

Scotland, 1708
Wood, leather, decorated with copper alloy studs
Bequeathed by Mr G.H. Ramsbottom through Art Fund
V&A: M.2713–1931

A crucial defensive element of Highland weaponry, the targe was effectively banned as part of the Act of Proscription following the Jacobite risings. In the 19th century it often reappeared within antiquarian displays of historic weapons, alongside other traditional Scottish arms including broadswords, dirks, pistols and Lochaber axes. Sometimes these weapons were acquired specifically for the purpose, but in the case of Blair Castle, they were provided by the Duke of Atholl's private army.

Dundee: Trade, Travel and Design

Dundee was a thriving industrial centre for many centuries, and its success was founded on its natural harbour, positioned on a major estuary. During the nineteenth century Dundee grew from a trading port to become a major force in shipbuilding, whaling and textiles. As a result, its economy was transformed into an international one based on interlinked industries with a dependency on design and innovation driving them forwards. The city's confidence and prosperity were symbolized in its Royal Arch, first built on the waterfront in 1844 to commemorate a visit by Queen Victoria and Prince Albert.

From the fourteenth century Dundee developed international links, particularly with Baltic and northern European ports. Already well known for textiles, with an established weaving industry dating back to the sixteenth century, Dundee saw its first 20 bales of raw jute unloaded at the city's docks in 1820. It was discovered that whale oil could be used to soften the raw jute fibre and make it workable by machine, and as a result jute production became predominant. Many of the city's firms changed production from linen to jute and, by the 1870s, 140,000 tons of raw jute were being imported annually through Dundee's docks to be transformed into woven fibre.

Dundee became known as 'Juteopolis' – the jute capital of the world. The industry's demand for whale oil helped stimulate the declining whaling industry and by the latter half of the nineteenth century the city was also the premier whaling port in Europe.

New worldwide markets opened up as the demand for jute products grew, stimulating Dundee's shipbuilding industry. Internationally, trading companies began looking for larger and faster vessels to replace the slower brigs and schooners, leading to the development of swift clippers and bulk-cargo barques. Many of these vessels were designed and built in Dundee, with local yards such as Caledon and Gourlay Brothers (the latter being pioneers in the design and use of the screw propeller) competing against larger firms on the Clyde and regularly winning contracts.

Gradually, ship production became concentrated in fewer, more specialized and larger yards with the development of metal-hulled steamships, and then motor vessels. The design innovation and quality of the Dundee yards, especially in iron shipbuilding, gained worldwide recognition. At the industry's height in the late nineteenth century, 200 ships were produced in the city per year, including Robert Falcon Scott's RRS *Discovery*, designed especially for polar exploration.

As a result of such industrial success, Dundee expanded fourfold in the nineteenth century, and up to 50,000 people were employed in its textile mills alone. However, jute production declined significantly from the 1920s onwards, mainly due to fierce competition from the Indian jute industry. Although jute is no longer processed in Dundee, its effects still resonate. The skills learned by the workforce, including nimbleness, a fine eye for detail and precision work, on top of a strong work ethic, helped to attract new manufacturing industries such as Levi, NCR and Michelin to the city. The American watchmakers Timex famously assembled the ZX Spectrum (one of the first home computers in the UK) in Dundee in 1982, helping to lay the ground for Dundee's excellence today in digital and especially game design.

JULIE MCCOMBIE

→ **Jute sack**

Dundee, 1960s
Printed jute
DUNDEE CITY COUNCIL (DUNDEE'S ART GALLERIES AND MUSEUMS): 998–152–3

That Dundee was able to become such an important centre of jute manufacture was aided by its existing textile industry. The Dundee weavers adapted their skills to this new versatile fabric, which was strong and durable as well as inexpensive. Its uses included sacking, ropes, boot linings, aprons, carpets, tents, roofing felts, satchels, linoleum backing, sandbags, sailcloth, oven cloths, horse covers, cattle bedding, electric cable and even parachutes.

1968 — 69

PAK TOSS.A

PRODUCE OF PAKISTAN

C

400 LBS

E.P.J.M.C.

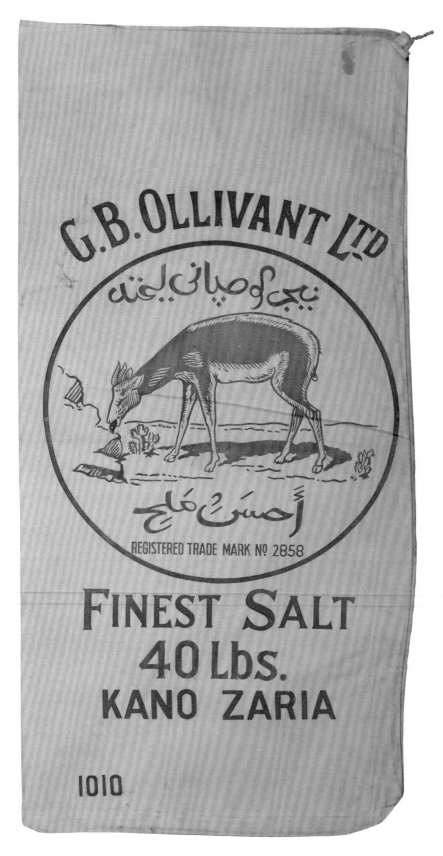

← **Cotton sample sack for G.B. Ollivant Ltd, made by A. & S. Henry & Co.**

Dundee, c.1965
Printed cotton
DUNDEE CITY COUNCIL (DUNDEE'S ART
GALLERIES AND MUSEUMS): 1973–884–2

The Manchester-based A. & S. Henry & Co. opened a branch in Dundee in 1858 to deal with the expanding jute industry. Factories were later established across the city to manufacture and print cotton and jute sacks and bags. This sample sack was produced for G.B. Ollivant Ltd, part of the United Africa group of Unilever. It traded African agricultural products for manufactured goods and provisions such as salt. It depicts the company's trademark colour for Dendritic Finest salt: an antelope licking salt.

↗ **Dundee Harbour and Docks, including the Royal Arch, photographed by Alexander Wilson**

Dundee, 1880s

Taken by the Dundee-based amateur photographer Alexander Wilson (a jute mill supervisor for over 20 years), this photograph shows the Royal Arch, constructed in 1848 within the city's harbour. It replaced a wooden arch erected to mark the visit of Queen Victoria and Prince Albert in 1844. The new stone arch was designed by John Thomas Rochead, designer of the Wallace Monument near Stirling. It was demolished in 1964 to reclaim land for the new Tay Road Bridge.

→ **Model of the *Lawhill*, by an amateur modelmaker**

Wood, paint
DUNDEE CITY COUNCIL (DUNDEE'S ART
GALLERIES AND MUSEUMS): 2012–64–1

The *Lawhill* was built in the Dundee yard of the Caledon Shipbuilding and Engineering Company for Captain Charles Barrie. A steel-hulled, 'bald headed' (without royal sails over the top-gallant sails) barque, it was designed specifically for the jute industry and was the sister ship to the *Juteopolis* of 1891. The *Lawhill* was launched in the following year, but made only two voyages carrying jute before the business became unprofitable, and it shifted to other cargoes. After an active career of 56 years it was broken up in 1959.

Shipbuilding and Maritime Trade

With its focus on innovative design and engineering excellence, the Clyde became the greatest shipbuilding river in the world in the late nineteenth century. Stunningly beautiful Atlantic liners, mighty battleships, highly technical specialist ships and thousands of cheap cargo tramps were produced there. Dundee, Leith and Aberdeen were also important centres of shipbuilding alongside the Clyde, during a period of dominance from 1850 to 1950. Scots played a pivotal role in the development of maritime trade, including the formation of the Cunard Line and many other shipping companies.

At its height in the early twentieth century the Scottish shipbuilding industry produced one fifth of the world's ships. This success was built on a combination of engineering excellence and entrepreneurial spirit that enabled steamship technology to develop at an astonishing rate on the Clyde. One of the key men driving this development was Robert Napier, whose devotion to quality created powerful and reliable marine engines that he marketed with considerable flair. When Samuel Cunard came to Britain in 1838 to order ships for his transatlantic passenger service it was Napier who won the contract. On the back of this success he established a shipyard at Govan, which became an important training ground for future engineers and shipbuilders. Napier concentrated on building warships and passenger liners. These were the most complex and lucrative types of contract, and a number of other yards followed the same model, including Fairfield in Govan, John Brown's at Clydebank and Scotts of Greenock. Some yards specialized in sailing ships or dredgers, while others churned out hundreds of cargo ships.

Shipyards on the east coast also earned a name for themselves. The Aberdeen yards of Alexander Hall & Co. and Duthie were renowned for building fast sailing ships and developed the 'Aberdeen bow' that epitomized the era of the clipper ship. In Dundee the shipyards built robust ships for the whaling industry that also made them ideal for polar exploration, as is seen in Captain Robert Falcon Scott's *Discovery*.

Design innovation gave Scottish shipbuilders their edge, with new developments in scientific research being rapidly adopted for practical shipbuilding. In 1883 the University of Glasgow established the world's first chair of naval architecture and Denny Brothers in Dumbarton built the first commercial ship model testing tank. The aesthetics of ships also benefited from the vibrant culture of artistic creativity in Scotland. Architects such as James Miller were commissioned to design liners such as the *Lusitania* and the interior designers Wylie & Lochhead fitted out hundreds of ships.

Design was very much a collaboration between shipbuilders and shipowners. Shipping companies worked closely with naval architects to get the best ships to carry the right cargo at the right speed and which looked the part, especially for passenger ships seeking to attract customers. The many Scottish firms such as the Ben Line, William Burrell and Son and the Aberdeen Line operated trade routes throughout the world and ensured a steady flow of orders for the shipyards.

The Great Depression in the 1930s threatened Scottish shipping and shipbuilding, but the maiden voyage of the *Queen Mary* ocean liner in 1936 offered new hope as a symbol of elegance and a supreme example of Clyde-built excellence. However, in the 1960s and 1970s shipping changed beyond all recognition. Commercial flights did away with the need for liners, and cargo was carried in massive supertankers and container ships. Scottish shipping companies could not keep pace and the shipbuilders lacked the space and competitiveness to tap into these new markets. Within 20 years a world-beating industry had virtually disappeared. But the construction of the Queen Elizabeth-class aircraft carriers at Rosyth in the early twenty-first century shows that quality and innovation are still very much alive in the Scottish shipbuilding industry. MARTIN BELLAMY

→ **Design for the engines of the *Palermo*, by David Kirkaldy for Robert Napier**

Glasgow, 1841
Ink and watercolour on paper
GLASGOW MUSEUMS AND LIBRARIES
COLLECTIONS: 1913.10.B

These engines produced by Robert Napier were specially designed for marine use. Instead of being located above the pistons, the beams were placed low down at the side to produce a compact and powerful engine. These engines were fitted into the wooden hull of the *Palermo*, built in Greenock. The engineering drawings produced by Napier's chief draughtsman, David Kirkaldy, were so beautiful that some were exhibited at the Royal Academy, London.

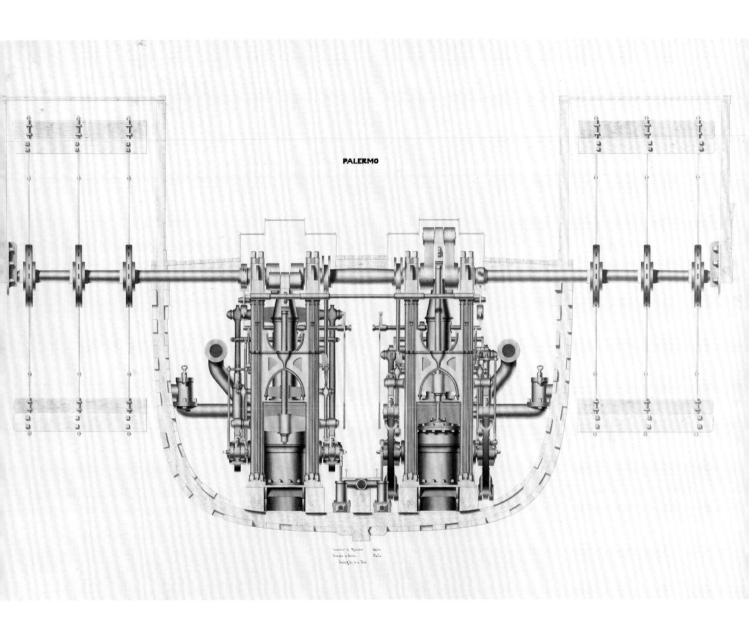

PALERMO

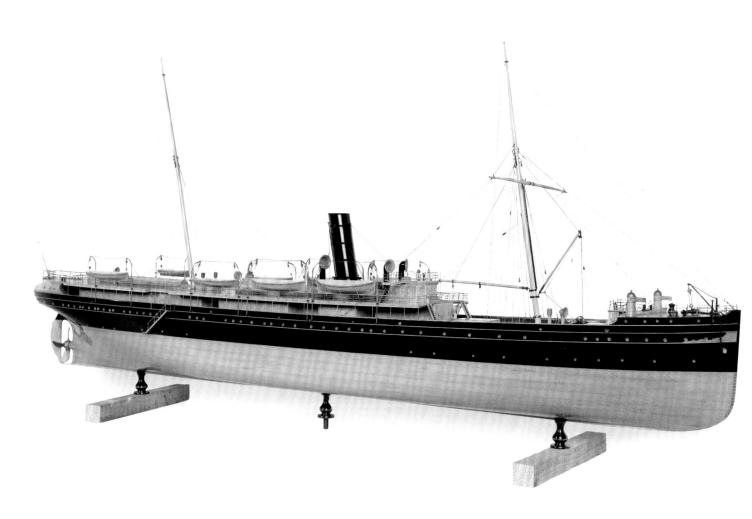

**↑ Model of the *Saikio Maru*,
steamship built in 1888 by the
London and Glasgow Shipbuilding
Co. for Nippon Yusen Kaisha, Japan**

Glasgow, *c.*1888
Wood, metal
GLASGOW MUSEUMS AND LIBRARIES
COLLECTIONS: T.1957.11.A

Scottish shipbuilding was regarded as
the best in the world, and Scots were
highly influential in developing Japanese
shipping and shipbuilding. Many Japanese
students studied on the Clyde and Scottish
expertise and finance helped to establish
Japanese yards and companies. *Saikio
Maru* was one of six ships ordered in
Glasgow in 1887 by the shipping company
Nippon Yusen Kaisha to train Japanese
engineers on site in the process of ordering and building ships.

→ **Shipping advertisements from *Scotland's Industrial Souvenir*, vol. 2, edited by Alan J. Woodward**

Published by Bemrose and Sons Ltd in Derby and London, 1905
Printed paper
HISTORIC ENVIRONMENT
SCOTLAND: DP144389

The Scottish contribution to international shipping was immense. As well as homegrown ventures such as the Aberdeen Line, Scots played an important role in establishing and running companies such as the Japanese Nippon Yusen Kaisha and the British–North American Cunard Line. *Scotland's Industrial Souvenir* was a lavish trade catalogue used to advertise Scotland's industrial might to the world.

↙ **Model of the *Stornoway*, clipper ship built in 1850 by Alexander Hall & Co., model made by James Henderson**

Aberdeen, 1959
Wood, metal and cord
ABERDEEN ART GALLERY &
MUSEUMS COLLECTIONS:
ABDMS003125

Aberdeen became a centre for the construction of fast sailing ships in the mid-19th century. The raking 'Aberdeen bow' improved speed and performance by creating a very slender hull shape that cut through the water. The design was first developed in Aberdeen but was quickly adopted as a standard feature of all clipper ships. The *Stornoway* was built for the Scottish trading company Jardine Matheson as a tea clipper.

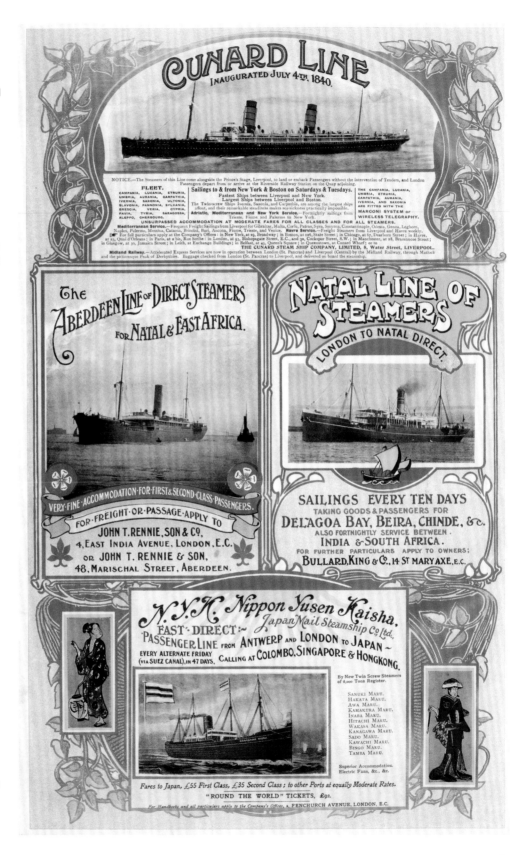

Scots and India

From the inception of the British East India Company (EIC) onwards into the twentieth century, thousands of Scottish men and women travelled to India. There they lived and worked as administrators, soldiers, merchants, scientists, educators, surveyors, architects and artists.

Though the EIC's monopoly (1600–1813) effectively prevented any nationalized Scottish organizations from trading with the East Indies, individual Scots in the Company's service nevertheless worked to their countrymen's advantage. Irrespective of the actual ratio of Scots engaged in the India trade to their English, Welsh and Irish counterparts, the expansion of Scottish influence in India – and the influence of India on Scotland – was owed in part to savvy networking.

Over the eighteenth century the extraordinary wealth of returning Scottish 'nabobs' (Company servants who had amassed fortunes in India) changed the social, cultural and political landscape of Scotland. Beyond building vast estates and houses filled with exotic treasures, their extensive finances contributed to the integration of Scotland's upper classes into London's elite circles of imperial power.

Into the nineteenth century industries built on trade with India transformed Scotland into a manufacturing powerhouse:

from the jute industry of Dundee to Turkey Red production in the Vale of Leven. While Scotland's universities promoted the study and exchange of Indian culture – the UK's first Indian Students Association was founded in Edinburgh in 1875 – Scottish designers appropriated Indian motifs so effectively that in some cases the patterns became better known by their Scottish connections than by their Indian origins (see pp. 50–51).

In India itself, Scottish entrepreneurs built some of the world's largest shipping companies, including the legendary British India line. Scottish planters and traders pioneered some of India's earliest tea plantations and jute mills in Calcutta (Kolkata). Scottish architects such as George Wittet designed such iconic monuments as the Gateway of India, Bombay (Mumbai), while Scottish missionaries established some of the country's leading educational institutions, including the Scottish Church College in Calcutta and Elphinstone College in Bombay (named after the Scot Mountstuart Elphinstone, Governor from 1819 to 1827).

Today some scholars argue that it was partly the extension of local Scottish networks into India, and the building of close-knit communities around the Scottish experience there, that led to regenerated ideas of a Scottish national identity. Thus, while generations of Scots undoubtedly left their mark on India's past, India would change Scotland's future. AVALON FOTHERINGHAM

→ **Cashmere cap**

Ludhiana, Punjab, c.1855
Embroidered wool
V&A: 8078 (IS)

The 1855 acquisition note for this cap reads simply 'Cashmere Cap – Scotch Style'. Apparently modelled on a Glengarry bonnet, it is embroidered with Kashmir shawl motifs. Whether this modified Glengarry was intended as a tourist novelty or for local use is uncertain; Scottish regiments had long been deployed across India, and it is possible that such caps became popular in the region after Captain Colin Mackenzie instituted the Glengarry as the uniform cap of the Ludhiana Sikh Regiment in 1848.

→ Fabric sample made by John Orr Ewing and Co.

Dumbarton, *c*.1860–80
Dyed and printed cotton
Given by the Society of Dyers & Colourists
V&A: T.133:20–1976

Between the late 18th and mid-20th centuries the Turkey Red industry of the Glasgow region produced millions of lengths of bright-red alizarin-dyed cloth for export abroad. India became one of the primary consumers of Scottish Turkey Red textiles, and surviving pattern swatches attest to the efforts of the industry to appeal to Indian tastes. Manufacturers created an extensive range of patterns imitating Indian motifs and techniques in graphic print, such as this piece featuring a Kashmir shawl-style design.

← **Throne chair,**
designed by Robert Home

Lucknow, Awadh, c.1820
Wood with gilt brass and gilt gesso, later
velvet upholstery
Given by the 5th Earl Amherst of Arracan
V&A: IS.6–1991

In 1790, at the age of 38, the Scottish artist
Robert Home sailed for India. Twenty-four
years later, having built an impressive
reputation as a painter, Home was invited to
Lucknow to serve as court artist to Nawab
Ghazi-ud-din Haidar of Oudh (Awadh). In
this role Home designed many of the court's
royal trappings, integrating both Mughal and
European aesthetics. This chair exemplifies
this integration: its form is European, while
it features the twin-fish and punch dagger
insignia of Awadh.

→ *Huqqa*, **designed by Hamilton & Co.**

Kolkata, West Bengal, c.1867
Silver and blackened zinc alloy overlaid with
silver (*bidri*-ware)
V&A: 2510:1, 2 & 3 (IS)

Robert Hamilton of Edinburgh first
established his silver business in Calcutta
(Kolkata) in 1808. Taking on partners in 1811,
Hamilton & Co. thrived, opening branches
in Delhi, Simla and Bombay (Mumbai). The
company specialized in fine silver products
in a hybrid of Indian and British tastes for the
upper classes of both spheres. This show-
piece *huqqa,* or smoking pipe, was exhibited
by the company at the Paris Exposition
Universelle (International Exhibition) of
1867. By the time it closed in 1973, Hamilton
& Co. had become a Calcutta institution.

Scottish Export Ceramics

In the late nineteenth century, at a time when the craze for Chinese blue-and-white porcelain was at its pinnacle in Britain, Scotland was one of the major European exporters of household ceramics to Asia. Producing a diversity of exotic patterns not previously seen in Britain, with pattern names printed in foreign scripts, Scottish potteries made use of clever marketing and improvements in marine transport to ensure the worldwide success of their export goods.

J. & M.P. Bell & Co. Ltd and R. Cochran & Co. were two of the largest and best-known potteries in Glasgow. They produced utilitarian and decorative wares for local and foreign markets, and both received recognition at international exhibitions. R. Cochran & Co. (later known as the Britannia Pottery) had originally started out in 1777 as the Verreville glassworks, making crystal for domestic and North American markets before expanding into the production of durable and affordable ceramics with similarly transatlantic reach. Bell's was of more recent origins, founded in 1842 and particularly popular among western Scottish middle classes for its hand-painted porcelain tea and dessert services.

Both companies reached an apogee in the last decades of the nineteenth century. Cochran & Co. continued to design for fast-growing markets in North America (including Canada), while Bell's specialized in South-East Asia, exporting its wares on steamships running between Glasgow and Rangoon (Yangon). Bell's designed ceramics specifically for these South-East Asian markets. Vessel shapes included rice dishes and large platters used for communal dining in this part of the Muslim world. Patterns featured popular South-East Asian fruits and birds or motifs associated with Islam. Numerous patterns were named after local place names, while some pattern names were printed in Malay on the reverse. Over 37 new patterns were registered from 1887 to 1906, most of them created using two-colour transfer-printing.

The success of both potteries was due to a combination of marketing acumen and entrepreneurship, an appreciation of a particular cultural context, and the ability to design products that suited specific consumers' needs and tastes. SAU FONG CHAN

→ **Plate, 'China' pattern, by R. Cochran & Co.**

Glasgow, c.1880–90
Lead-glazed earthenware, transfer-printed in underglaze purple
V&A: C.92–2007

This plate is decorated with a scene from a Chinese drama, *Romance of the West Chamber*. The pattern was directly copied from a Chinese original. A Kangxi period (1662–1722) porcelain plate with the same scene was exhibited at the Bethnal Green Museum, London, in 1876, during the period when the collecting of Chinese blue-and-white porcelain was fashionable. That earlier plate is now held by the British Museum, London.

← **Plate, 'Buah Nanas' pattern, by J. & M.P. Bell & Co. Ltd**

Glasgow, *c.*1888
Lead-glazed earthenware, transfer-printed in underglaze red and blue
V&A: C.85–2007

'Buah Nanas', meaning 'Pineapple' in Malay, was one of a series of new patterns deliberately designed for Malay-speaking Muslim communities. It combines pineapples, the tropical fruit local to South-East Asia, with a crescent moon, the symbol of Islam. Keen to adapt its products to appeal to local markets, Bell's printed the pattern name in Malay, both in Roman script and in *Jawi* (the Malay form of Arabic script), a language that was widely used by South-East Asian traders.

→ **Plate, 'Makassar' pattern, by J. & M.P. Bell & Co. Ltd**

Glasgow, *c.*1890
Lead-glazed earthenware, transfer-printed in underglaze green and red
V&A: C.88–2007

Like most of Bell's export wares, this plate is printed in two colours using a transfer-printing technique. This involved printing an identical design onto tissue papers in a range of colours, and then transferring these onto pottery. Simple variations in design were achieved by reversing the colour scheme. The two-colour transfer-printed pattern was a design innovation introduced by Bell's. 'Makassar' refers to the largest city in South Sulawesi, an important trading centre of eastern Indonesia.

Floorcloth and Linoleum

'I have seen our floorcloth and linoleum beyond the first cataract of the Nile; and I have seen it in the mosques of Constantinople.' (Michael Baker Nairn, *c.*1900)

Attractive, hard-wearing and affordable, linoleum was a revolutionary product when it was invented by the Englishman Frederick Walton in 1863. Kirkcaldy became one of the most important centres for its design, manufacture and export. There, firms such as Michael Nairn & Co. and Barry, Ostlere and Shepherd designed and produced linoleum for settings ranging from the shop floor of Les Grands Magasins du Louvre in Paris to the public rooms of the *Aquitania* ocean liner.

In 1848 Michael Nairn opened a factory in Kirkcaldy to produce floorcloth, a waterproof floor covering made from canvas heavily treated with oil, and used in bathrooms and hallways from the eighteenth century. Although mocked locally as 'Nairn's Folly', the Kirkcaldy factory was ideally located to produce floorcloth (and later linoleum) because of a long-established local weaving industry and ready access to the necessary raw materials (flax, jute and oil) through its harbour. Nairn defied expectations with his display at the 1862 London International Exhibition, with an *Art Journal* critic stating that 'the Scottish firm is without any

real rival whatever … floorcloth can now be produced with all the richness … of a velvet-pile carpet'.

As soon as Walton's patent expired in 1877, Nairn's began producing linoleum. Far superior to floorcloth because of its thickness, durability and greater water resistance, linoleum was produced by mixing oxidized linseed oil with ground cork dust, rosin, gum and pigments to create a 'cement'. This was pressed between heavy rollers onto a canvas backing, which was then hung to dry and printed with decorative designs. The variety of designs available, often imitating far more expensive floor coverings such as granite, moiré, marble and carpet, appealed to a wide range of consumers. Linoleum flooded the market, remaining the world's most popular floor covering for the next 100 years. The Kirkcaldy linoleum companies employed a network of export agents and opened additional factories in Britain and internationally to meet demand and avoid tariffs.

Although synthetic vinyl products largely replaced linoleum from the 1960s, linoleum's popularity has increased in recent years because of its environmental credentials. Forbo-Nairn in Kirkcaldy is now the only factory in the UK still designing and manufacturing linoleum, with its Marmoleum Modular range made from 97 per cent natural raw materials. MEREDITH MORE

← **'Linoleum Nairn', poster, printed by Banks & Co.**

Edinburgh, *c.*1890
Printed paper
KIRKCALDY GALLERIES (FIFE CULTURAL TRUST, ON BEHALF OF FIFE COUNCIL), FIFER:2013.8

This poster proudly illustrates the medals won by Nairn's at International Exhibitions. These were crucially important events for attracting publicity and new customers abroad. Made for the French market, the poster employs some artistic licence in the representation of the company's factories, showing them all on one site, projecting the impression that Nairn's was a large, established outfit.

→ Sample of floorcloth
for a national hospital

Kirkcaldy, *c.*1880
Floorcloth
KIRKCALDY GALLERIES (FIFE CULTURAL
TRUST, ON BEHALF OF FIFE COUNCIL),
FIFER:2017.5

Floorcloth and linoleum were hard-wearing,
comfortable and easy to clean, which made
them ideally suited to use in public buildings
such as hospitals, schools, nurseries, government offices, hotels and banks, where, over the
course of the 19th century, safety and hygiene
were considered increasingly important. This
sample of floorcloth was designed for use in a
hospital, with a pattern imitating mosaic tiles.

↘ Sample of inlaid linoleum,
by Barry, Ostlere and Shepherd

Kirkcaldy, *c.*1900
Linoleum
KIRKCALDY GALLERIES (FIFE CULTURAL
TRUST, ON BEHALF OF FIFE COUNCIL),
FIFER:2017.16

Although the flat base colour of linoleum did
not wear, its printed decoration was not so
long-lasting. To remedy this, Walton invented a
machine for inlaid linoleum that automatically
stitched together sheets of different colours to
create geometric designs. Barry, Ostlere and
Shepherd secured the licence to use Walton's
machine and later made major improvements
to it. Constantly developing new designs in
order to widen market appeal, by 1907 the
company was advertising inlaid designs with
carpet, tile or wood effects.

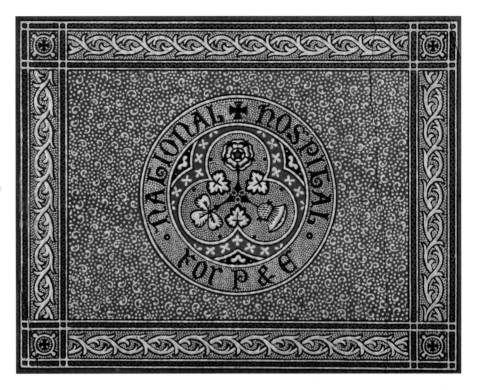

Alexander 'Greek' Thomson

In the nineteenth century the developing industrial and commercial success of Scotland led to the expansion of its cities. No more so was this the case than in Glasgow, which became one of the industrial powerhouses of the British Empire. The city's prosperity and growth created the conditions in which architecture flourished, the most original and visionary examples of which were by Alexander 'Greek' Thomson (1817–75), who was born in Balfron in Stirlingshire and who lived and worked in Glasgow throughout his life.

Nicknamed 'Greek' for his interest in ancient and particularly Grecian architectural forms and motifs, Thomson responded in an original way to every building type that the modernizing city required, designing urban terraces and tenements, warehouses and office buildings, churches and villas. Irrespective of building type, Thomson's architecture is distinguished by its rich historic eclecticism, brought into harmony by his genius with proportion and rhythm.

Wider radical developments of the period were well suited to Thomson's design individuality. In 1843 the Disruption, a schism in the national Church of Scotland that created the Free Church of Scotland, brought a wave of new church building. Thomson's design for Caledonia Road Church, with its massive podium surmounted by a temple front, offset with a severe steeple to one side, was as forceful in its design as the historical events that brought about its commissioning. The changing city was reflected too in the commissioning of villas, such as Holmwood House (1857–58 and c.1865), designed by Thomson for the mill owner James Couper. Its interior is theatrical in its polychromatic decoration, including friezes reproducing scenes from Homer's *Iliad*.

Later in his career Thomson began to experiment with industrial materials, especially in his commercial buildings. His Egyptian Halls in Union Street (1870–72), built using cast iron and stone, features on the top floor a continuous glazed screen set behind columns with Egyptian-style lotus-flower capitals. And in his 1868 (unbuilt) proposals for new tenement housing in the oldest part of Glasgow around the High Street, his designs included innovations in ventilation and glazing that anticipated future ideas of sustainability in architecture. PHILIP LONG

↑ **Capital from the interior of St Vincent Street Church, by Alexander 'Greek' Thomson**

Glasgow, c.1859

Thomson took great care over the design of his interiors, paying as much attention to their detail and architectural arrangement as to his external designs. For the interior of the St Vincent Street Church, Thomson worked with the Glaswegian artist and designer Daniel Cottier, whose art-furnishing business had branches in Edinburgh, Glasgow and London, and then later in New York and Australia.

→ Design for Caledonia Road Church, elevation to Cathcart Road, showing front and side of church with pitched roof campanile, by Alexander 'Greek' Thomson

Glasgow, c.1856–57
Pen and ink with grey wash on paper
GLASGOW MUSEUMS AND LIBRARIES
COLLECTIONS, THE MITCHELL LIBRARY,
SPECIAL COLLECTIONS: 898034

Thomson designed four churches, of which Caledonia Road was the first, for the United Presbyterian Church. He proposed an alternative model to the prevailing Gothic taste in church architecture: the Greek temple, but in a thoroughly modernized form suited to the type of worship for which it was designed. Thomson's drawing shows the long elevation of this church, on the Cathcart Road side. The building is now an isolated ruin, following a fire in 1965.

↘ Holmwood House, designed by Alexander 'Greek' Thomson, plate LXVIII from *Villa and Cottage Architecture*

Published in London and Glasgow by Blackie & Son, 1868
Printed book, with engraved illustrations
V&A: NATIONAL ART LIBRARY,
38041800930984

From early on in his career Thomson received commissions for villas from Glasgow merchants and industrialists who were moving out of the city. His early villa designs explored a variety of styles; from the mid-1850s he adopted the Grecian emphasis of his urban projects, but combined this with asymmetry to create a completely new style. Holmwood House is acknowledged as Thomson's masterpiece of villa architecture, in which he designed every single element of its decoration, inside as well as out.

Exhibitions, Aestheticism and Exports: The 'London Brethren'

From the late 1860s a generation of talented Scottish designers, mainly active in London, pioneered Aestheticism, a literary and artistic movement that emphasized visual and sensual qualities. They included Bruce J. Talbert (1838–81), John Moyr Smith (1839–1912) and the entrepreneur and art dealer Daniel Cottier (1838–91). Their activities helped to promote Aestheticism in Britain as well as in Europe, the USA and Australia.

Talbert was born in Dundee, where he was apprenticed to a woodcarver and an architect, and moved to Glasgow in about 1856. Cottier and Moyr Smith were born in Glasgow; Cottier trained as a stained-glass designer and in 1864 established a stained glass and decorating business. Moyr Smith trained as an architect, probably meeting Cottier through the Glasgow Architectural Society, which brought them into contact with one of Scotland's most original architects, Alexander 'Greek' Thomson (see pp. 76–77). In the 1860s the work of Cottier, Moyr Smith and Talbert showed the influence of Thomson's architecture and polychromatic interiors, which drew on ancient Greek, Egyptian and Assyrian sources. The young designers soon emigrated, becoming what Thomson referred to as the 'London brethren'.

In 1867–68 Talbert published *Gothic Forms Applied to Furniture, Metal Work and Decoration for Domestic Purposes*. The attractive 'Modern Gothic' designs revealed Talbert's growing interest in Japanese art and influenced furniture designers and makers for many years, in Britain and in the USA, where they were later published. Talbert's designs also achieved wide exposure through international exhibitions; at the Paris Exposition Universelle in 1878 the cabinetmaker Jackson & Graham displayed the 'Juno' cabinet, which was awarded the Grand Prix d'Honneur for the British Section and purchased by the Khedive of Egypt (and which is now in the collection of the V&A). In the 1870s Talbert designed furniture, stained glass, metalwork, textiles, carpets and wallpapers for a number of leading firms. Following his premature death, from chronic alcoholism, one obituarist claimed Talbert was 'probably the most original and remarkable of furniture designers which this aesthetic age has produced'.

Cottier & Co. supplied interiors and stained glass in the Aesthetic taste for private and public commissions throughout Britain, diversifying into furniture manufacture and ceramic

→ **Chair, made by Cottier & Co.**

London, *c.*1870–75
Mahogany, ebonized, painted and gilded, with replacement upholstery
V&A: W.89–1982

Cottier's debt to Alexander 'Greek' Thomson, with whom he collaborated in Glasgow, is evident in the design of this chair, the form and surface decoration of which are derived from Greek and Egyptian prototypes. Moyr Smith also incorporated elements of Thomson's architecture into some of his furniture designs. This chair probably formed part of a suite that was made for an unidentified domestic interior scheme undertaken by Cottier & Co. in the 1870s.

decoration to cater to growing public demand. This work reflected the style practised by Thomson, which was inspired by Greek and other ancient cultures, as well as the influence of William Morris (1834–96) and his circle, and the 'Anglo-Japanese' furniture devised by the architect–designer E.W. Godwin (1833–81). In 1873 Cottier travelled to New York to establish a branch of his firm, and a Sydney branch, Lyon, Cottier & Co., opened with a business partner. Cottier also developed an art dealing business, championing the work of contemporary Dutch, French and American artists. He lived increasingly in the USA, where his firm had many wealthy clients, and it is credited with introducing and promoting the Aesthetic style there and in Australia.

In London, Moyr Smith originally worked in the studio of Christopher Dresser (1834–1904; see pp. 82–85), and as an independent designer supplied designs for furniture, ceramics and metalwork to a number of manufacturers, including series of pictorial tiles for Minton. A gifted draughtsman, he enjoyed success as an illustrator, many of his chromolithographed illustrations appearing in children's books in Britain and the USA; he also edited a magazine, *Decoration*. In the late 1870s Moyr Smith worked on the lavish interiors of the new Holloway Sanatorium in Virginia Water, Surrey, for which Cottier & Co. made stained glass, indicating the connections that existed among the 'London brethren'. MAX DONNELLY

↗ **Tiles, designed by John Moyr Smith and made by Minton's China Works**

Stoke-on-Trent, *c*.1874
Earthenware, dust-pressed, with transfer-printed decoration
Mrs G.M. Spear Bequest
V&A: C.15 TO J–1971

Moyr Smith was a prolific designer of tiles for Minton. Some of his designs were used to decorate objects at Minton's Art Pottery Studio in London, whereas tiles such as these, from the 'Shakespeare' series, were mass produced in Stoke-on-Trent. Tiles from these series were incorporated into fireplaces and also used to embellish furniture and other items for the Aesthetic home, such as jardinières (plant containers), stoves and trivets.

↓ Cabinet, designed by Bruce J. Talbert and made by Holland & Sons

London, 1867
Walnut with other woods, part gilded, with electrotype panel (copper gilt), *champlevé* enamel roundels, silvered and enamelled copper alloy, glass and silk velvet
Given by Paul F. Brandt
V&A: CIRC.286–1955

This cabinet was one of a number of items of furniture designed by Talbert for display at the 1867 Exposition Universelle (International Exhibition) in Paris, where it formed part of a prize-winning ensemble. Its rich materials and ornamentation lent it a sensuous quality in tune with Aestheticism, while a literary theme was introduced by an electrotype panel depicting the story of the Sleeping Beauty from Alfred, Lord Tennyson's poem, *The Day-Dream* (1842).

Christopher Dresser: Design Reform and Industry

In the early nineteenth century, as Britain continued to industrialize, many became aware that well-designed products gave manufacturers an edge in the face of increasing global competition. The British government attempted to reform the training of designers for industry by opening Government Schools of Design from 1837. One star pupil, Christopher Dresser (1834–1904), became Britain's first independent industrial designer. Dresser's inventive designs, for a multitude of manufacturers from Europe to the USA, earned him international recognition.

Dresser was born in Glasgow, where his father, an English excise officer, had been posted. In 1847, aged just thirteen, he entered the Government School of Design in London, where his precocious talent blossomed over the next seven years. As part of his training Dresser learned to analyse plant specimens, developing a deep interest in botany. He supplied a plate depicting geometrically arranged flowers for *The Grammar of Ornament* (1856), an influential design manual by his mentor Owen Jones (1809–74), and Dresser's botanical researches were acknowledged in 1860 when he was awarded a doctorate from the University of Jena in Germany. In the 1860s Dr Dresser, as he advertised himself, established a reputation as a commercial designer, running a large London studio.

As a designer, Dresser had several key strengths: an ability to understand the properties of materials and the processes of production, and skill in adapting his designs and aesthetic ideas to them. He forged a new style based on his botanical knowledge and a diverse range of historic and international sources, including Egyptian, Greek and Gothic art as well as the arts of Asia and – unusually for the time – Peru. Early clients included leading firms, such as the ceramic manufacturer Minton in Stoke-on-Trent, and the cast-iron producer, Coalbrookdale Co., Shropshire. In time, Dresser's studio supplied designs to scores of businesses across Britain, western Europe and the USA, for everything from textiles, wallpapers, carpets, linoleum and lace to furniture, metalwork, ceramics, glass, stained glass and bookbindings. Dresser also devised complete interior schemes.

A turning point occurred when Dresser became the first European designer to visit Japan, where he studied arts and industries for four months from 1876 to 1877. He greatly admired the simplicity of Japanese objects and on his return developed the groundbreaking designs for metalwork, ceramics and glass on which much of his subsequent reputation rests. In order to realize these designs Dresser worked closely with innovative and experimental manufacturers such as the Linthorpe Art Pottery, Middlesbrough, which he helped to establish in 1879. The resulting objects emphasized the qualities of particular materials and methods of manufacture, and many still appear surprisingly modern in contrast with much Victorian design. Some of these products were retailed in the showroom in New Bond Street, London, of the Art Furnishers' Alliance, a short-lived venture of which Dresser acted as art adviser from 1881 to 1883.

Dresser tirelessly promoted his theories through lectures, articles and books, and further extended his influence by acting as a consultant and adviser for governments, museums, manufacturers and retailers, and as a juror and critic at international exhibitions in Britain, Europe and the USA. From the mid-1870s he began to stipulate that manufacturers put his name on his designs, sometimes in the form of a facsimile signature. This 'branding', as it would be called today, reassured consumers that they were buying well-designed products, helping to raise Dresser's profile and elevate the status of the professional industrial designer. MAX DONNELLY

→ **Vase, 'Clutha' glass, designed by Christopher Dresser, made by James Couper & Sons**

Glasgow, c.1890
Glass, streaked and bubbled with silver flecks
V&A: C.52–1972

This vase is from a range retailed under the name 'Clutha', the ancient name of the River Clyde in Glasgow, where it was made. Dresser's glass designs drew on ancient Roman and Middle Eastern forms, while the manufacturing process, inspired by the work of Japanese craftsmen, exploited the accidental effects produced by bubbles and random streaks. 'Clutha' glass was retailed through Liberty & Co. in London and the etched mark on the underside states it was 'DESIGNED BY C.D.'

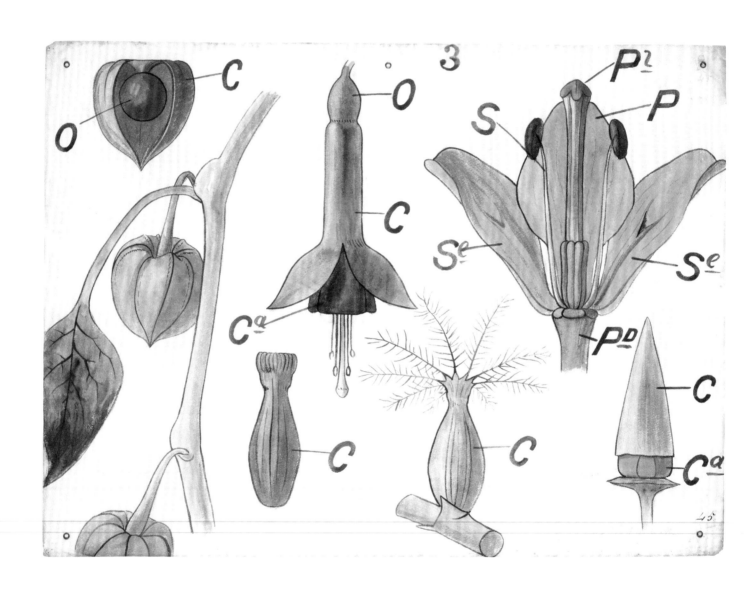

↑ Diagram, by Christopher Dresser

London, *c.*1855
Watercolour and body-colour on paper
drawing, laid on canvas
V&A: 3968

Beginning his career in botany and teaching,
Dresser was appointed as a lecturer in botany
at the Government School of Design in London
in 1854. Diagrams such as this, made to
illustrate lectures, reveal his fascination with
plant structure and growth. Dresser believed
that by understanding and assimilating the
basic patterns upon which natural forms were
constructed, it was possible to create designs
suitable for industrial production.

→ Claret jug, designed by Christopher Dresser, mounts made by Stephen Smith & Sons Ltd

London, 1879–80
Glass and silver
V&A: CIRC.416–1967

Dresser's ability to extrude the abstract qualities of design from a range of cultural sources is evident in this jug. The broad base is loosely modelled on the form of an Islamic or Chinese vase, while the handle is based on that of a Japanese vessel. Dresser detected 'a simplicity of execution, and a boldness of design' in Japanese metalwork, and even the monogram engraved on the lid resembles a Japanese *mon* or family emblem.

↘ Teapot, designed by Christopher Dresser, made by James Dixon & Sons

Sheffield, *c.*1879
Electroplated nickel silver and ebony
Purchased with generous support of the National Heritage Memorial Fund, Art Fund, the American Friends of the V&A and an anonymous donor, the Friends of the V&A, the J. Paul Getty Jr. Charitable Trust and a private consortium led by John S.M. Scott
V&A: M.4–2006

This astonishing teapot, made shortly after Dresser's return from Japan, was described by its manufacturer as 'English Japanese' in style. With its abstracted forms and undecorated surfaces it counts among the most radical of Dresser's designs. Dresser sold about 37 designs to Dixon's between 1879 and 1882, although not all were put into production and only one other example of this teapot is known. The underside is marked with Dresser's facsimile signature.

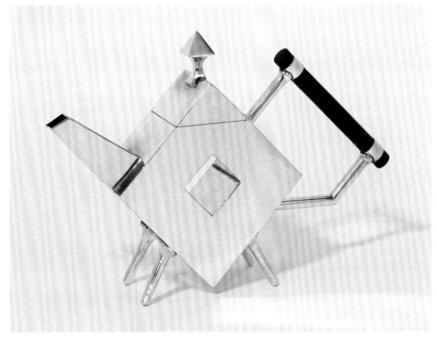

Industrialization and Urban Design in Glasgow

With the onset of the Industrial Revolution, Scotland rapidly urbanized. From 1841 to 1911 the population of the city of Glasgow nearly trebled in size to 784,000, and during this time two-thirds of the city's inhabitants lived in one- or two-room houses. The scale of overcrowding brought serious health, sanitary and social problems, and policies and programmes of improvement had to be put in place to alleviate the appalling living conditions.

There were several cholera outbreaks and typhoid epidemics in Glasgow from the 1830s and one report spoke of the 'large amounts of filth, crime, misery and disease' in the city. From about the 1860s, however, a civic spirit took hold in the municipal authorities, who began to tackle this urban crisis head-on. In 1859 Glasgow Corporation completed the project to pipe fresh water from Loch Katrine to the city, in 1862 a policing system to control numbers in individual houses – 'ticketing' – was introduced, in 1867 a municipal gas supply was set up and in 1869 the first municipal fever hospital was opened.

Many other forward-looking policies were put in place, including the institution in 1866 of the Glasgow City Improvement Trust. This body was set up by an Act of Parliament with 'the right to alter and reconstruct the more densely built areas of the city'. Thus, the first big slum clearance of Glasgow's history began. The overcrowded and insanitary closes leading off Glasgow's original medieval High Street were cleared and sandstone tenements built. The trustees commissioned the photographer Thomas Annan to record the buildings in the old streets and closes in 1868–71 before they were demolished. The work of replacing the slums took some 40 years, with many areas remaining gap sites for long periods.

It was from the 1890s onwards that the monumental red sandstone Glasgow Improvement tenements, still prominent today, began to take shape. They include many buildings on the High Street and Albion Street, and the Hope Street tenements designed by the architects Honeyman, Keppie and Mackintosh. These new improved tenements replaced the former squalid conditions with more and larger rooms per dwelling, running water and inside toilets. JOHNNY RODGER

↑ **Photograph of Close No. 11, Bridgegate, Glasgow, from** *The Old Streets and Closes of Glasgow* **(1900), by an unknown photographer**

Glasgow, 1897
Photogravure
V&A: 187–1976

The Old Streets and Closes of Glasgow (1868–71), containing Thomas Annan's photographs, was republished in 1900 by MacLehose, after Annan's death. More views in a similar style were added, including this photograph representing one of the long, dark, narrow closes that formerly led off the city's main streets to houses deep in the plots. In contrast, the new tenements were built as perimeter blocks that faced and had entrances directly onto those main streets.

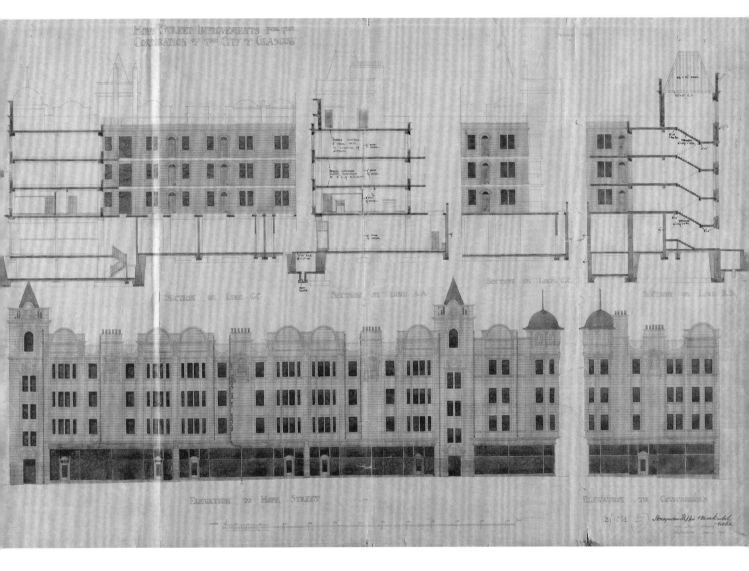

↑ Design for improvements to tenements on Hope Street, Glasgow, by Honeyman, Keppie and Mackintosh

Glasgow, 1906
Photomechanical reproduction and wash, with ink inscriptions
GLASGOW MUSEUMS AND LIBRARIES
COLLECTIONS: B4/12/2/1234

These elevations and sections for a bold red sandstone tenement running to the north-west corner of Hope Street were designed for the Glasgow City Improvement Department (formerly Trust) as part of a street-widening project. Railed access galleries to the rear and an open flat roof with a drying area and wash houses would bring light and fresh air to improve the inhabitants' health and sanitary conditions. Baroque carvings, pediments and a parapet presented a palatial street frontage.

Patrick Geddes:
Three Drawings Towards a Poetics of the City

'Town plans are no mere diagrams, they are a system of hiero-glyphics in which man has written the history of civilisation, and the more tangled their apparent confusion, the more we may be rewarded in deciphering it.'
(Patrick Geddes, *The City in Evolution*, 1915)

Patrick Geddes (1854–1932) was convinced that the city had inscribed in it the knowledge that constitutes civilization. He proposed the citizen survey as a way for people to accumulate this knowledge, via a process of self-determination and participation within the city. He advocated what he called 'conservative surgery' as a form of urban renewal that erased as little inscription as possible, applying this to his work in Edinburgh's Old Town (beginning in 1886) and in India (beginning in 1915).

Geddes, born in Ballater, Aberdeenshire, described himself as a sociologist, was a student of Thomas Henry Huxley, and became a professor of botany at Dundee (1888–1919) and later a professor of sociology at Bombay (Mumbai) in 1919–25. He was one of the founders of the town planning movement in the UK. Geddes was not a designer of cities; he was a designer of ideas about cities. He posited that the city shaped its publics, and the problem was how to understand the relation between cities and societies, and between people and the places they build in order to live well in them. These ideas took the form of an extraordinary collection of lecture diagrams. In the drawing tagged with the head of Medusa (*Evils Organic and Social*), folded into eight card-sized lecture notes, diagrams and keywords – note the neologism 'civicise', to make civic – set out the landmarks of his thought.

Geddes argued through his drawings that the city is the precondition for social and political life, without which representative democracy is not possible. The city gives shape to the public, literally and metaphorically. The multitude of individuals are constituted as a public by the city spaces they inhabit; in this respect his ideas anticipated those of the political theorist Hannah Arendt. His thought is relevant to today's policy debates about well-being in the built environment because he sought to define, through city form, the 'good life'. LORENS HOLM

↑ *Evils Organic and Social* (Diagram depicting aspects of society, social and individual life, and their interrelations), by Patrick Geddes
Pencil and colour pencil on paper
ARCHIVES AND SPECIAL COLLECTIONS, UNIVERSITY OF STRATHCLYDE LIBRARY: T-GED 22/2/18.2

For Geddes, the most fundamental template for social life was geographical; livelihoods, upon which social groups are based, correlate to the landform of the city region. Geddes's city section (top) is based on Edinburgh and the Royal Mile; his valley section (bottom) is based on Dundee in the Tay Valley. The valley section relates social formations to livelihoods to regional resources and their extraction. The letters M W H S P and F stand for miner, woodsman, hunter, shepherd, peasant and fisher.

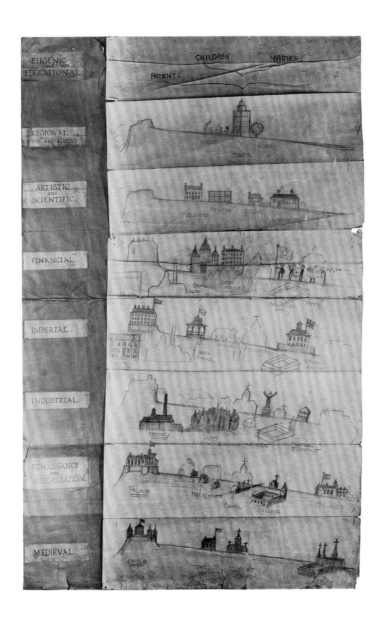

Photograph of original drawing
ARCHIVES AND SPECIAL COLLECTIONS, UNIVERSITY OF STRATHCLYDE LIBRARY: T-GED 22/2/24

This drawing repeats the section of Edinburgh in a quasi-historical sequence of narratives from medieval times to an idyllic present. Each narrative locates public institutions along a line between power and its implementation in the world. In the imperial register, a barracks represents military power, while public life is represented by the bandstand. In the industrial register, the slum or dwelling place of the labourer is positioned between the factory and the grave of the political economist Adam Smith.

↓ *Perspective view of the Mound from Ramsay Garden to Bank Street showing improvements proposed by Patrick Geddes,* by George Shaw Aitken

Edinburgh, 1893
Watercolour and pencil on paper
ARCHIVES AND SPECIAL COLLECTIONS, UNIVERSITY OF STRATHCLYDE LIBRARY: T-GED-22/1/502.1

From 1890 Geddes worked with the architect Stewart Henbest Capper on additions and renovations to Ramsay Lodge, including six new flats, to produce the eclectic turreted and balconied building that appears in the drawing more or less as it exists today. The Ramsay Garden Project was part of a larger programme of refurbishment and selective demolition (which Geddes called 'conservative surgery') to improve tenement housing by bringing light and open playspace into these dense working-class dwellings.

Railway and Bridge Design

One of the great achievements in Victorian Britain was the construction of its railways. A few years after Victoria became monarch in 1837, the line from Berwick-upon-Tweed to Edinburgh was complete. By the turn of the century all of Scotland's cities, most of its towns and many villages were linked, opening up the country to commerce and tourism. On the east coast this involved the design of two of the greatest engineering projects of the nineteenth century, the rail bridges across the Tay and the Forth.

The ambition to build a rail bridge across the Tay, reducing the travel distance between Edinburgh and Dundee and then Aberdeen, had begun in the 1850s. It was a complex design challenge, and construction eventually began in 1873 to the scheme of Thomas Bouch for a single-track crossing. Inspired by the innovative use of cast iron in Joseph Paxton's Crystal Palace in London and using a previously tested method, Bouch specified cast and wrought iron in a lattice-grid form. Brick piers were intended to support this, resting on bedrock, but the latter was found to be at a far greater depth as work on the bridge progressed out into the river. An alternative design was introduced: wrought-iron caissons (watertight chambers) were sunk onto the gravel layer of the riverbed and filled with concrete, upon which rested the piers, now in open-lattice iron to reduce weight.

The Tay Bridge opened in 1878 as the longest bridge in the world, and Queen Victoria crossed it in the following year on her way to Balmoral. Bouch received a knighthood and was made a burgess of Dundee. However, from the moment of the bridge's completion,

→ **Photograph of the original Tay Railway Bridge, Firth of Tay, by Valentine & Sons**

Dundee, 1879
Albumen print mounted on card with handwritten ink notation
Transferred from the British Museum
V&A: E.4945–2000

The Dundee company Valentine & Sons became known internationally for its photographic picture postcards, and this image shows the original Tay Bridge before the disaster of 1879. Valentines was subsequently commissioned to record the collapsed bridge in detail using photography, which was submitted as evidence of the bridge's design failure to the inquiry that followed.

TAY BRIDGE FROM NORTH.   969.   J.V.

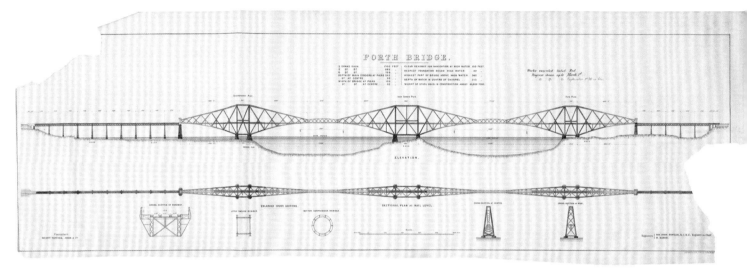

surveys revealed unacceptable movement and remedial work was required. During high gales on the night of 28 December 1879 the bridge collapsed and a train crossing it plunged into the water, killing all 75 passengers and crew. The subsequent inquiry found the bridge was 'badly designed, badly constructed and badly maintained' and that high winds had not been accounted for.

Bouch, engineer to the North British Railway, had simultaneously been working on bridging the Forth at Queensferry, joining the Lothians with Fife. Removed from the job after the Tay Bridge disaster, he was replaced by John Fowler and Benjamin Baker, whose design was the first major structure in Britain to be built of steel. Its vast diamond-shaped cantilevers were engineered not to fail: each of the four-column towers at their centre was seated on circular piers comprising enormous sunken caissons surmounted by granite. Over 2.4 km (8,000 feet) in length from shore to shore, the bridge required stupendous amounts of material and manpower for construction, the methods of which were innovative. With a superstructure weighing over 50,000 tons and utilizing 6.5 million rivets, the enormous quantity of steel needed was provided by the Bessemer process, developed in England in the 1850s as an inexpensive means of mass-producing the metal. A telephone cable was laid across the river to provide communications across the bridge's points of construction, which at its most intense involved about 4,600 men.

Completed in 1889, the Forth Bridge was opened in 1890 by the Prince of Wales (later King Edward VII). Aberdeen had been connected by rail in the 1850s, when at first the journey from London took 17½ hours. With the Forth Bridge in place (and a replacement across the Tay by 1887), rivalry between the different railway companies intensified as they competed to improve upon their timetables. Sensationalized by the press as the 'Race to the North', this competition received peak public interest in 1895, when on overnight runs the journey time from London to Aberdeen was reduced to 8½ hours. PHILIP LONG

↑ Elevation and section of the Forth Bridge, coloured to show dates of construction

United Kingdom, 1888
Lithograph and ink on paper
NETWORK RAIL CORPORATE ARCHIVE: NRCA110040

Fowler and Baker's Forth Bridge utilizes the principle of the cantilever, enabling structures supported at one end to reach out horizontally into space. The engineers designed three great four-tower cantilever structures, each 110 metres (362 feet) tall, supporting the central girders carrying the line. Fowler and Baker had both worked on the early Underground railways in London, but found fame together as the designers of the Forth Bridge, the engineering marvel of late Victorian Britain.

↗ Photograph of the Forth Bridge under construction, by Valentine & Sons

Queensferry, 1888
Albumen print
V&A: 590–1927

→ Photograph of the Forth Bridge soon after construction, by unknown photographer

Queensferry, 1890–99
Albumen print
V&A: PH.249–1902

The construction of the Forth Bridge began with the installation of foundations at three points across the river. Approach viaducts were required to the north and south, reaching out to the cantilevers; their tubular members were constructed in workshops on the riverside and then moved out to be riveted to the structure. Following testing, the first complete crossing was made by a two-carriage train carrying the chairmen of the rail companies involved.

The Arts and Crafts Movement in Scotland

In the latter part of the nineteenth century Scotland shared with the rest of the United Kingdom a growing concern over the effects of industrialization on society and on design. The Arts and Crafts Movement, with its ideal of unity across the arts, its wish to learn from the past, and the desire to remove barriers between so-called fine and applied disciplines, contributed to an extraordinary creative flourishing in Scotland and further afield in the years around 1900, illustrated here through the work of four designers.

In the 1890s The Glasgow School of Art was being reformed by its new Director, Francis Newbery, whose innovations included the establishment of workshops for the development of craft skills, as well as the appointment of practising artists and designers to teaching posts. Former student Jessie Marion King (1875–1949) was made Tutor in Book Decoration and Design, and was sought after commercially for her virtuoso graphic technique and dream-like imagery, for which the School was becoming internationally known. In 1899 King produced covers for the German publishers Globus Verlag, owned by the Berlin department store Wertheim,

which sought a range of designs for items termed by the owner as in 'the new Scottish style'. Shortly afterwards, King was chosen to illustrate a posthumous edition of *The Defence of Guenevere and Other Poems* by William Morris, the leader of the Arts and Crafts Movement. She created character scenes that were both flowing and tightly controlled, the perfect accompaniment to Morris's fascination with chivalric myth.

King's designs were included in the First International Exhibition of Modern Decorative Art, held in Turin in 1902, the Scottish section of which was Newbery's responsibility. Among the 50 chosen designers was the Aberdonian James Cromar Watt (1862–1940), who had begun his career as an architect. While making studies of medieval and classical buildings in Scotland and in Europe, Watt began to deal in works of art and developed an interest in ancient ceramics and precious metalwork. True to the Arts and Crafts ethos he taught himself hand-metalworking and enamelling and studied historic methods, becoming a specialist in the ancient technique of gold granulation, which he put to exquisite use in his plaques and highly decorated jewellery.

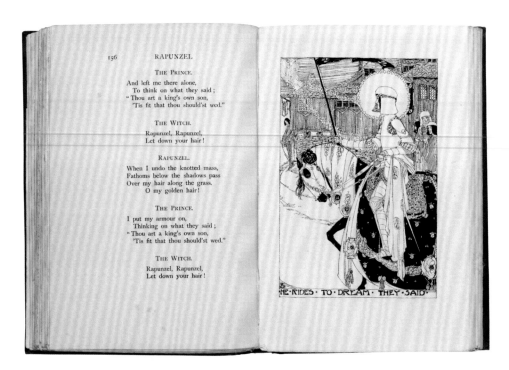

← **Illustration from *The Defence of Guenevere and Other Poems*, by William Morris, illustrated by Jessie M. King**

Published in London and New York, John Lane, The Bodley Head, 1904
Printed book
Donated by Veronica Babington Smith
V&A: NATIONAL ART LIBRARY, L.571–1971

The leader of the Arts and Crafts Movement, William Morris expressed his love of the medieval period in this collection of poems which begins with legends of King Arthur and his court. Morris lectured across Scotland in the late 1880s, when the young illustrator Jessie M. King may have heard him speak. King's numerous illustrations for this 1904 edition were produced following Morris's death in 1896.

**→ Snake bangle,
by James Cromar Watt**

Scotland, *c.*1905
9.37-carat gold, foiled enamel, opal
Purchased in 1992
ABERDEEN ART GALLERY & MUSEUMS
COLLECTIONS: ABDAG008791

Watt was a consummate craftsman,
whose study and first-hand knowledge of
decorative artefacts from the past informed
his style and techniques. In this elaborate
bangle, Watt combined techniques in which
he came to specialize: gold granulation
and the process of enamelling over a
foiled metal ground. He bequeathed a
large collection of historic objects he had
collected (including Asian and Venetian
work) to Aberdeen Art Gallery and National
Museums Scotland.

**→ Casket, designed by
Phoebe Anna Traquair for
Brook & Son**

Edinburgh, 1928–29
Silver with enamelled plaques
Phoebe Anna Traquair Bequest
V&A: M.599–1936

As with the other designers' work here,
Traquair's casket is imbued with historic
references. Each of the six enamel plaques
is contained within an octofoil frame, a
device typically used in Renaissance art.
Suggestive of a chivalric challenge, the
plaques are entitled 'The Awakening',
'Last Voyage', 'Storm', 'Calm', 'Morning'
and 'The Finished Task'.

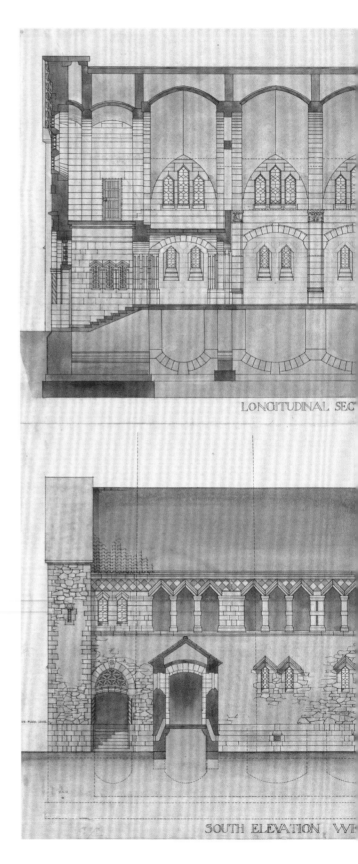

→ Longitudinal section and south elevation of the Cathedral Church of All Saints, Khartoum, Sudan, by Robert Weir Schultz

c.1906–12
Pen, ink and watercolour on paper
Given by Robert Weir Schultz
V&A: E.2310–1934

Schultz was strongly interested in historic architecture. From early in his career he travelled throughout the Mediterranean and the Middle East to study and draw. This wide cultural knowledge contributed to his selection as the architect for the new Anglican Cathedral in Khartoum. Although it was completed in 1912, Schultz continued to work on the building for many years, adding a tower in 1929 (not shown in this drawing).

LONGITUDINAL SEC

SOUTH ELEVATION W

At the heart of artistic life in Edinburgh during the same period, about 1900, was the Irish-born Phoebe Anna Traquair (1852–1936). Like Watt, she specialized in producing small-scale precious works, in embroidery, jewellery and book illumination, but she also designed murals for whole architectural interiors. The first of these (1885–86) decorated the Mortuary Chapel of the Royal Hospital for Sick Children, a commission received through Patrick Geddes (see pp. 88–89) and the newly formed philanthropic Edinburgh Social Union. Her mural scheme featured influential artists and writers of the period, including Edward Burne-Jones and John Ruskin. Enamelling became her favourite small-scale medium. For Robert Lorimer's Thistle Chapel at St Giles' Cathedral she designed the enamel armorial panels over the Knights' seats (1910–11), and throughout her work she was influenced by medieval and Renaissance periods and styles, seen in her silver casket inset with six enamel plaques that she bequeathed to the V&A.

A characteristic of the Arts and Crafts Movement was its focus in specific places or communities. King settled in the artists' colony of Kirkcudbright, while Traquair remained part of an intellectual and artistic milieu in Edinburgh. The Scottish-born architect Robert Weir Schultz (1860–1951), on the other hand, established his busy professional practice in London, building creative and collaborative links through membership of the Art Workers' Guild. Schultz's greatest patron was the Marquess of Bute, for whom he worked across Scotland on new buildings and restoration works. With the Marquess he shared an interest in Byzantine and Middle Eastern architecture, which led to commissions in that style, including St Andrew's Chapel in Westminster Cathedral and, remarkably, the Anglican Cathedral in Khartoum in Sudan, consecrated in 1912. PHILIP LONG

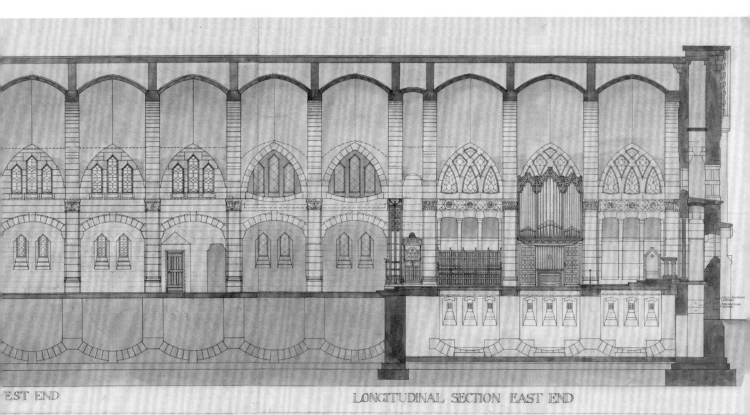

EST END LONGITUDINAL SECTION EAST END

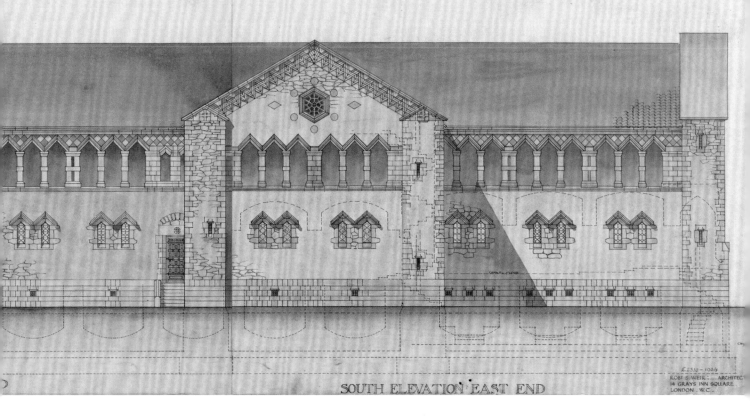

SOUTH ELEVATION EAST END

E.2510-1934
ROBT S WEIR···· ARCHITEC
14 GRAYS INN SQUARE
LONDON ·W.C·

Robert Lorimer: Design and Collaboration

In 1878 the young Robert Lorimer (1864–1929) moved with his family to Kellie Castle in Fife, an abandoned sixteenth-century tower house of medieval origins. Its restoration by his family was a formative influence on the future architect, who – whether on existing buildings or in his own architecture – took great care in his methods, materials, interior design and garden layout, true to the Arts and Crafts ideology in which he had trained.

Lorimer began his career working with the distinguished Scottish architect Sir Robert Rowand Anderson on the new Scottish National Portrait Gallery (opened in 1889), a building of Venetian Gothic style but of a purpose that exemplified the wider nineteenth-century interest in Scotland's heritage and achievement. Lorimer would continue in this vein, contributing in particular to the revival of interest in the country's vernacular design traditions. The young architect spent a brief period in London, working with George Frederick Bodley and learning of William Morris's work, before establishing his own practice in Edinburgh. There he brought together a group of artists, designers and craftsmen who he involved in his commissions and who together sent their work to the London Arts and Crafts exhibitions in the 1890s.

Lorimer became widely known for his restoration of historic houses, early in his career receiving the commission to work on Earlshall (near his family home at Kellie) from its new owner, a bleach merchant from Perth. Lorimer's sensitive treatment of the existing fabric (which included rescuing the extensive painted ceiling of its Long Gallery) and his respectful new design, extending to its elaborate topiary garden, led to wide success as a designer of country houses. He received numerous commissions in the years up to the First World War and, although in some instances this resulted in the demolition of earlier buildings (for example at Hill of Tarvit in Fife), it also resulted in important restorations, including Lennoxlove House, near Haddington (1912–14). Lorimer also designed on a smaller, more domestic scale, building in Colinton, on the edge of Edinburgh, a group of cottages (1893–c.1900) utilizing traditional materials, craft methods and integrated gardens, expressive of a domestic harmony true to his Arts and Crafts principles.

As the war approached the number of private commissions reduced, but Lorimer's reputation and his connections led to important, more public ones, notably the elaborate, exquisitely crafted chapel (1909–11) that he designed for the ancient order of the Knights of the Thistle at St Giles' Cathedral in Edinburgh. Following the war, Lorimer became a Principal Architect of the War Graves Commission, producing over 300 memorials around the world, including those to the Navy in Portsmouth, Plymouth and Chatham.

Towards the end of his life he was responsible for the design of the Scottish National War Memorial, commemorating those in the Scottish services killed in the Great War. Situated within the sensitive site of Edinburgh Castle, the project was subject to much debate and its original ambition was scaled down. Despite that, Lorimer's design retains a strength of form and composure appropriate to its purpose as a shrine. It is also distinguished throughout by the architect's collaboration with leading craftsmen of the day, including the sculptors Pilkington Jackson, Alice Meredith Williams and Phyllis Bone and the stained-glass artist Douglas Strachan, whose works movingly draw out the contributions of the individuals and regiments commemorated.

PHILIP LONG

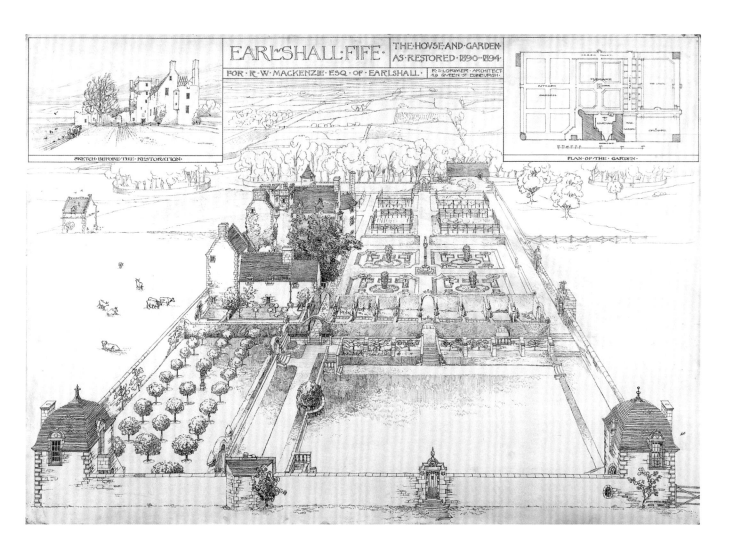

Within the drawing:

EARLSHALL · FIFE ·

THE HOUSE AND GARDEN AS RESTORED · 1890 – 1894

FOR · R · W · MACKENZIE · ESQ · OF · EARLSHALL ·

R · S · LORIMER · ARCHITECT 49 · QUEEN · ST · EDINBURGH ·

SKETCH · BEFORE · THE · RESTORATION ·

PLAN · OF · THE · GARDEN ·

↑ *Earlshall, Fife, the House and Garden*
as Restored by Robert Lorimer,
for R.W. Mackenzie Esq of Earlshall,
drawing by John Begg

Scotland, 1895
Pen and ink on paper
ROYAL SCOTTISH ACADEMY OF ART &
ARCHITECTURE (DIPLOMA COLLECTION):
1993.106

Lorimer was interested in garden design from a young age, drawing up the garden plan for Kellie Castle, his family home, aged 16. After laying out the garden at Earlshall he wrote, 'A garden is a sort of sanctuary, a chamber roofed by heaven … In the garden something of the golden age still lingers.' When elected to the Royal Scottish Academy, Lorimer chose this drawing by his friend, the Scottish architect John Begg, to represent his own work.

← **Fire basket, probably for Midfield House, Lasswade, designed by Robert Lorimer, made by Thomas Hadden**

Scotland, *c.*1914–18
Wrought iron
NATIONAL MUSEUMS SCOTLAND, K.2005.77

Lorimer's close collaborations with craftsmen working in particular materials included a long association with the ironworking firm of Thomas Hadden. Established in 1901, Hadden's firm produced decorative wrought iron to Lorimer's designs for private commissions, such as this fire basket, as well as for major public works such as the Thistle Chapel screens and the gates and steel casket of the shrine in the Scottish National War Memorial.

↓ **Scottish National War Memorial, designed by Robert Lorimer**

Edinburgh, 1927

Lorimer's design utilized a former barrack building, retaining its rubble stonework. He combined this with battlement detailing and niches set with sculptures representing Valour, Justice, Peace and Mercy, to convey the gravitas required of the national memorial. On opening, it was described as 'a Shrine wherein the artistic genius of Scotland has been caught and fixed for evermore just at the moment of its first proud and joyous rebound from four long years of struggle after struggle'.

Douglas Strachan

Douglas Strachan (1875–1950) was one of the finest Scottish stained-glass artists, with works in churches and public buildings across Scotland and beyond. As well as individual windows, he completed large schemes for the Peace Palace in The Hague, the Scottish National War Memorial in Edinburgh and Marischal College in Aberdeen. His work is striking for its beautiful use of varied types and colours of glass, and an intelligent approach to iconography and symbolism.

Born in Aberdeen, Strachan studied at Gray's School of Art in the city after having been an apprentice lithographer. He was a political cartoonist in Manchester (1895–97), but returned to Aberdeen in 1898 to work as a portrait and mural painter. He won his first window commission in 1899 for the city's Kirk of St Nicholas, and designed his first window for the University (in King's College Chapel) in 1903.

↑ **Cartoon for the Cruickshank Window at Marischal College, by Douglas Strachan**

Scotland, c.1905
Watercolour on paper
UNIVERSITY OF ABERDEEN COLLECTION: ABDUA: 103045

The Cruickshank Window consists of three groups of three lights. From the left, they portray the earth sciences, the higher or heavenly sciences, and the human sciences of healing and the study of society. Shorter windows above relate to the sciences depicted below, but take their inspiration from the Biblical Creation. Appropriately for a university library, Strachan's design is a sophisticated scheme linking the achievements of scientific investigation with an appreciation of the sacred and poetic understandings of Christianity.

In 1906 the University's Marischal College was extended to house modern teaching and research spaces. Strachan was commissioned to fill the nine great lights of the library that lay above the main entrance to the College, in memory of the Professor of Mathematics and Librarian, John Cruickshank.

A member of the Aberdeen Ecclesiological Society, Strachan had a rich understanding of the historical role of stained glass and the liturgical symbolism of colour. He therefore made a subtle use of the movement of sunlight through the day such that colours would shine brilliantly or remain soft and muted as the light changed. He made striking use of different types and thicknesses of glass and painting and etching techniques, giving an effect that reflected the best modern design in the Arts and Crafts tradition.

From 1909 to 1913 Strachan taught at Edinburgh College of Art, shortly afterwards winning the competition to design the British Empire's contribution to the Peace Palace in The Hague. The profile that this gave him led to the commission to design the windows of the Scottish National War Memorial and over 350 other commissions. These included the St Dunstan Window for St Paul's Cathedral in London (destroyed during the Second World War) and Glasgow Cathedral, the cartoons for which are in the V&A collection. NEIL CURTIS

↑ 'Holy Spirit' (upper panel) and
← 'Physics' (lower panel), from the
**Cruickshank Window, designed by
Douglas Strachan for Marischal College**
Scotland, 1906 · Leaded glass

UNIVERSITY OF ABERDEEN COLLECTION:
ABDUA: 64093.005 AND ABDUA: 64094.014

The main feature of the Cruickshank Window is the series of tall standing figures, each depicting a scientific discipline. This section is the central panel of the window. It depicts Physics in a purple robe, with the naked figures of Mathematics and Astronomy contemplating the heavens and the earth. The smaller window above has the Holy Spirit over the 'nebulous state' of swirling matter at the Creation, with the Aristotelian motto 'The whole is more than the sum of the parts'.

The Glasgow Style

When Charles Rennie Mackintosh (1868–1928), Herbert McNair (1868–1955), Margaret Macdonald Mackintosh (1864–1933) and Frances Macdonald McNair (1873–1921) exhibited at the First International Exhibition of Modern Decorative Art in Turin in 1902, *The Studio* declared, 'Brilliant in its young strength is that of Scotland.' Celebrated internationally, the work of 'The Four' established a design vocabulary known as the Glasgow Style, which from the 1880s to the 1920s was applied across the decorative arts by a multitude of designers, mostly trained at The Glasgow School of Art.

Featured in design journals such as *The Studio* and *Dekorative Kunst,* and having exhibited at the Eighth Vienna Secession Exhibition of 1900, by 1902 The Four were already operating within European artistic circles. For Turin, Mackintosh submitted an entry to the competition for a house for an art lover – a compelling exercise in the concept of the 'total work of art' that won a special prize from the jury. Often considered the Scottish interpretation of the international Art Nouveau movement, the Glasgow Style combined eclectic influences, from the Pre-Raphaelites and European symbolists to Celtic imagery and Japanese art. The stylized, geometric motifs recurrent in The Four's designs, for graphics, textiles, furniture, metalwork and interiors, often derived from the natural world: the rose, the lily, the peacock feather and the raven. Despite foreign acclaim, especially in Germany and Austria, The Four's radical new style was not embraced enthusiastically by their home city, where they were known as the 'Spook School' because of the elongated, ghoul-like figures of their early designs. In 1888 and 1901 the Glasgow International Exhibitions gave little prominence to The Four; in 1901 Mackintosh's designs for exhibition buildings were rejected in favour of fantastical, historicist schemes.

Truly nurturing the style within the city, however, was The Glasgow School of Art. Founded by local manufacturers in 1845 as one of the centralized Government Schools of Design, it was independent from 1901, becoming one of Europe's leading art and design schools following radical reforms instigated by Francis Newbery. Appointed Director in 1885, he believed that students should learn to design in and through the use of materials and so employed professional craftspeople as teachers. As well as fine art and architecture, students could study textiles, wallpapers, metalwork, pottery, wood- and stonecarving, embroidery, mosaics

↑ **North wall of Hall 10, Eighth Exhibition of the Vienna Secession, from *Ver Sacrum*, no. 24, 1900**

Vienna, 1900

The Four exhibited a harmonious 'total work of art' at the Eighth Vienna Secession Exhibition. Painted all white, the scheme was dominated by two ethereal figurative gesso panels designed for Miss Cranston's tearooms: 'The Wassail' by Mackintosh and 'The May Queen' by Margaret Macdonald Mackintosh. Although the exhibition did not secure The Four many commissions, it did confirm their reputation in European artistic circles, leading to invitations to exhibit in Dresden (1901) and Turin (1902).

→ **Bookcase, designed by George Logan, made by Wylie & Lochhead Ltd for its pavilion at the Glasgow International Exhibition, 1901**

Glasgow, 1901
Mahogany, stained and leaded glass, mother-of-pearl, white metal mounts, leather inserts
V&A: W.23–1972

Employing soft, muted colours and organic motifs, Wylie & Lochhead's 1901 exhibition pavilion presented a more 'homely' version of the Glasgow Style. It appealed to middle-class consumers keen to support local modern design, but unwilling to live in an inflexible 'total work of art'. The characteristic 'Glasgow rose' motif on this bookcase, displayed in the pavilion's 'Rossetti' library, also featured on the library's carpet, ceiling and curtains, representing a more commercial, marketable version of the style.

← **Banner, designed and embroidered by Jessie Newbery and Ann Macbeth for Professor Rucker at the British Association for the Advancement of Science**

Glasgow, 1901
Hessian with appliqué linen, embroidered with metal threads and coloured silks
Lent by the British Association for the Advancement of Science
V&A: LOAN:BRITISH ASSOC.1–2004

This double-sided banner was designed and made collaboratively by Jessie Newbery and her student Ann Macbeth, who later succeeded her as Head of the Embroidery Department at The Glasgow School of Art. Macbeth worked the side showing a stylized Glasgow coat of arms, with Newbery responsible for the reverse, shown here. Macbeth's elegant design, use of soft greens and pinks, and simple but perfectly executed linen embroidery technique clearly reflect the influence of Newbery's teaching.

and enamels, bookbinding, colour printing, poster design and engraving. The School considered architects, artists and industrial designers equal, encouraging the cross-fertilization of ideas. Newbery was Director when Mackintosh took evening classes in 1888–90 and was responsible for introducing Mackintosh and McNair to the Macdonald sisters. Encouraging their originality from the start, Newbery helped The Four to exhibit and gain international scholarships, and also introduced them to sympathetic patrons. It was Newbery who introduced Mackintosh to the tearoom proprietor Miss Catherine Cranston (see p. 108) in 1896, and who championed Mackintosh's design for the new School building, acknowledged as his masterwork.

Crucial for the development of the style was Newbery's encouragement of women in the arts. Going against standard practice, all subjects except life drawing were taught in mixed classes, and women could study all disciplines except architecture. By 1908 there were ten female teachers, including Newbery's wife, Jessie, who ran the Embroidery Department. Jessie Newbery helped raise the status of embroidery with her new approach to teaching, which encouraged the students to create their own designs. Her own work also inspired students, combining whimsical verses with abstracted, natural forms such as roses, pea pods and pea flowers.

Although The Four's radical style was not fully accepted by Glasgow, it nonetheless developed thanks to the progressive outlook and teaching of The Glasgow School of Art. Until about the 1920s students and teachers at the School, many of whom designed for commercial Glasgow firms such as Wylie & Lochhead, continued to work within the Glasgow Style, enabling its dissemination across Britain, Europe and America.

MEREDITH MORE

Charles Rennie Mackintosh and the Oak Room

Many things combine to make the Art Nouveau-era interiors designed by the Glasgow architect Charles Rennie Mackintosh a special, resonant experience: simplicity; spatial and proportional harmony; rhythm through the repeats of vertical and horizontal lines, shapes and motifs; contrasts; the use of shadow and light; and bursts of sparing but richly coloured elements. Furniture, furnishings and fittings, tailored perfectly, complete the whole. Mackintosh was responsible for every detail, creating otherworldly interiors as a *Gesamtkunstwerk*: 'a total work of art'.

The Oak Room, an imposing wood-panelled tearoom interior, was commissioned in 1907 by his greatest patron, the Glasgow entrepreneur and Temperance restaurateur Miss Catherine Cranston. Theirs was an important collaboration for Mackintosh's stylistic evolution over a twenty-one-year period. Her premises – a place for the middle-classes to eat, drink and socialize while keeping away from 'the demon drink' of alcohol – had a unique selling point alongside their reputation for quality: Mackintosh's avant-garde artistic interiors.

Miss Cranston's four tearoom complexes in Glasgow city centre chart the growing sophistication of Mackintosh's design language and abstraction of ideas: mysterious new art stencilled murals for rooms at Buchanan Street (1896–97); furniture, including his now iconic, high-backed chair for Argyle Street (1898); and a range of individually themed rooms at Ingram Street (1900–11). The street-front remodelling and luxurious, conceptual interiors of The Willow Tea Rooms on Sauchiehall Street, completed in late 1903, herald the emergence of his obsession with geometry and squares. This is the only tearoom that remains in situ today. Mackintosh's last tearoom interior was a brightly coloured premonition of Art Deco, a basement extension to the Willow called 'The Dug-Out', completed in 1917.

Completed in 1908, at the creative height of Mackintosh's career, the Oak Room is the largest of the Ingram Street tearooms. It marks an important point between two of his internationally significant architectural masterworks: Scotland Street Public School, designed and built between 1903 and 1906, and the second phase of The Glasgow School of Art (1907–9). Many specialist contractors were employed to realize Mackintosh's design. The joiners McCall & Sons panelled the entire tearoom in oak and constructed a mezzanine balcony around three sides. This subdivision maximized the number of covers, creating an interior with a central full-height, light-filled space and cosily intimate peripheral areas on both upper and lower floors. Mackintosh manipulated the psychological impact of this enclosed central space by extending the lines of the solid balustrade panels across the window recesses of the long wall.

→ **Sideboard for the Oak Room,
designed by Charles Rennie Mackintosh,
made by Francis Smith**

Glasgow, 1907
Oak, glass
GLASGOW MUSEUMS AND LIBRARIES
COLLECTIONS: E.1982.60

This sideboard is the only piece of furniture
directly attributable to the Oak Room. The
original sketch design includes many annotations by Mackintosh indicating how the cabinet
related to other features within the room. The
indigo-blue enamelled squares at the back
of the cabinet aligned with the squares in the
slatted stair screen, while the wavy lathe frill is
a repeat of that along the edges of the balcony.

↙ **Model of the Oak Room,
reconstruction of overpainted panelled
interior as removed in 1971, longitudinal
section looking east**

2004–5
Model: card and laser copy photographs
Room: stained and polished oak, pine,
composite wood, enamelled opalescent glass,
flashed glass, leaded coloured and mirrored
glass, blown glass, cast iron, painted steel,
lacquered brass, textile, cement
GLASGOW MUSEUMS AND LIBRARIES
COLLECTIONS: ISTR.10 COLLECTION

Mackintosh's interiors for Ingram Street were
removed in 1971 so the premises (modified in
the 1950s into a shop unit) could be converted
into a hotel. Before their removal all the parts
were numbered and recorded; they comprise
over 700 individual sections of wood, with
additional fittings and furniture. This model,
the first 'virtual' reconstruction of those components, was made as part of a photographic
survey and conservation assessment by
Glasgow Museums. That work helped to inform
the conservation and full-scale reassembly
and restoration undertaken between 2015 and
2018 of the room, as designed by Mackintosh
(1907–8); it is now installed in V&A Dundee.

A large staircase leading up to the balcony level introduces a new set of vertical rhythms into the room. Simple balustrades pierced with ovals seamlessly segue into parallel slatted stair-screens that airily conceal a second staircase to the basement directly beneath – an ingenious design. Centrally positioned in the southernmost part of the room under the mezzanine, this area is delineated by a repeating motif: a waist-height blue-enamelled glass square, which appears at the same height in the adjacent cash-desk, the entrance door and the porch.

All the walls are clad with warm-hued, dark-stained oak panelling, providing the rhythmic heartbeat for the musicality of Mackintosh's applied decoration. He added rich colour at carefully placed intervals. Pairs of pale-green translucent blown-glass teardop lampshades hang between the central upper verticals of each 'tree'. Along the underside of the mezzanine balcony, simple trapezoid leaded-glass lampshades add streaks of pink and blue. In addition to the zoned area of blue-glass squares, an inverted teardrop shape regularly placed into the perimeter walls of the stepped wooden panelling provides further colour. Eye-searing enamelled opalescent indigo blues are introduced at head height along the solid walls, while across the lower window walls is a translucent glass, its colours softly moving between pink, purple and blue with changes in daylight. A unifying double-band of flat wavy lathe intersects the indigo glass across the innermost walls.

Though no meaning was stated by Mackintosh, the stylized forms he employed within the room suggest a forest of trees around a calming central glade. Here the feature-panel elements of tall tree-like structures stretching from floor to ceiling are confined to this central full-height area. Tree canopies are inferred by the use of horizontal wavy lathe across the balcony line, its undulating line emphasized by the specific positioning of brass basket-weave lampshades, one suspended in front of each 'tree'. When daylight wanes, the lamps shoot shadows out across the balcony face to create upward-reaching branches.

Furniture and furnishings designed and positioned to accentuate and harmonize would have completed the scheme. With many of the freestanding elements now lost, the fully furnished interior can only be imagined. Yet the experience of the Oak Room as an unfurnished space allows a better understanding of how Mackintosh structured and layered his interiors, and how he orchestrated visual and imaginative responses to his design.

ALISON BROWN

← **The Glasgow School of Art Library, photograph by Bedford Lemere**

*c.*1910

The volumetric and structural articulation of The Glasgow School of Art Library clearly shows Mackintosh building upon ideas he explored earlier through the Oak Room: the full-height tree forms; subdivision of the overall height by the three-sided mezzanine; decorative interplay of curved forms and colour along the balcony front; and evolution of the brass and glass lampshade design.

↑ **The Oak Room, looking north-east**

1940s

This photograph by Thomas Howarth is one of the few to survive showing the tearoom in use. Taken in the 1940s, when the complex was run as Cooper's Tea Rooms, it shows Mackintosh's pendant light fittings of brass and pale-green blown glass, and the leaded-glass trapezium shades under the mezzanine balcony, all in their original locations.

Scotland's Celtic Revival

The Celtic Revival developed in Scotland due to a growing interest among antiquarians in the origins of the Gaelic people. In the mid-nineteenth century reproductions were made of Pictish symbol stones, important archaeological finds of British and Irish metalwork, and medieval manuscripts such as the Book of Kells (*c*.800). A new fashion developed for Celtic ornamentation on jewellery, silverware and other objects, and continued to inspire Scottish designers well into the twentieth century.

While many associate Scotland's Celtic Revival with Charles Rennie Mackintosh and the Glasgow Style, the movement was spearheaded in Edinburgh by the biologist, sociologist and utopian visionary Patrick Geddes. In the mid-1890s Geddes commissioned artists to produce decorative schemes for public buildings, as well as designs and illustrations for his avant-garde journal *The Evergreen*. The leading artist in his circle was Dundee-born John Duncan, whose work manifests a profound knowledge of Celtic myth, European symbolism and theosophy. As well as being an innovative designer, Duncan was an influential teacher and encouraged students such as Helen Hay to reinterpret the stylized animals, spirals and interlace of Celtic art.

The Hebridean island of Iona was an important centre for the Celtic Revival and provided the inspiration for much of Duncan's work. It was there, at the turn of the twentieth century, that Alexander and Euphemia Ritchie set up their craft industry, Iona Celtic Art. They specialized in repoussé brasswork and also designed jewellery, silverware and bookbindings – all decorated with Celtic designs based on local medieval crosses and grave slabs. To meet demand, they commissioned manufacturers such as W.B. Darby in Birmingham to cast the most popular designs.

Celtic design enjoyed a second revival after the Second World War under the guidance of George Bain, who attempted to establish a College of Celtic Cultures in the Scottish Highlands at Drumnadrochit in Glenurquhart. In his influential book *Celtic Art: The Methods of Construction* (1951), Bain analysed and synthesized repeated patterns found in insular art, producing the first comprehensive guide for the modern designer.

It was through the assimilation and adaptation of Celtic ornamentation that Scottish designers were able to express their national identity in a modern and original way. Today Celtic art is part of mainstream culture, reworked by designers all over the world. FRANCES FOWLE

← **Quaich, designed by John Duncan, made by James Ramsay**

Dundee, 1900
Silver
DUNDEE CITY COUNCIL (DUNDEE'S ART
GALLERIES AND MUSEUMS): 2004–135

This traditional toasting cup, or loving cup, was designed by John Duncan, a leading figure in the Scottish Celtic Revival. The cup has a raised octagonal panelled body and pierced handles with Celtic knotwork designs, representing the sun and the moon. Known for his collaborations with Patrick Geddes in Edinburgh, Duncan also had a studio in Dundee during the late 1890s and taught Celtic design at both Dundee Technical Institute and University College, Edinburgh.

↓ Firescreen, designed and made by Alexander Ritchie

Iona, c.1900–14
Repoussé brass panels set in carved oak frame
PRIVATE COLLECTION

This carved wooden screen has inset brass panels designed by Ritchie with stylized trees of life and foliated cross designs, copied from medieval grave slabs on the island of Iona. The central panel shows one of Ritchie's favourite motifs, a birlinn or West Highland galley, symbolizing life's journey. The inscription in Gaelic reads: 'Tuig thusa am bàta agus tuigidh am bàta thu' ('Understand the boat and the boat will understand you').

→ **'Hebridean' rug, designed by George Bain, made by Quayle and Tranter Ltd**

Kidderminster, *c.*1949
Machine-woven carpet
V&A: T.579–1995

A trained artist and illustrator, Bain made painstaking copies of Celtic designs found on Pictish stones, metalwork and insular manuscripts, which he incorporated into his own work. The stylized forms of the Book of Kells were the inspiration for the birds and human figures in this rich polychrome rug. The design also includes a repeated Viking ship motif, probably based on West Highland grave slabs, as well as sea dragons, shells, Celtic spirals and interlace.

The Orkney Chair

With its simple wooden frame and high straw back, the Orkney chair is a highly distinctive piece of furniture. Its form and materials reveal its vernacular origins, specific to the conditions and natural resources of Orkney. Yet the Orkney chair as we know it is really the product of a 20-year period at the turn of the twentieth century, in which it became a standardized, fashionable design that achieved international popularity.

The tradition of straw-working on Orkney goes back to the Bronze Age. An obvious choice of material to work with on the naturally treeless islands, straw was used for centuries to make goods ranging from baskets to clothing. Crofters and fishermen used indigenous black oat straw, dried, coiled and sewn together with bent-grass cord, to make simple low stools and curved-backed chairs. These pieces were of a type with close parallels in Denmark, highlighting the strong cultural and trading links between the Northern Isles and Scandinavia.

In the 1870s the Kirkwall joiner David Kirkness began making straw-backed chairs, initially as a sideline, but within 20 years they had become the main product of his workshop. He achieved this success in part by producing four standard designs, of which the hooded chair was the most expensive, and by replacing the boarded seat with a woven seagrass seat dropped into an open timber frame: this enabled different parts of the chairs to be made separately and the work to be outsourced for more efficient production.

Kirkness's chairs also benefited from the contemporary taste for Arts and Crafts furniture when they were exhibited at the Edinburgh International Exhibition of 1890. Enthusiastically promoted by the Scottish Home Industries Association, his chairs appealed strongly to the handmade aesthetic, as well as to a romantic idea of the Scottish islands. Orkney chairs were ordered from Liberty & Co. of London, and from Canada, Australia and South Africa. Copies could be found in the Netherlands and, in Britain, they were acquired by clients no less distinguished than King Edward VII. JOANNA NORMAN

→ **Hooded chair, probably made by David Kirkness**

Orkney, *c.* 1900–20
White pine, straw (probably black oat) sewn with bent grass; rush
V&A: W.11–2017

The 'heided stül', as it was known locally, was the most expensive of David Kirkness's models of Orkney chair. Its hooded back and low seat are said to have originated as a means of protecting the sitter from draughts and maximizing fireside heat in a croft. Kirkness's use of straw and bent grass continued the tradition of making Orkney chairs from indigenous materials, although Kirkness replaced the traditional driftwood with more reliable commercially supplied pine or oak.

Shetland Knitting: From Local Tradition to High Fashion

Shetland knitting in Fair Isle pattern and lace has been produced for centuries by generations of enterprising subsistence crofters who live on the islands. Shetland wool is valued for its natural warmth, strength, fineness and softness. Queen Victoria's love of lace and the charismatic 1920s image of the young Prince of Wales (later King Edward VIII) in a colourful 'gansey' made these garments highly desirable, a trend that has endured to the present day.

Knitted garments were produced from the seventeenth century by Shetlanders, usually women, children or the elderly, who knitted at home when not tending their animals or crops. Initially made for local use on the sea or on the croft and for barter with passing ships, garments were increasingly exported as part of the fishing trade with continental Europe. In the nineteenth century Shetland and Fair Isle knitting developed into an organized industry.

Fair Isle garments ranged from 'keps' (caps) and stockings to 'ganseys' (jumpers or vests) and even purses. Shetland lace pieces, created from about the 1830s using an open-knit technique, included hosiery and 'haps' (shawls), which found a ready fashionable market. Royal approval created new demand for these intricate designs, particularly from the 1920s when Fair Isle sweaters became the preferred golf-course attire for Edward, Prince of Wales. In 1922 his sister Princess Mary was gifted from Unst two Fair Isle jumpers and a 'spider lace' shawl for her wedding. The latter was so delicate it could be drawn through a finger ring.

The motifs used in Shetland knitting have often been passed down through many generations. Some Fair Isle motifs were probably inspired by eighteenth- and nineteenth-century textiles from the Baltic and, into the twentieth century, from trade with British colonies. The design of Shetland lace shawls often includes the Paisley pine cone motif in direct imitation of woven shawls (see pp. 50–51).

Recent decades have seen the continued popularity and reimagining of Shetland knitted garments, particularly in brightly coloured Fair Isle style. In the 1970s the Fair Isle-style tank top was rediscovered by punks and skinheads attracted to its DIY ethic and unisex designs, while into the twenty-first century both Fair Isle and openwork knitted lace have been reinterpreted by fashion designers including Vivienne Westwood and Alexander McQueen. MHAIRI MAXWELL

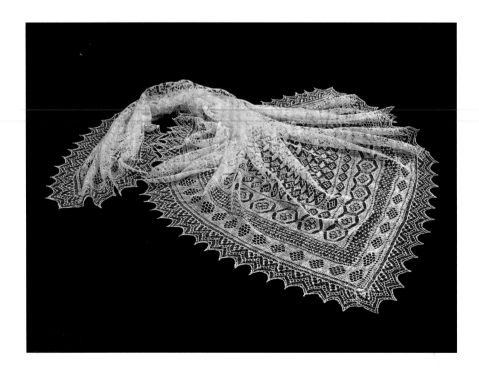

← Shetland shawl or 'hap'

Shetland, 1900–29
Knitted Shetland wool
Given by Mrs C.E. Johnson
V&A: T.42–1967

This fine Shetland lace 'hap' comprises delicate openwork of interlocking diamonds, at times only one-ply thick, and a border of four different bands with an edging of pointed scallops. For her coronation Queen Victoria received a gift of lace from an astute Shetland businessman; impressed, she commissioned more. This example, made approximately 100 years later, is testament to its enduring fashionable appeal.

← Portrait of the Prince of Wales, the future King Edward VIII, after John St Helier Lander

Published in *Illustrated London News*,
23 November 1925
Colour photogravure
NATIONAL PORTRAIT GALLERY, LONDON:
D34119

This widely published photogravure shows a relaxed Prince of Wales, the future King Edward VIII, wearing a knitted Fair Isle jumper while on holiday in Biarritz. This artificially inked image created a demand for more colourful knits, which Shetlanders had to fulfil by using imported dyes (including indigo and madder) and wool. The publicity also encouraged the imitation of Fair Isle knits by textile producers in the Scottish Borders and further south.

↓ Fair Isle jumper, worn for golfing by General Sir Walter Kirke, GBC, CMG, DSO, DL, JP

Shetland, 1920s
Hand-knitted two-ply wool
Given by Mrs M. Kirke
V&A: T.185–1982

Fair Isle jumpers such as these were the height of 1920s and 1930s sporting fashion. This is a typical example knitted in the round and featuring repeating motifs such as the anchor and cross. Traditionally, four interchangeable colours would be used, as in this jumper. These colours were probably created using plant-based dyes in yellows and browns, derived from local lichen.

The Borders Knitwear Industry

Characterized by invention and determination coupled with ingenuity, design and engineering, the Scottish Borders has been at the centre of the British knitwear industry for some 300 years. From the emergence in 1682 of the first hand-powered mechanical knitting frames in East Lothian for the production of stockings, to the development of the broad frame for undergarments in 1826, the expansion of the Scottish hosiery industry was centred on the town of Hawick.

It was within the context of immense political and social upheaval that the invention of the first mechanical knitting frame by William Lee took place in 1589. However, it took until 1682 before a small number of Lee's adapted frames for the manufacture of silk hose were introduced in Scotland. The Acts of Union of 1707 and the foundation of the Board of Trustees in 1727 acted as impetus for the encouragement of Scottish manufacture, supported by the pioneering work of master hosiers including several generations of the Pringle family. With the formation of the Hawick Framework Knitters Society in 1840, representing some 1,200 frames, Hawick's position was established as a centre for the manufacture of hosiery.

Nineteenth-century engineering developments, combined with a concentration of a highly skilled workforce, made it possible for the industry to adapt to changing markets and customer demands. Examples such as the innovative 'seamless gore' – developed by Pringle in 1895 – which removed uncomfortable seams from ladies' combinations, secured the Borders' reputation as makers of high-quality, fully fashioned hosiery of 'Hawick goods'. Industrialization brought better communication, and railway links built in 1849 and 1862 connected the Borders to Edinburgh and Carlisle, enabling access to greater markets. By the early 1900s well-known producers such as Pesco of Hawick diversified to outerwear in materials traditionally associated with hosiery and undergarments. Department stores, such as Marshall and Snelgrove of Oxford Street in London, opened branches in fashionable spa towns such as Harrogate to respond to the growing appeal of women's leisure outerwear, popularizing such garments as wool and silk 'steamer coats' made in the Borders.

Over the first part of the twentieth century the two World Wars significantly altered the direction of the hosiery industry. In the 1920s designers such as Coco Chanel had new ideas about knitwear inspired by functionality as well as silhouette, and

young European designers such as Otto Weisz, the lead designer at Pringle in Hawick, had resettled in Britain during the 1930s. Technical advances in new lightweight cashmere allowed Weisz to design for an expanding American market for smart afternoon and evening-wear, which, with its attention to fashion detail and styling, was known as the 'dressmaker style'. In the 1950s and 1960s advertising promoted the cashmere industry, including men's outerwear by companies such as Peter Scott and Pringle of Scotland. The 'Strathspey twin-set in powder blue' was regularly seen in society magazines, such as *Harper's Bazaar* and *Country Life*, and the introduction of intarsia patterns in cashmere and fine wool created new opportunities for the knitwear industry in the Scottish Borders. ALISON HARLEY

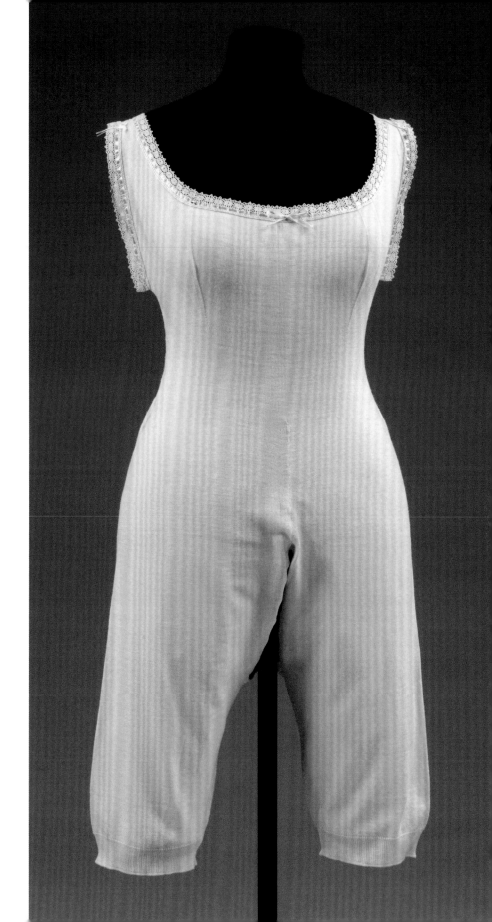

→ Combinations, made by Elliot of Hawick, retailed by Marshall and Snelgrove, London

Hawick, c.1906
Knitted wool, machine-made lace, satin ribbon
Worn and given by Heather Firbank
V&A: T.134–1960

By combining a chemise and drawers into one garment, 'combinations' reduced garment layers, reflecting the simpler silhouettes fashionable in the first decade of the 20th century. These ladies' combinations have 'kilt legs', one of at least a dozen styles produced by the Hawick hosiery industry and available in British department stores. The label states that they are made from 'unshrinkable pure wool', achieved through mechanized washing, pressing and hand-finishing. This process produced high-quality undergarments that could be regularly laundered without losing their original shape and size.

← Ski ensembles designed by Pringle of Scotland and Croydor of Switzerland, modelled at Pringle charity fashion show at The Savoy, London

c.1968

In response to changing markets and fashion in the 1950s, Hawick's skilled and knowledgeable hosiery industry adopted intarsia techniques for knitted pattern and colour. These opened up exciting possibilities for knitwear, such as this ski ensemble by Pringle of Scotland, shown in a 1968 charity fashion show in London. Pringle collections showcased the design of fashionable cashmere knitwear, including innovative printed cashmeres developed by Robert Stewart, Head of Printed Textiles at The Glasgow School of Art from 1946 to 1976.

Speedo

In 1914 Scottish émigré Alexander MacRae (1888–1938) founded MacRae Knitting Mills in Sydney, Australia. The factory initially manufactured underwear, but after the First World War MacRae saw the opportunity to branch into a new market. Renamed Speedo in 1929, MacRae's company became the worldwide pioneer of performance-enhancing swimwear. His company's tight-fitting, hydrodynamic designs not only transformed competitive swimming: they also challenged contemporary morals.

Australian beach culture first began to flourish in the 1920s, when a more relaxed attitude to mixed bathing and the promotion of health and fitness created a market for modern swimsuit styles. In response to this, MacRae designed the revolutionary Racer-back swimsuit for bathing, swimming and surfing. Its fitted shape exposed the back and shoulders, which, as a contemporary company catalogue claimed, made it instantly appealing to the 'sun baker' as it gave 'maximum body exposure'. Banned on some beaches for being too revealing, the Racer-back soon became the height of fashion and was often awarded as the prize for winning a swimming club race or 'beach beauty' competition.

The Racer-back garnered international attention when the Swedish swimmer Arne Borg broke a world record when wearing it in 1927. Much faster times were achievable in the suit because of its design: the inverted back straps allowed freer movement of the arms and shoulders. Racer-backs were also made from cotton or silk rather than the traditional wool, as MacRae realized that these fabrics were far lighter and would reduce water drag.

Under MacRae's leadership Speedo continued to invite controversy into the 1930s, with the Australian swimmer Claire Dennis almost disqualified at the 1932 Olympics because her swimsuit was deemed to show too much shoulder. Similarly, a stir was created at the 1936 Olympics when Speedo moved away from the traditional one-piece by dressing the men's Australian team in swimming shorts.

MacRae died in 1938 but Speedo continued to innovate by experimenting with new materials and styles. To this day more Olympic swimming gold medals have been won wearing Speedo than any other brand. MEREDITH MORE

→ **Arne Borg wearing a Racer-back swimsuit, photographed by Sidney Riley and used as promotional material for Speedo Racer-back swimsuits**

Brisbane, 1927
Gelatin silver print
MUSEUM OF APPLIED ARTS AND SCIENCES, SYDNEY: 95/232/1

The Swedish swimmer Arne Borg broke 32 world records and won 5 Olympic medals during the 1920s. Borg always wore Speedo swimsuits when competing in Australia and allowed Speedo to use his celebrity to promote the Racer-back design to a broader public. This advertisement especially highlights the suit's back straps, which helped Borg to achieve such impressive speeds.

→ Racer-back swimsuit, by Speedo

Sydney, 1930s
Cotton
LEICESTERSHIRE COUNTY
COUNCIL MUSEUMS SERVICE:
X.C145.2013

As part of its hydrodynamic design, the Racer-back costume also featured a patented half-skirt attachment. This stretched across only the front of the suit, replacing the 'ungainly full skirt' that at the time was a normal feature on both men's and women's swimsuits for protecting modesty. The half-skirt provided the necessary coverage, but allowed much greater freedom of movement and limited 'unpleasant ballooning' of the fabric under water.

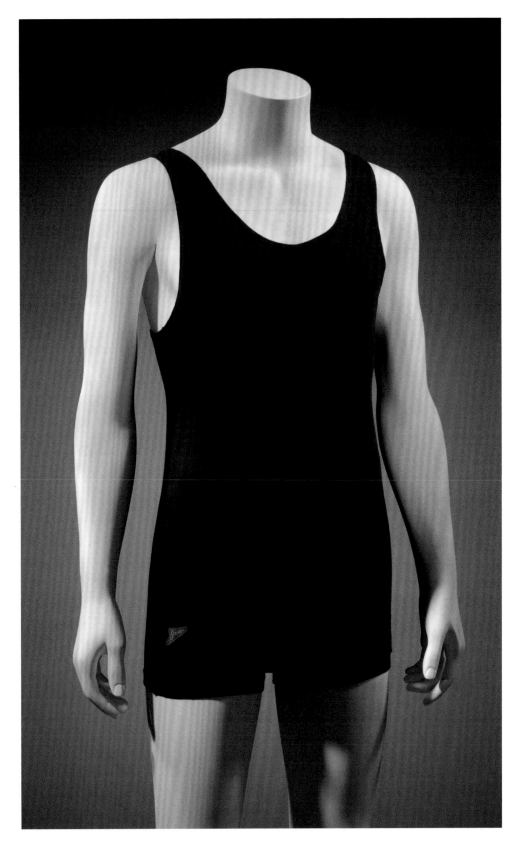

Glass in the 20th Century:
The Ysart Family, Innovation and Design

Originally from Spain, the Ysart family had a significant impact on the development of Scottish glass throughout much of the twentieth century. They introduced a range of colourful decorative glass known as Monart Ware in Perth in 1924, which continued in production until 1961. Salvador Ysart had worked in France during the evolution of the Nancy movement, famous for its striking and highly influential Art Nouveau glass, and came to Edinburgh in 1915 with his four sons to teach apprentices. After he moved to the John Moncrieff glassworks in Perth, followed by his sons in the 1920s, a collaboration with the owner's wife saw the production of glassware to order for prestigious retailers, particularly Liberty in London, where it was highly successful.

The designs of Monart Ware were collaborations between Isabel Moncrieff and Paul Ysart, Salvador's oldest son. In addition, influenced by antique examples, Paul Ysart rediscovered the lampworking skills required to produce a range of paperweights. After the Second World War he continued to make both Monart Ware and paperweights at Moncrieff's while the rest of the family set up the Vasart factory in Perth, producing ranges that were similar but aimed more at the gift trade.

In 1963 Paul Ysart moved to Caithness Glass in Wick, where Domhnall O'Broin, from Eire, had recently started producing a modern range of decorative glass, with forms inspired by Scandinavian design and colours influenced by the Scottish landscape. Paul was employed there as the training officer but continued to make paperweights on his own account, leading to the introduction of Caithness Glass's first range of abstract paperweights in 1969. Caithness added a range of engraved glassware in 1968, hiring engravers who had studied at Edinburgh College of Art, such as Denis Mann and David Gulland. Paul left Caithness in 1970 to set up his own studio nearby before finally retiring in 1979, while Caithness Glass continues to operate today and is now based in Crieff, near Perth.

The Ysart family, combined with education at Edinburgh College of Art, were significant in establishing the importance of Scottish glassmaking and design over 60 years. Several glassworks were founded by Ysart apprentices. A direct design ancestry from Ysart influence, with a continuation of the lampworking skills rediscovered by Paul Ysart, can still be found among contemporary glassmakers, alongside other external influences such as scientific glassblowing, computer design and auto-cutting (using water jet cutters that are computer-controlled). FRANK ANDREWS

↑ *Ducks on a Pond* **paperweight,**
by Paul Ysart

Scotland, *c.*1965
Glass
PRIVATE COLLECTION

Paul Ysart's *Ducks on a Pond* paperweight pays tongue-in-cheek homage to a 19th-century paperweight representing swans on a pond. He had to rediscover the technique (which was lost at the time) for making this type of paperweight, which features lampwork ducks, a lily and rocks under the water surface, all encased in clear glass.

→ **Vases, designed by Salvador or Paul Ysart with Isabel Moncrieff, made by Salvador Ysart or his sons at John Moncrieff & Co. (North British Glassworks)**

Perth, 1924–61
Glass with aventurine gold or copper inclusions
Miss Catherine S. Reid Bequest
(LEFT TO RIGHT) V&A: CIRC.252–1976,
CIRC.251–1976, CIRC.243–1976;
(FAR RIGHT) V&A: CIRC.26–1975

Monart Ware is distinguished by its diversity of forms, sizes and colours. In this group, the small green vase is a typical example of Monart production using Kugler enamels (colours marvered onto the glass), lavished with aventurine glass to give a golden appearance, while the large vase on the right shows how Paul Ysart maintained a two-colour design even when Kugler colours were unavailable from Germany after the Second World War. Unusually for factory-made glass, all Monart Ware was free-blown, without moulds. No colour books survive, but labels with colour numbers into the 500s are known, indicating the very wide range of colours employed.

→ **'Lochshiel' vase in 'Moss' glass, 'Stroma' decanter in clear glass and 'Morven' decanter in 'Soot' glass, designed by Domhnall O'Broin for Caithness Glass Ltd**

Wick, 1961–65
Glass
(LEFT TO RIGHT) V&A: CIRC.197–1966,
CIRC.1169&A–1967, CIRC.1167&A–1967

While working at Waterford Glass in Ireland, Domhnall O'Broin was sent on study visits to Scandinavia between 1952 and 1954. Then, in 1955, he studied glass design at Edinburgh College of Art. The ranges he designed for Caithness reflect this Scandinavian influence combined with the colours of the Scottish landscape. These modernist designs were a huge break from traditional British glassware and successfully competed with continental glass, defining O'Broin as one of the 20th century's leading glass designers.

Donald Brothers

From the 1830s Donald Brothers was one of the many Dundee manufacturers of coarse linen and jute for sacking and carpet backing. Anticipating the decline of these industries, in the 1890s the firm began to explore more artistic uses for the rough yarns that were readily available, shifting its focus towards woven furnishing fabrics. From the 1930s to the 1970s Donald Brothers specialized in a wide range of upmarket woven and printed textiles.

One of Donald Brothers' first furnishing fabrics was 'Antique Canvas', woven with a rough yarn made from a mixture of jute and linen fibres. When the fabric was dyed, the colour appeared differently on the two fibres, increasing its textural effects. Used extensively from the late 1890s until 1914 as a wallcovering in British and American art galleries and museums, it was also popular with the American Arts and Crafts designer Gustav Stickley, who thought its 'natural' appearance enhanced the wood, leather and copper of his 'Craftsman' interiors.

Constantly adapting to changing markets, Donald Brothers expanded its output in the period after the First World War with a wide range of fabrics designed to complement modern architecture and interiors. Collaboration with freelance designers including Marion Dorn and Robert Stewart produced colourful, modern patterns that injected liveliness into these sometimes severe settings.

The firm was particularly successful during the 1950s and 1960s under the directorship of respected textile designers and adept businessmen William Robertson and Peter Simpson. Having worked in New York at JOFA, a textile firm that distributed Donald Brothers fabrics to architects across the United States, Simpson brought in new international contacts, from clients to freelance designers. By this time, more than half of Donald Brothers' output was exported, largely to America and Canada, but also to Scandinavia, New Zealand, Australia and Switzerland. Simpson and Robertson continually sought inspiration for patterns and textures when travelling, photographing examples of local design and techniques and later filing them in a large cabinet constantly used by the company's small internal design team.

Despite this success, Donald Brothers experienced financial problems from 1976 and was bought by William Halley and Sons, which in turn closed down in 2004. Although Dundee's textiles industry may have declined, it continues in a specialist way. Local firms continue to innovate, from Wemyss Fabrics, which relocated to Dundee in 2006, to Scott and Fyfe in Tayport, specializing in advanced technical textiles, and Halley Stevenson, which designs and manufactures waxed cottons and weatherproof fabrics.

MEREDITH MORE

↑ **'Glendale' woven fabrics, designed by William Robertson and Peter Simpson for Donald Bros. Ltd, retailed as 'Old Glamis Fabrics'**

Dundee, 1964
Linen blended with rayon and cotton
Given by the Council of Industrial Design
V&A: CIRC.116&A TO T–1965

In the 1960s Robertson and Simpson advocated the firm's return to richly textured woven fabrics, like those that had originally made Donald Brothers' name. Their 'Cawdor', 'Orlando' and 'Glendale' ranges, which would appear quite utilitarian were it not for their vibrant, jarring colours, were all awarded Design Council Awards by the Council of Industrial Design.

↑ Design for 'Cyprus' furnishing fabric, studio of Donald Bros. Ltd

United Kingdom, c.1936
Pencil, bodycolour and kaolinite
V&A: E.197–1994

→ 'Cyprus' furnishing fabric, designed by Marion Dorn, made by Donald Bros. Ltd

Dundee, 1936
Reversible jacquard woven cotton
V&A: CIRC.521–1954

Designed to complement a modern interior, 'Cyprus' was woven in harmonious tones of blue, white and cream, and includes some of Marion Dorn's signature motifs: stylized ivy trails, Ionic pillars and birds. When working with a freelance designer such as Dorn, Donald Brothers transferred the designer's sketch onto a series of point papers. These were instructions for the weaver: each horizontal square represented a warp thread, each vertical square a weft thread, and each weave a different colour.

Edinburgh Weavers

'Modern painters should really work in textiles ... as nowhere else are the qualities they are after available in such diversification.' (Alastair Morton, 'Contemporary Design in Furnishing Textiles', lecture notes, 1961)

For 30 years Edinburgh Weavers was led by the visionary artist–designer Alastair Morton (1910–63). The third generation in a family of Scottish textile innovators, Alastair succeeded his grandfather Alexander, who had founded the Arts and Crafts textile firm Alexander Morton & Co., and his father, John, the inventor of 'unfadeable' Sundour dyes. In 1928 John Morton established Edinburgh Weavers, a small, experimental branch of Morton Sundour Fabrics. Three years later 21-year-old Alastair took it over, moving the workshop to Carlisle, and transforming it into what the art historian Nikolaus Pevsner called a 'laboratory for textile art'.

An accomplished artist as well as a skilled weaver, Alastair Morton believed that a good textile was equal to a good painting, and he sought to prove that the huge variety of textural effects achievable in textiles made them a worthy medium for modern artists. Edinburgh Weavers first experimented with artist-designed textiles in its 1937 collection of 'Constructivist Fabrics'. Designs were commissioned from Alastair's artist friends, including Ashley Havinden, Ben Nicholson and Barbara Hepworth, which were then adapted for weaving by technical specialists, and often by Alastair himself. Many of these designs closely mirrored the artists' works, and so Alastair tried to replicate their colours and textures in his choice of yarns, weave structures and colourways. In the 1930s Edinburgh Weavers also began collaborating with professional freelance designers such as Marion Dorn, Hans Tisdall and Marian Mahler. In most cases Edinburgh Weavers would ask the freelance designer to create a pattern for a particular fabric they had developed, but occasionally the designer would be invited to send a sketch along with suggestions for fabrics and colours.

In the 1940s Alastair took the opportunity to study handweaving with Ethel Mairet at Gospels at Ditchling in Sussex. This informal but rigorous training allowed him to experiment with weave structures and exposed him to the widest possible variety of yarns, from the familiar cotton and rayon to less common natural fibres such as raffia, jute and sisal. Following this experience, Alastair always made prototypes on the handloom when designing his own textiles. He regularly took samples of his handweaving to the Carlisle studio to see if the effects could be replicated on jacquard looms.

Inactive during the Second World War due to government restrictions and yarn shortages, Edinburgh Weavers was not fully revived until the 1950s, when it launched another collection of artist textiles, designed by a new generation including William Gear, Keith Vaughan and William Scott. By this time Edinburgh Weavers was producing as many screen-printed textiles as woven ones in order to appeal to a broader market, so for each design a decision had to be made about the most suitable technique. The textures achieved by printing fabrics could be just as interesting as those created on the loom, however, with Edinburgh Weavers making particular use of slubby spun fabrics and grainy printing effects. Edinburgh Weavers was one of the first textile firms to use screen-printing, choosing this technique rather than roller-printing as it was more economical for the short runs of fabric the firm produced. It also allowed more freedom to innovate, and made possible the unusually large double and single repeats for which Edinburgh Weavers became known.

By embracing modern art and experimenting with materials and techniques, Edinburgh Weavers created some of the world's most innovative furnishing fabrics between the 1930s and 1960s. Ever consistent was Alastair Morton's belief that 'whether woven or printed, the pattern must grow from the texture and weave of the cloth. The cloth always comes first.' MEREDITH MORE

→ **Detail of 'Caird', furnishing fabric designed by Alastair Morton, made by Edinburgh Weavers**

Carlisle, 1956
Machine-woven cotton (dobby-woven warp-spaced cotton sheer)
Given by Edinburgh Weavers Ltd
V&A: CIRC.683–1956

Although not often credited, Alastair Morton designed many of Edinburgh Weavers' most successful and experimental textiles. This machine-woven fabric was based on one of his handwoven prototypes, with the finished textile revealing how this unconventional working method helped to create fabrics with surprising textures.

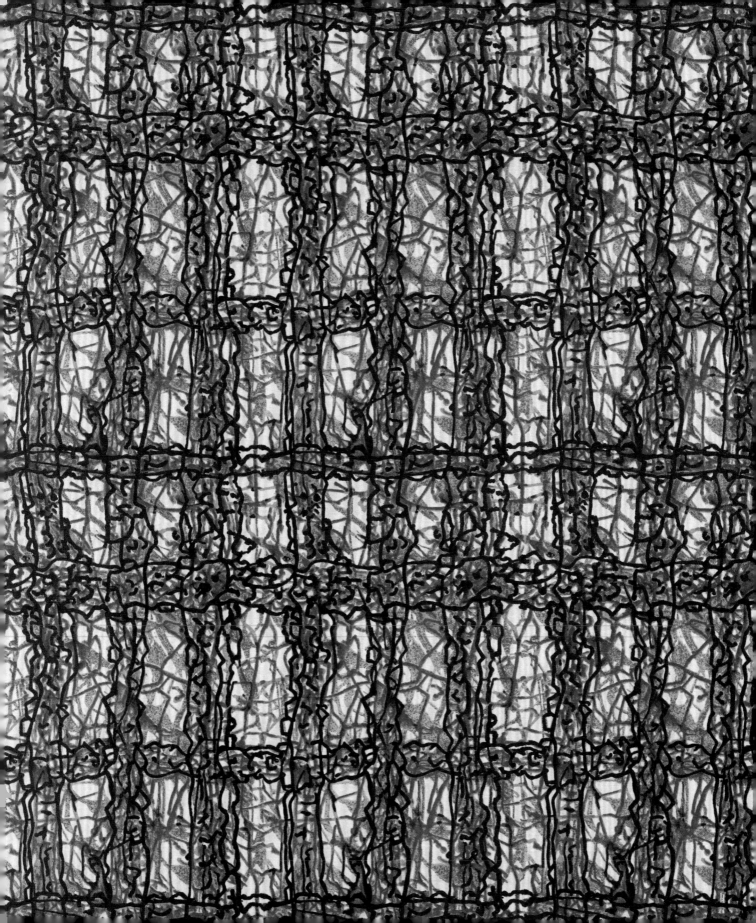

← 'Brittany', furnishing fabric designed by William Gear, made by Edinburgh Weavers

Carlisle, 1955
Screen-printed cotton crepe
V&A: CIRC.192–1955

In October 1953 an exhibition called 'Painting into Textiles' at the Institute of Contemporary Arts, London, aimed to encourage collaboration between contemporary artists and textile firms. Struck by the work of the Scottish abstract artist William Gear, Alastair Morton purchased three of Gear's exhibited designs. The finished textile for 'Brittany' sensitively replicates the painterly effects of Gear's watered-down pigments and also the particular tones of olive green, black and pink that appeared in his original design.

→ 'Skara Brae', furnishing fabric designed by William Scott, made by Edinburgh Weavers

Carlisle, 1958
Screen-printed slubby cotton tweed
Given by Edinburgh Weavers Ltd
V&A: CIRC.266–1960

Edinburgh Weavers collaborated on both printed and woven textiles with William Scott, another internationally acclaimed artist with Scottish connections. The colours, textures and abstract compositions of Scott's work translated so well into textiles that Alastair Morton created some fabrics directly from his paintings. Scott also provided designs specifically for textiles, including 'Skara Brae'. The subject and rugged texture of this fabric were influenced by the landscape of Orkney, an island that inspired both Morton and Scott.

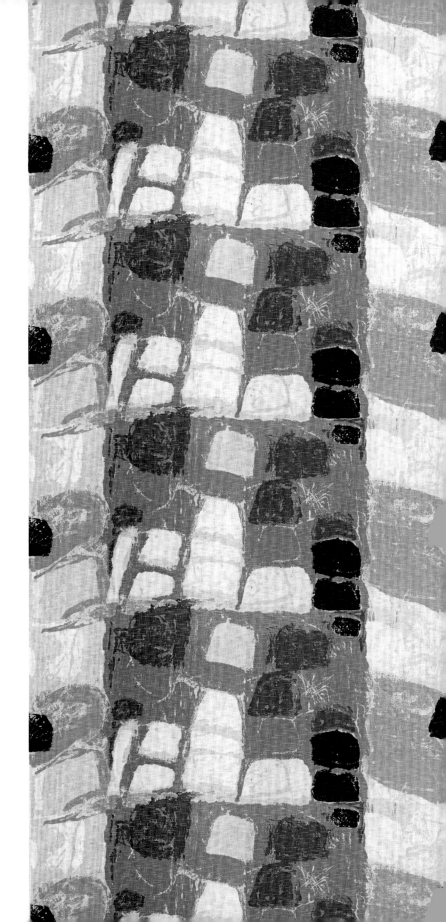

Bernat Klein

Bernat Klein (1924–2014) was born in Senta, Serbia, and after a period of study at the Bezalel School of Art and Craft in Jerusalem, arrived in Britain in 1945 to study textile technology at Leeds University. In 1949 he was employed as a designer with Munrospun of Edinburgh. The company relocated its design department in 1951 to Galashiels in the Scottish Borders, where Klein was to set up his textile design and manufacturing company Colourcraft in 1952. As an advocate of 'good design', Klein created several design-led companies until his retirement from business in 1992.

As a designer, artist and industrialist Bernat Klein brought colour, flair and ingenuity to the Scottish Borders textile industry. By the early 1960s Klein's couture textiles were captivating the Paris and London fashion houses, and generating curiosity among the international fashion press. His highly original textiles cleverly combined colour and texture through his innovative production method of space-dyeing, developed through dipping individual hanks of brushed mohair yarn to create dispersed and balanced colour. Klein's imaginative use of asymmetric and non-repeating weaving patterns interwoven with these multi-coloured yarns and unusual materials such as velvet ribbon redefined Scottish textiles. In his book *Eye for Colour* (1965) Klein particularly cited the French painter Georges Seurat and his technique of Pointillism as the early inspiration for his couture textiles. Through his oil paintings first shown in London in 1966, Klein continually explored the close connection between colour, texture, materials and landscape, the relationship of which permeated his textile collections from couture and ready-to-wear fashion to interiors.

Klein's exploration of colour remained a feature of his design thinking and creative process. Early in his career he introduced working methods such as colour boards, a complex system of numbering and naming each colour. The series of six *Personal Colour Guides* (1965) offered guidance for the consumer in their choice of coordinated colour in textile collections for fashion, which Klein and his wife, Margaret, had developed into a mail order business by 1973. His influence as a design consultant extended into commissions from the Department of the Environment developing coordinated colour and interior collections for government buildings, including the V&A.

Klein's design identity, personality and admiration of Scandinavian design are unreservedly celebrated within his family home, High Sunderland in Selkirk, designed in 1957 by the modernist architect Peter Womersley (1923–93). Influenced by events early in his career such as the 1951 Festival of Britain, and later through his extensive textile and colour consultancy work as Bernat Klein Design Consultants Ltd, established in 1966, Klein was open to new ideas and approaches to design. He also took much from his personal relationship with his adoptive Scotland, which provided continual inspiration in colour and texture throughout his lifetime. ALISON HARLEY

← **Samples of *Aspen* furnishing fabrics, designed by Bernat Klein for Margo Fabrics Ltd**

United Kingdom, 1969
Wool, viscose and cotton, backed with acrylic
Given by the manufacturer
V&A: CIRC.721–1969

From 1966 to 1992 Klein developed successful ranges of upholstery collections with a number of Scandinavian and British companies. The textile collection of *Aspen, Larch, Rowan, Spruce* was designed for Margo Fabrics, with each of its colourways intended to appeal to a domestic and international mass market that Klein sought to reach through 'good design'. It won the Council of Industrial Design Award in 1969.

→ **Suit, designed by Edwin Hardy Amies, made with fabric designed by Bernat Klein**

London and Scotland, *c.*1960s
Mohair tweed and wool jersey
Given by Mrs Gould
V&A: T.82:1, 2–1992

The design of the jacket and skirt suit shows the originality of the couture mohair tweed, which Bernat Klein developed in the early 1960s through his innovative space-dyeing process. The design simplicity of the Hardy Amies silhouette complements Bernat Klein's brushed lightweight mohair in a blue and turquoise colourway, which is offset by a single-colour knitted jersey bodice and contrasting buttons.

Basil Spence

Basil Spence (1907–76) became a household name in Britain as the designer of the new Coventry Cathedral, built after the Second World War, and as a public spokesperson for his profession. His admiration of earlier architecture and his own flair for Modernist design were put to excellent use in a great range of buildings both public and private, including airports, army barracks, university campuses, housing and churches.

Born in Bombay (Mumbai) in 1907, Spence was brought to Scotland as a child. After studying in Edinburgh he worked under the renowned architect Sir Edwin Lutyens, assisting on the designs for the Viceroy's House, New Delhi. Like Lutyens, Spence became highly adept at responding to differing clients' desires, and his work in Scotland in the 1930s was characterized by his openness to tradition and innovations of the past, as well as to new ways of doing things. The Great Depression meant building work was limited and Spence supplemented his practice with exhibition design. His creative flair and receptiveness to lightweight, advanced materials enabled him to produce exhibition stands that impressed with their spirit of modernity. Particularly outstanding was his ICI pavilion at the Empire Exhibition, Glasgow, in 1938. With its interlocking curved towers joined together by shiny cupro-nickel tubes and with surface decoration by the Scottish sculptor Thomas Whalen, it was one of the most eye-catching moments in an event characterized by Modernist design.

Spence was a camouflage artist during the Second World War, and afterwards worked on two of the most significant regeneration projects in the country. In the same year, 1951, that he produced the Sea and Ships Pavilion on London's South Bank and the Exhibition of Industrial Power in Glasgow, both for the Festival of Britain, he won the most important commission of his career, for the new Coventry Cathedral, following the destruction of the medieval building in the first air raids on Britain of 1940.

From the moment his winning design was announced it was widely commented on. Much of this comment was critical: to general opinion his vision did not pay sufficient homage to the historical forms it was replacing; to the design profession his plan was unrevolutionary. But more than any other architect of his generation, Spence made room in his work for fellow artists and designers, fostering young talent as well as providing commissions for established figures. The new cathedral's open vaulted

↑ **ICI Pavilion at the Empire Exhibition, designed by Basil Spence**

Glasgow, 1938

Spence was commissioned to produce three pavilions at the vast Empire Exhibition held in Glasgow's Bellahouston Park in 1938. The pavilion for Imperial Chemical Industries (ICI) was intended to reflect the company's status as one of the largest chemical producers in the world. Spence's Modernist building comprised three pylons representing earth, air and water; at its centre was a 60-metre (200-feet) high beam of light symbolizing fire.

→ **Sea and Ships Pavilion at the Festival of Britain, by Basil Spence**

South Bank, London, 1951

As part of the Festival of Britain that was held on London's South Bank, Spence created the Sea and Ships Pavilion. He utilized a dramatic framework of steel towers and gantries from which were suspended large-scale, cutaway models of ships and engines through which visitors could walk. With all the theatricality of an industrial shipyard and the modernity of a Constructivist sculpture, Spence's design brilliantly conveyed Britain's prowess as a forward-looking maritime nation.

← *Interior perspective of Coventry Cathedral from the south towards the altar,* **by Basil Spence**

London, 1951
Oil on canvas with graphite underdrawing
HISTORIC ENVIRONMENT SCOTLAND (SIR BASIL SPENCE ARCHIVE): DP004288

For Coventry Cathedral, Spence commissioned work from artists he had recently encountered at the Festival of Britain. John Piper designed stained glass and vestments, the young Elisabeth Frink an eagle-shaped lectern, and Ralph Beyer (who had escaped from Nazi Germany in 1937) large-scale inscribed stone tablets. This early presentation drawing, which includes Graham Sutherland's intended full-height tapestry on the altar wall, demonstrates Spence's concern to integrate the creative work of others in his design from the outset.

↓ *South-west elevation of Hutchesontown Area C, Gorbals, Glasgow,* **by Spence, Glover and Ferguson**

London and Edinburgh, 1958
Photomechanical process with graphite
HISTORIC ENVIRONMENT SCOTLAND (SPENCE, GLOVER AND FERGUSON COLLECTION): DP026799

Fundamental to Spence's designs for high-rise flats to replace tenement housing in a deprived area of central Glasgow were large communal balconies that would enable residents to hang out their laundry while their children played outside. Describing his slablike design to the local commissioning authorities, Spence said, 'on Tuesdays, when all the washing's out, it'll be like a great ship in full sail', referencing Glasgow's famous Clyde-side shipbuilding history.

space, full-height sidelights, intimate chapels, sensitive relationship with the fragmented remains of the medieval original, and especially its integrated art and design work continue to resonate with people today.

The attention that Coventry brought helped Spence's practice to expand, with offices in both London and Edinburgh, and to win commissions around the world. From early in his career Spence had worked on housing projects, and opportunities to design for differing communities came in the 1960s and 1970s for the new university campus for Sussex, the Hyde Park Cavalry Barracks in London, and for Glasgow residents in the Gorbals. The Gorbals slum tenement district was being redeveloped and Spence contributed the boldly modern Hutchesontown C towers, high-rise flats with generous communal balconies. Although the buildings were welcomed by their first residents, the maintenance required was underestimated and, coupled with wider problems of social deprivation, they fell out of favour. The Hutchesontown C towers were demolished in 1993, sharing the fate of similar housing around the world; nonetheless the majority of Spence's prodigious output remains in daily use today. PHILIP LONG

Gillespie, Kidd & Coia: Designing for a New Liturgy

The development of new towns in Scotland in the 1950s and 1960s, providing a modern and spacious environment for people frequently relocating from the congested and poorer housing conditions of inner cities, required the design of all types of social and community amenities. Ecclesiastical architecture became the specialized contribution of the Glasgow-based practice Gillespie, Kidd & Coia, whose work stands out in post-war Scottish design for its poetic Modernist approach.

Under the direction of partner Jack Coia – born in England to Italian parents and raised in Scotland – the practice succeeded in winning a commission for a new church in 1931 from the Archbishop of Glasgow. From then on, the Roman Catholic Church became the firm's most important client, vital to its future creative success. In 1938 Gillespie, Kidd & Coia produced the Roman Catholic pavilion at the Empire Exhibition, and was part of architect Thomas Tait's team that masterplanned the exhibition in Glasgow's Bellahouston Park. But it was after the Second World War, with the addition of the younger leading talents Isi Metzstein and Andy MacMillan, that the practice began to produce work embracing Modernist principles that made an outstanding contribution to twentieth-century architecture in Britain.

Metzstein, who had come to Glasgow from Berlin on the *Kindertransport* prior to the outbreak of the war, took evening classes in architecture at The Glasgow School of Art. There he met Glasgow-born MacMillan, who worked for the East Kilbride Development Corporation before joining Metzstein in Jack Coia's practice in 1954. The first work of the newly energized firm was the church of St Paul's in Glenrothes in Fife, like East Kilbride one of the country's earliest post-war new towns. Formed of angular planes in white-painted brick, and with a western elevation of a wooden glazed screen, the church rises to double height over the sanctuary. Overhead, windows focus light down onto the altar, a dramatic meditative illumination of the simple interior and a characteristic of Metzstein and MacMillan's later work.

Favouring cast concrete and brick, they used the latter to extraordinary effect in the keeplike, high-walled St Bride's in East Kilbride, completed in 1964. The church's external monolithic form is relieved by highly inventive brick detailing, whether in its 'light cannons' directing light into the interior, or in the vertical

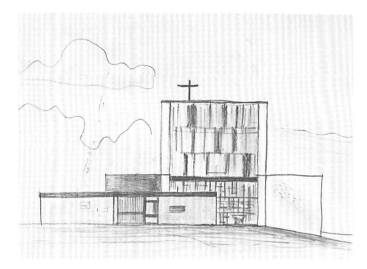

↑ **Design for St Paul's Church, Glenrothes, by Gillespie, Kidd & Coia**

Glasgow, c.1955–70
Coloured pencils on tracing paper
THE GLASGOW SCHOOL OF ART: GKC_CG_3–8–1

In this sketch for a small-scale Roman Catholic church in the new town of Glenrothes, the influence of Modernist art and architecture is clear in the rectilinear forms and geometric colour-accented glazing reminiscent of the work of the Dutch De Stijl artist Piet Mondrian. The designers' vision was to create a lectern-shaped building, symbolic of the spreading of the Gospel.

→ **St Bride's Church, East Kilbride, designed by Gillespie, Kidd & Coia**

1964

As Metzstein and MacMillan's church design for Gillespie, Kidd & Coia developed, they mastered an approach characterized by single-volume interiors contained within adventurously sculptural buildings. The red-brick St Bride's is unmistakeably modern in form, but at the same time acknowledges the influence that medieval church building had on the two architects, especially the brick-built Roman Catholic cathedral of Albi in southern France.

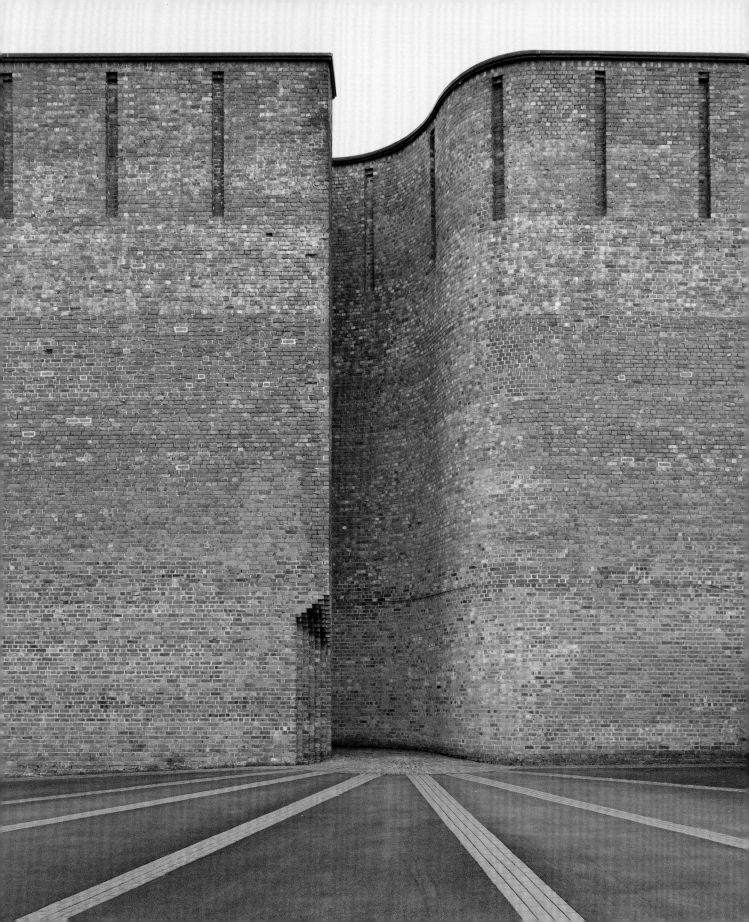

brick patterning of its north side, reminiscent of the elevation of Charles Rennie Mackintosh's earlier Glasgow School of Art library with its towering bays.

Gillespie, Kidd & Coia's campanile for St Bride's no longer remains, and indeed a considerable number of the practice's buildings have been demolished. In a tragically ruinous state is their most ambitious project, St Peter's Seminary at Cardross near Helensburgh, completed in 1966, but closed in 1980. Indebted to Le Corbusier's cast-concrete Dominican priory of Sainte Marie de la Tourette, near Lyon, St Peter's was to provide for the practical and spiritual needs of the community of Roman Catholic priests in training, with a combination of spaces for large congregations and monastic-like cells. In a private woodland setting, the design, distinguished by rough cast concrete, stepped terracing, boldly formed external stair-cases and service vents, cantilevered structures and funnelled natural light, was unapologetically modern, Brutalist in approach and spiritual in atmosphere. Even in its abandoned, perilous state, and in part because of it, St Peter's impresses as one of the most romantically bold Modernist buildings of the twentieth century. PHILIP LONG

→ **View through the chapel to the sanctuary of St Peter's Seminary, Cardross, designed by Gillespie, Kidd & Coia**

1966

↓ **Model of St Peter's Seminary, Cardross, designed by Gillespie, Kidd & Coia, made by students of the Mackintosh School of Architecture, their design tutor Mark Baines, and modelmaking technician Suzanne Dunscombe**

Glasgow, 1995–96
Foamex (plastic) card sprayed white
MACKINTOSH SCHOOL OF ARCHITECTURE, THE GLASGOW SCHOOL OF ART

In the higher levels of the residential block at St Peter's, the accommodation was stepped in, allowing internal balcony corridors to look down through glazed screens on to the refectory and the chapel below. Fourteen years after St Peter's was completed, it went out of use as a seminary and was abandoned, to the frustration of the architects. Metzstein declared, 'I can certainly say that if they try to pull it down, I'll have the last laugh. The building would be almost as difficult to demolish as it was to build!'

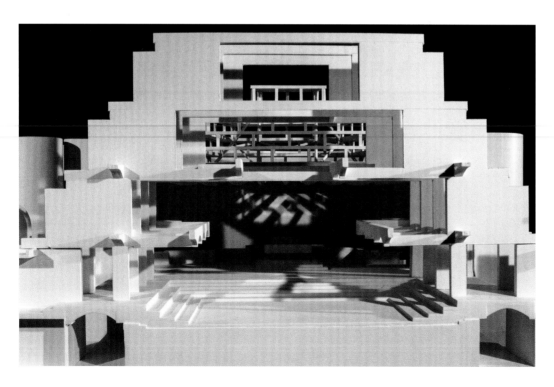

Energy and Power in Scotland: The Last 250 Years

Water and steam power have dominated energy and power generation in Scotland over the last 250 years. Scotland's abundance of fast-flowing water has provided the most significant energy source, leading to innovations in design and engineering that enabled the development of industries from textile manufacture to iron founding, and technologies from the pumping of water from coal mines to the engines that drove Clyde-built steam ships.

The eighteenth century saw significant developments in water and steam power and consequent benefits for manufacturing and design industries. The abundance of fast-flowing water enabled the mechanization of textile production in the late eighteenth century, taking manufacture out of the home and into mills such as New Lanark on the River Clyde. James Watt's 1765 improvements to the Newcomen steam engine, first introduced into a Scottish colliery to pump water in 1719, powered the Industrial Revolution into the nineteenth century. Manufactured by the firm of Boulton and Watt, the steam engine provided energy and power to the tin and then coal mining industries; paper, flour, cotton and iron mills; and distilleries, canals and waterworks.

Fort Augustus Abbey, built in 1891, was the home of the first-ever public hydroelectric supply in Scotland. Five years later, the first large-scale hydro plant was commissioned at Foyers to provide cheap electricity for the aluminium smelting industry; it operated until 1971. The remarkable Cruachan Power Station commissioned in 1965 and designed by Sir Edward MacColl, with its turbine hall located in Ben Cruachan itself, was the first pumped storage hydro system in the world. From the early 1900s electricity generation through coal-fired steam power also developed at the Pinkston and Yoker power stations in Glasgow, Pinkston powering the Glasgow Corporation Tramway network.

Fossil fuel and nuclear-produced energy dominated the industry in the latter half of the twentieth century, supplying the modern industrial age of mass manufacturing, transport and aviation. Key to industrial expansion was the Scottish offshore oil and gas sector, as the largest supplier of oil and the second-largest supplier of gas in the European Union. However, in 2016 the last coal-fired power station, at Longannet, closed, confirming the move to a lower-carbon energy economy and the need for new design solutions for renewable energy sources.

MARKUS MUELLER

↑ 'Festival of Britain, Exhibition of Industrial Power' poster, by Reginald Mount

United Kingdom, 1951
Colour offset lithograph
V&A: E.306–2011

Coordinated by Basil Spence, leading a team of five architects, the Exhibition of Industrial Power at Glasgow consisted of six halls representing Britain's history of engineering and energy production. It included a model of a hydroelectric power station, a vast mural of a coalface and a 20,000-gallon (90,900-litre) waterfall. The final room, the Hall of the Future, housed a million-volt machine that demonstrated the theory of nuclear fission, heralding the future of energy production.

→ **Arrangement of Sphere Elevation, Dounreay, Building No. D1100, by the United Kingdom Atomic Energy Authority**

United Kingdom, 1955
Digital scan of original drawing
NUCLEAR DECOMMISSIONING
AUTHORITY & DOUNREAY SITE
RESTORATION LTD

↘ **Construction of the Dounreay Fast Reactor sphere, by Motherwell Bridge & Engineering Company Ltd**

Caithness, 1956

Led by Motherwell Bridge & Engineering Company's chief designer, James McLean, the Dounreay Fast Reactor housing was designed as a sphere to tolerate the greatest possible build-up of pressure within, with no weak points. The sphere's construction was groundbreaking, requiring steel plates to be built up from a concrete raft and welded in situ to ensure a completely sealed environment. The first fast reactor in the world to supply energy to a national grid in 1962, it was shut down in 1977.

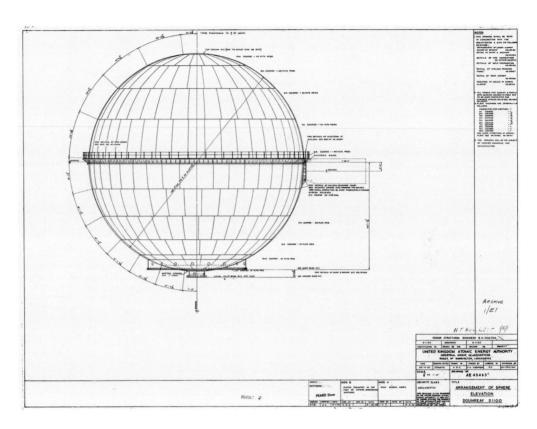

Design for Pantomime

'The national theatre of Scotland is pantomime,' declared the actor and director Lewis Casson in the 1920s. Today over 20 professional productions fill Scottish theatres each Christmas season, generating over £5.7 million of income. Known for its extravagant sets and costumes, pantomime thrives on spectacle, transporting audiences from cold winter nights to tropical islands, royal balls and enchanted woodlands.

Scottish pantomime has a rich and diverse history, and its performance in Glasgow was first recorded in 1751. While titles such as *Harlequin Pantomime and the Dutchman Bitt* have given way to the twentieth century's *Cinderella*, pantomime's key conventions of audience participation, good triumphing over evil and grand transformation sequences remain popular.

According to one of Scotland's most respected pantomime performers Stanley Baxter, 'The whole process of pantomime as you put the thing together is like piecing together a mosaic, until you finally finish the fresco, the finished job.' Script writer, designer and director work collaboratively to conjure up underwater kingdoms, oriental palaces and rural landscapes. Designers are required to create a vast array of environments and effects, with the end of Act One often concluding in a stunning transformation sequence created by a combination of stage machinery, pyrotechnics, lighting and sound.

Pantomime's dazzling sets and costumes often require shows produced at the largest venues to tour in subsequent seasons to recoup large initial outlay costs. Terry Parsons's sumptuous pantomimes of the 1980s, including 1985's *Aladdin* starring Baxter as the Dame, played the King's Theatre in both Edinburgh and Glasgow, before finishing at the Sunderland Empire. The three local authorities shared the shows' high production costs, including £20,000 for Baxter's costumes alone.

While similar in nature to its English counterpart, Scottish pantomime has its own set of traditions and practices. At the King's Theatre, Glasgow, for example, the audience shout 'Bring doon the cloot' to summon the song sheet at the end of Act Two. Titles are often Scottified, such as *Dick McWhittington*, and narratives may be localized to reflect their Scottish setting. In the 1960s the producers Howard & Wyndham enjoyed great success with *A Wish for Jamie* and its sequels. Set in the Highlands and featuring a miniature military tattoo as its Act One finale, the pantomime starred tenor Kenneth McKellar as Jamie with actor–comedian Rikki Fulton as the Dame and popular Principal Boy Fay Lenore as Donald. SIMON SLADEN

← Costume designs for the Ugly Sisters in *Cinderella*, performed at the King's Theatre, Edinburgh, designed by Anthony Holland

Edinburgh, 1979
Pencil, watercolour and ink on paper
V&A: S.543–2000, S.544–2000

Cinderella's Ugly Sisters provide designers with the opportunity to explore contrasts between the two characters in order to create an immediate impact as soon as they appear on stage. When Stanley Baxter and actor Angus Lennie played the roles, designer Anthony Holland created a series of pairings to highlight the difference in the performers' stature and physique. These included a beetroot and a carrot, and silver bell and four-tier wedding cake ballgowns, the latter designed so that Baxter could disappear through a trapdoor while the cake remained on stage. The Sisters' opening costumes, representing a tube of Smarties and a packet of Jelly Tots, reference pantomime's practice of throwing confectionery and the use of contemporary products and brands as design inspiration.

↑ Set model for the finale of *Aladdin*, performed at the King's Theatre, Edinburgh, designed by Terry Parsons

Edinburgh, 1985
Ink and watercolour on board
MUSEUMS GALLERIES EDINBURGH,
CITY OF EDINBURGH COUNCIL

Widely regarded as the leading 20th-century pantomime set designer, Terry Parsons has created over 70 productions, describing his approach as 'beautifully vulgar' because of his enthusiastic use of glitter. Parsons designed three pantomimes starring Stanley Baxter, working collaboratively with Baxter and the writer Russel Lane over 12 months in each case to create the final production. Traditionally the most extravagant scene, Parsons's finale or 'walkdown' for *Aladdin* featured a willow pattern backdrop as the cast walked down the steps to take their final bows.

John Byrne and Scottish Theatre in the 1970s

The 1970s was unquestionably a high point for Scottish theatre. Theatre censorship in the UK had been lifted in 1968, Arts Council funding was available, the Fringe Festival was in full swing, and theatres such as the Traverse in Edinburgh were seeking out work by Scottish playwrights. This decade brought with it exciting opportunities for the artist John Byrne, who was drawn to the world of theatre at this progressive moment, and began working as a set designer and playwright.

In 1972 Byrne designed a pair of giant wellington boots for the set of Billy Connolly's *The Great Northern Welly Boot Show*, a comedy–musical inspired by the Upper Clyde Shipbuilders' 'work-in' protest that saved the shipyards from closure. In the audience was the playwright John McGrath, who asked Byrne to design his socialist play, *The Cheviot, the Stag and the Black, Black Oil*, produced by the small company 7:84 (Scotland). Byrne's set for *The Cheviot* was designed for the play's performance from 1973 in village halls across the Highlands: it took the form of a

pop-up book that could be easily transported between venues on the top of the company's van. Specifically addressed to Highland audiences, the play used familiar songs and drew on Scotland's tradition of variety theatre and music hall to convey an urgent political message: that the discovery of North Sea oil would lead to a new Highland Clearance.

Byrne's own celebrated play, *The Slab Boys*, was first shown at the Traverse Theatre in 1978. Part of a trilogy, it was based closely on Byrne's experiences of working as a 'slab boy' at the carpet manufacturers A.F. Stoddard in Paisley in the 1950s, where it was his menial job to grind and mix paint for the pattern designers. Describing what motivated him to write the play, Byrne said: 'I'd seen sentimental things about Scotland. I'd seen puerile comedies about Scotland. But I'd never seen plays about people like me.'

In his work as a playwright and theatre designer Byrne was one of the first to speak directly to working-class Scottish audiences, striving to capture contemporary Scotland on stage.

MEREDITH MORE

← **Pop-up set for** *The Cheviot, the Stag and the Black, Black Oil*, **by John Byrne**

Scotland, *c.*1973
Painted cardboard
NATIONAL LIBRARY OF SCOTLAND: ACC. 13037

Byrne's pop-up book set had five openings so that the actors needed only to turn the page to reveal a new scene. The first opening, showing an idealized Highland landscape, was used for most of the play, but others showed a humble Highlander's croft, a poppy-strewn war memorial and a Native American tipi. The style of images was based on children's book illustrations, its naivety deliberately belying the play's political messages.

↑ **Poster for** *The Slab Boys Trilogy* (*Cuttin' a Rug*, *Still Life* **and** *The Slab Boys*), **performed at the Traverse Theatre, Edinburgh, 1982, by John Byrne**

Scotland, 1982
Printed ink on paper
V&A: S.3183–1995

Byrne's poster highlights the importance of drawing to his creative process, as a way of constructing 'living and breathing' characters. Although Byrne did not design the set for the first (1978) production of *The Slab Boys*, he did design several of the revivals, including this production of the whole trilogy at the Traverse in 1982. Byrne was most content when he was in control of all aspects of the production, including designing the set, costumes and promotional materials.

Design at the Citizens Theatre

From 1971 until 2003 the Citizens Theatre in Glasgow was run by the triumvirate of the playwright and translator Robert David MacDonald, the director Giles Havergal, and the designer and director Philip Prowse. For more than 30 years the three collaborated to produce imaginative, daring theatre for as wide an audience as possible, achieving particular critical acclaim in the 1970s and early 1980s.

First opened in 1878 as the Royal Princess's Theatre, performing pantomime and variety, the theatre was renamed in 1945 when it became the new home of the recently established Citizens Company. Taken over in 1970 by Havergal and Prowse, who were joined by MacDonald a year later, the theatre faced a significant challenge in its location in the Gorbals slums. To tackle this, and to fulfil the crucial role, as they saw it, of being a local theatre for a local community, they instigated a single price point of 50 pence per ticket. Even when forced to raise prices subsequently, they continued to offer a free preview before the opening of each new production, as well as reduced rates for students, children, senior citizens and the unemployed.

Citizens' productions were innovative and daring: plays were chosen for their timelessness, not for their familiarity. Alongside classic repertoire such as Shakespeare ran obscure European dramas from Goldoni to Goethe, translated and reinterpreted by Robert David MacDonald, as well as his own plays. Philip Prowse designed productions on a tiny budget, taking this less as a constraint and more as a stimulus to create striking, sumptuous but inexpensive sets and costumes that attracted audiences and inspired a younger generation of theatre designers. Award-winning Trisha Biggar and Bunny Christie both cite the extraordinary design creativity of Prowse and the Citizens as one of their key inspirations and influences. Biggar worked as wardrobe mistress at the Citizens before becoming a highly successful costume designer, including for the *Star Wars* prequel films (1999–2005). Christie's innovative designs for theatre productions, including *The Curious Incident of the Dog in the Night-Time,* have also won numerous awards. JOANNA NORMAN

↑ **Glenda Jackson in *Phedra*, produced at the Old Vic Theatre in London, 1984; costume designed by Philip Prowse**

Phedra was produced by Colin Brough, who commissioned from Robert David MacDonald a new translation of Jean Racine's 17th-century play *Phèdre*. Directed and designed by Philip Prowse, *Phedra* starred Glenda Jackson in the title role. Prowse designed two costumes for Jackson, one of which is now in the V&A. His lavish designs for these costumes and the play's sets were strongly influenced by the Baroque style of 17th-century France, combined with draperies reminiscent of ancient Greece.

→ **Poster for *Semi-Monde* by Noël Coward, performed at the Citizens Theatre, Glasgow**
Glasgow, 1977
Offset lithograph
V&A: S.3163–1995

Although written by Noël Coward in 1926, *Semi-Monde* received its premiere only in 1977 at the Citizens Theatre. Daring in its portrayal of ambiguous sexuality, the play's first performance brought London theatre critics to the Gorbals for a production remarked upon particularly for its costumes: lavish cocktail and evening dresses. Prowse's design was also praised by *The Stage* as having 'brilliantly telescoped the diffuse action onto a single mirrored set'.

GLASGOW CITIZENS THEAT RE PRESENTS THE CITIZENS COMPANY IN SEMI MONDE BY NOEL COWARD SEPTEM BER 9 - OCTOBER I GORBA LS GLASGOW 041 429 0022

Bill Gibb

When British *Vogue* crowned Bill Gibb Designer of the Year in 1970, it represented a volte-face in fashion. Gone were the structured minidresses and block colours of the 1960s; instead, Gibb offered looser, flowing garments of layered patterns and fabrics, creating an eclectic, romantic look that chimed with the hippie aesthetic. In the same year, he won the Dress of the Year award of the Fashion Museum, Bath. Only two years out of college, he was already revolutionizing fashion.

Born in an Aberdeenshire farming village, Bill Gibb (1943–88) studied in London at St Martin's School of Art and the Royal College of Art. The year 1967 first brought him to notice as one of six designers contributing to the London Look Award in New York, sponsored by Yardley; the same year saw his first, short-lived attempt at setting up a business, the boutique Alice Paul, in collaboration with Annie and Alice Russell.

Gibb's designs, developed for the fashion house Baccarat and from 1972 for his own line, continually sought inspiration in the past. His fascination with history and his extensive drawing activity dated from childhood: work on a new collection frequently led him to the British Museum and the V&A and always began with a sketch and swatches of fabric. His eclectic influences ranged from the Renaissance, folk dress and Indian saris to William Morris and the natural world. At the same time, he had an excellent understanding of cut, pattern, colour and texture, developing close relationships with collaborators such as Nives Losani, his trusted pattern cutter, and Kaffe Fassett, whose knitted designs he frequently incorporated into his collections.

Gibb recognized the power of endorsement from well-known figures such as the actress Elizabeth Taylor and the model Twiggy, a particular devotee of his designs. But the large numbers of different fabrics and the handcrafting techniques that Gibb's garments entailed meant that despite such backing, his short career, and sadly life, were plagued by financial crisis. Nonetheless, throughout the 1970s, Gibb's clothes offered a richness of texture, palette and silhouette, a romantic reimagining of history and a world of storytelling and fantasy. JOANNA NORMAN

↑ **Design with fabric samples, by Bill Gibb**

Probably London, *c.* 1970
Felt-tip pen, pencil and biro pen on paper with fabric samples pinned to the paper
V&A: E.123–1978

Annotations on this design note that it appeared in articles in *The Sunday Times* in 1969 and in *Vogue* in 1970. Both publications celebrated the startling newness of Gibb's combination of fabrics and patterns. The design and attached fabric samples exemplify this in mixing a pleated tartan skirt with a laced knitted waistcoat and printed blouse.

→ **Evening dress, designed by Bill Gibb**

Made with 'Tana' lawn, 'Nimbus' voile and 'Country' cotton fabrics designed by Susan Collier and Sarah Campbell for Liberty & Co. Ltd · London, 1972
Printed cotton trimmed with leather, plastic, lined with silk
V&A: T.94–1981

Gibb often combined a range of fabrics to create a unique layered effect, always crediting those who had produced each element. In this evening dress he used three different fabrics designed by Susan Collier and Sarah Campbell for Liberty & Co., adding leather streamers and motifs as trimmings. Its flowing skirt creating a loose, romantic effect and its puffed sleeves evoking an earlier period, the dress was worn by the singer Sandie Shaw.

James Stirling

From early in his career James Stirling (1926–92) passionately and provocatively engaged with style, concept and technology in his architecture, interplaying these traits in new ways. Two particular works by Stirling's practices – the Faculty of Engineering at Leicester University and the Neue Staatsgalerie in Stuttgart, Germany – are landmarks of post-war architecture, reflecting wider architectural preoccupations of the times and influencing generations of younger designers.

Born in Glasgow, Stirling studied in Liverpool and in 1956 set up in practice with his fellow Scot James Gowan, who had designed the gravity-defying Skylon at the Festival of Britain on the South Bank in 1951. Stirling and Gowan's shared interest in industrial and pre-twentieth-century architecture and in the Modernist forms of Le Corbusier resulted in designs of fantastic vigour and individuality, most famously at Leicester University. Their design for the university's engineering department comprises two elements: ground-hugging workshops surmounted by angled, crystalline skylights, and an adjacent glass-clad tower rising on stilts through the revealed form of the faculty's lecture theatre. Gowan quietly referred to the work as a project in the 'engineering style', underestimating the influence that its virtuoso composition of dynamic forms and materials of ceramic glazing, steel and glass would have on subsequent generations.

Stirling's partnership with Gowan was short-lived and in 1971 he began an association with Michael Wilford, expanding the practice to include galleries, theatres, libraries and museums. In 1984 they completed the Neue Staatsgalerie following an international competition. Its references to historic German museum buildings, juxtaposition of sharply coloured steel elements with warm travertine and sandstone, and series of ramps and massive curved glazed screens led the critic Charles Jencks to refer to it as one of the first buildings of Postmodernism.

Stirling's completed work for the Neue Staatsgalerie has the drama of a theatre set. Along with his design for Leicester, it confirms the architect's belief, expressed in 1979, 'that shapes of a building should indicate – perhaps display – the usage and way of life of its occupants, and it is therefore likely to be rich and varied in its appearance, and its expression is unlikely to be simple'. PHILIP LONG

→ Leicester University Faculty of Engineering, designed by James Stirling and James Gowan

Leicester, 1963

Stirling and Gowan's design for the engineering faculty at Leicester University responded to a very specific brief. The lower workshop space had to be open to partitioning to allow alterations to be made according to changing experiments, and lit by north lights so sensitive machinery was not affected by direct sunlight. The height of the adjoining tower had to be at least 30.5 metres (100 feet) to provide a water tank to feed down to hydraulic demonstrations at ground-floor level.

↙ Neue Staatsgalerie, designed by James Stirling, Michael Wilford and Associates

Stuttgart, 1984

The commission for a new gallery was part of a political initiative to revitalize Stuttgart. Constructed on a sloping site adjacent to the Alte Staatsgalerie, Stirling's design created new spaces for the institution's modern collections, but also responded brilliantly to the challenge of connecting the old and new with an outdoor architectural promenade between the two buildings. Different colours were used indoors and out for specific purposes, such as bright pink and blue pipes indicating circulation routes.

Eduardo Paolozzi

The relationship between design and art is complex. Art might be said to be a creative means to record and explore our world, provoking and inspiring us. Design, too, requires similar insight, utilizing creativity to enrich our environment and solve practical needs. In Scotland's history, as in others, moments where the practices of art and design intersect have been among the richest. This is the case with the artist Eduardo Paolozzi (1924–2005), who carried his diverse interests into the multidisciplinary way in which he worked, including in design.

The range of sources which inspired Paolozzi – whether in his robotic sculpture, or the combination of popular and classical imagery in his printmaking and textile designs – shows a depth of inquisitiveness and a passion for life that can be traced back to his earliest days. Born in the port of Leith, near Edinburgh, Eduardo was the child of immigrants, part of the important Italian Scots community there. His father made radios for every room in their home, a source of information that Paolozzi depended on throughout his career. The family business was a confectionery shop and so there was a ready supply of fascinating magazines and wrapping papers, which the young Eduardo cut up and pasted into scrapbooks.

Paolozzi's ambition initially was to become a commercial artist, and he studied briefly at Edinburgh College of Art before being first interned as an enemy alien, after Italy declared war

→ Mosaics in Tottenham Court Road underground station, by Eduardo Paolozzi

London, 1982–84

Paolozzi's work for Tottenham Court Road underground station was a major undertaking. Made of coloured glass mosaic, the entire scheme covered 950m². Paolozzi took his inspiration from the local area above ground in the heart of London, and from his wider interests in mechanization and popular culture. A programme of restoration and repair of the mosaics – undertaken while the station underwent huge expansion to prepare for the arrival of the Elizabeth line – was completed in 2017.

← Ceiling panels for Cleish Castle in Eduardo Paolozzi's studio

c.1972

Painted ceilings were a distinctive characteristic of Scottish houses and castles from about 1540 to 1640 (see p. 22), when they were superseded by decorative plasterwork. Paolozzi's designs for Cleish Castle continued this tradition: his relief panels, commissioned by the then owner and architect Michael Spens, were set back into the coffered ceiling space. For the design, Paolozzi took inspiration from a 1927 German magazine illustration, representing organ music in the form of a visual pattern.

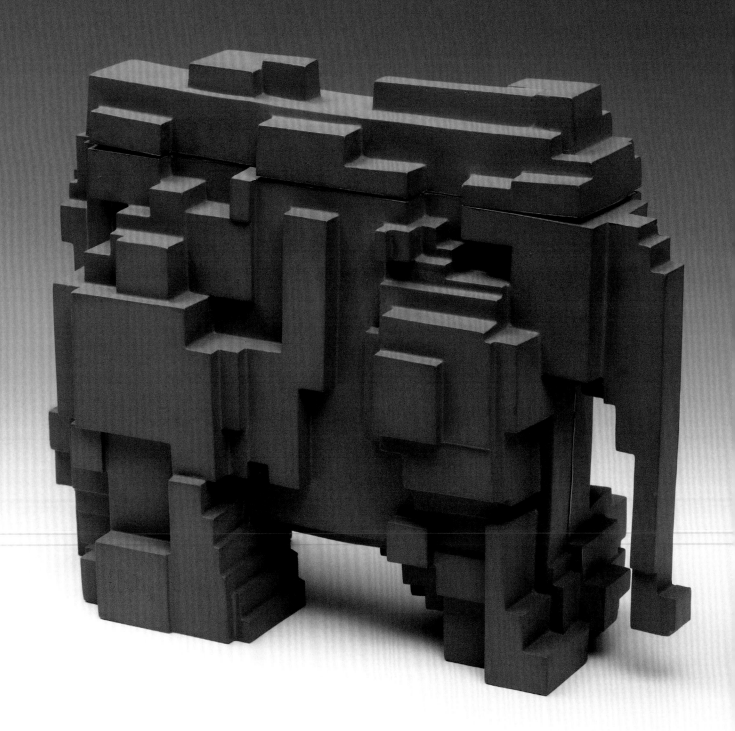

on Britain in 1940, and subsequently called up for war service. While in training he was inspired by the French painter Amédée Ozenfant's book, *Foundations of Modern Art* (1931), which introduced him not only to modern art, but which 'showed aeroplanes, and Zulus and Greek architecture all in one volume'. He committed to becoming an artist, moving to London after the war, and for a while spending some time in Paris. There he learned first-hand from the artist Jean Arp about the Dada and Surrealists' use of collage as a means of image-making using an unconventional range of sources and innovative graphic techniques.

Settling in London, he associated with artists, architects and designers who shared his interests in modern art, literature and popular culture, becoming a founder member with them of the Independent Group. At the Group's first event, held at the Institute of Contemporary Arts (ICA) in London in 1952, Paolozzi presented a rapidly changing slide show without commentary, juxtaposing images from across culture and history, which formed the basis for his series of 'Bunk' collages and which has been recognized as a vital moment in the development of Pop Art. As he began to exhibit his art, he also received commissions, including a fountain for the 1951 Festival of Britain on the South Bank.

Further design projects followed, including ceramics for Wedgwood, textile designs for the French fashion house Lanvin, tapestries and ceiling reliefs for Cleish Castle, near Kinross, and elaborate doors for the Hunterian Art Gallery, University of Glasgow. In 1980 he was commissioned to decorate Tottenham Court Road underground station, London, producing an ambitious scheme of brightly coloured mosaics through which many people became familiar with his work. Of that project, he said: 'My alphabet of images for Tottenham Court Road reflects my interpretation of the past, present and future of the area. Specific representational elements are interwoven with geometrical and musical rhythm lines – metaphors exist on many levels simultaneously. The cross section of the camera refers to local shops as well as to tourists; an engine/ethnographic mask evokes not only the British Museum but also the diversity of backgrounds of local inhabitants and the automotive traffic above ground.' PHILIP LONG

← Promotional case for a Nairn Floors catalogue for 1972–73, designed by Eduardo Paolozzi

United Kingdom, 1972 · PVC and polystyrene
V&A: W.94–1978

Commissioned by Nairn Floors Ltd of Kirkcaldy to promote its products among the architectural profession, Paolozzi's geometrically shaped elephant has a removable lid, allowing the company's product brochures to be stored inside. It was produced in an edition of 3,000. The elephant's complex moulding, and that of its interior, were developed by Paolozzi working with a plastics engineer.

↑ 'Djerba' evening ensemble, designed by Jules-François Crahay and Eduardo Paolozzi for Lanvin

Paris, 1971
Printed wool etamine, silk, plastic and chrome, lined with white silk crepoline
Given by Lanvin
V&A: T.304 TO B–1971

Head Designer for Lanvin from 1964 to 1984, Crahay commissioned the fabric for this dress having seen Paolozzi's print series 'Moonstrips Empire News', on which it is based. 'Djerba' was presented as an informal evening dress for the countryside as part of Lanvin's Spring/ Summer 1971 collection. Rather than accept royalties, Paolozzi asked Lanvin to donate an example of the ensemble to the V&A. The same print series inspired a set of ceramic plate designs by Paolozzi for Wedgwood, also in the V&A.

Buffalo Style: Designing Identity

During the 1980s Dundee-born Ray Petri (1948–89), founder and mentor of the Buffalo collective, played a pivotal role in defining the style and identity of the decade. Consumed by Generation X through the pages of *The Face*, *i-D* and *Arena* magazines, Petri's creative direction as a stylist elevated youth culture, embraced diversity and celebrated difference. His visionary thinking challenged prejudices and had a global impact on men's fashion, influencing international designers.

Buffalo was a collective of like-minded people assembled and mentored by Ray Petri in the early 1980s. They included photographers (Jamie Morgan, Cameron McVey, Mark Lebon), stylists (Mitzi Lorenz), film-makers (Jean-Baptiste Mondino) and singers (Neneh Cherry, Nick Kamen). The name Buffalo referenced Bob Marley's song 'Buffalo Soldier' and the Wild West, a perfect emblem for this free-spirited movement, which challenged the corporate world of fashion and highlighted its exclusivity. Perhaps Petri's greatest achievement was providing a platform to black and mixed-race models, such as Naomi Campbell, who were not then represented by model agencies.

The Buffalo look, a unique mix of high and low fashion – tailored jackets, felt hats, US military surplus garments, and sportswear – was influenced by Petri's love of reggae and soul music and a razor-sharp eye for juxtaposing influences from Native American Indian culture to Olympic athletes. His ideas demanded that fashion is nothing without style and attitude. By casting individuals with strong identities, pulling fashion from diverse sources and directing every aspect of photo shoots, Petri invented the role of fashion stylist.

One of his iconic silhouettes was of Nick Kamen in a length of leather wrapped like a kilt, paired with Dr Martens boots. It blurred gender conventions but made perfect sense to Petri, whose Scottish roots dictated that men wearing kilts were inherently masculine. These DIY styles went on to inspire Jean Paul Gaultier's Men in Skirts collection.

Petri's vision brought racial, sexual and social politics openly into the world of fashion, a legacy that gave us metrosexuality and is seen today in gender-fluid fashion. SARAH SAUNDERS

→ **Front cover of *The Face* (March 1985, issue 59), with photograph by Jamie Morgan, styled by Ray Petri**

Published by Wagadon Ltd, London, 1985
Printed magazine
V&A: NATIONAL ART LIBRARY, 38041800870131

This striking cover of *The Face* features a defining image of the Buffalo collective. The fierce photograph of the young teen Felix Howard by the photographer Jamie Morgan was styled by Ray Petri. Felix wears a herringbone jacket, polo neck jumper and a cowboy hat collaged with the word 'KILLER', referencing Jamaican slang. It was through 'killer' front pages such as this that Buffalo proved you don't need money or designer clothes to create style that oozes attitude and self-expression.

THE FACE No. 59 ● MARCH 1985 85p US $2.75

THE FACE

KILLER

SAM SHEPARD AND JESSICA LANGE
HOLLYWOOD"S HOT COUPLE

Alison Moyet
Andy Warhol
Lovers rock
Pogues ◆ Brazil
Mel Smith

Photo: Jamie Morgan

HARD

Comic Book Design

Comics have long been one of Scotland's major cultural exports, and Scottish comics creators are some of the most successful in the business. Comics encompass many elements of design. Once the script is completed, roughs (thumbnail sketches and page breakdowns) are produced, leading to pencilled pages, then inking, colouring and lettering. Then there is the cover and the branding and, finally, printing. Each stage requires highly skilled artists and designers, and while many comics are now produced digitally, the core skills remain largely the same.

The best-known Scottish comics publisher is D.C. Thomson, based in Dundee. This company has defined the look of British comics since the mid-1930s, with characters such as Oor Wullie and The Broons, Dennis the Menace, Desperate Dan and hundreds of others. Until that point British comics had been dominated by the English publisher Amalgamated Press, whose comics typically featured images arranged in a grid with several lines of descriptive text underneath. New influences in the form of American newspaper strips and comic books, imported into Britain at that time, and the advent of *Mickey Mouse Weekly* (1936), containing a combination of American reprints and new British material, exemplified a different 'American style' with less text and greater reliance on sequence, action, word balloons and visual humour. This American style was adopted by D.C. Thomson's *The Dandy* (1937–2012) and *The Beano* (1938–), and by artists such as Dudley D. Watkins and James Crichton. Unlike American comics though, British comics usually adopted an anthology format, allowing many genres to thrive.

American imports were banned in the 1940s and 1950s, partly as a wider form of economic protectionism, responding to the danger to British industries posed by the war, but also because imports that benefited the war effort were prioritized over entertainment. As a result smaller publishers such as Foldes Press in Edinburgh and Cartoon Art Productions in Glasgow, along with D.C. Thomson, produced comics that copied, and sometimes parodied, American examples. They often masqueraded as American products, emulating their format and design elements, and even displaying a price in cents to make them look authentic. In the late 1950s and early 1960s comics were at the height of their popularity and artists including Leo Baxendale, David Law and Ken Reid offered an even more spirited style of fun in

D.C. Thomson comics, delighting in compositional chaos. These styles soon dominated British humour comics, and were developed by the likes of David Sutherland. Alongside the humour and superhero comics were westerns, science-fiction, school stories, romance and war stories.

In the late 1960s and into the 1970s the influence of Spanish, Italian and French comics was increasingly evident, as were themes for an older readership. The photo-story appeared, based on the design of the Italian *fumetti* tradition of photo-comics. Comics studios in Dundee and Glasgow, run by the brothers Jock and Bill McCail, nurtured artists such as Sydney Jordan, who enjoyed considerable success with his science-fiction newspaper strip *Jeff Hawke* (1955–74). Ian Kennedy became renowned for striking colour paintings, especially of aircraft, which appeared in war comics, for example *Commando* (1961–). By the 1980s America was again the touchstone for a generation of Scottish comics creators such as Alan Grant, who wrote for *2000AD* and *Batman*. Cam Kennedy, who drew *Judge Dredd* and *Star Wars*, worked with Alan Grant to produce the definitive comic adaptations of Robert Louis Stevenson's nineteenth-century novella *The Strange Case of Dr Jekyll and Mr Hyde* and his adventure story *Kidnapped*. Grant Morrison was similarly inspired by Scottish gothic literature and art when he conceived the best-selling Batman graphic novel *Arkham Asylum* (1989).

By the 1990s the influence of Japanese manga was evident in the artwork of Frank Quitely, who brought together a rather

→ **Artwork for Dennis the Menace strip for publication in *The Beano*, by David Law**

Dundee, 1960
Paper, pencil, ink, white-out
D.C. THOMSON & CO. LTD, DUNDEE

David Law's strips were particularly masterful in how he employed design elements of perspective, colour and sequence to create a tension between the quite rigid format of the page and the anarchy contained therein. The use of 'sound effects' to shape the action and draw the eye of the reader through the composition is a particularly effective visual and narrative strategy.

strange combination of influences, including Dudley D. Watkins and Katsuhiro Otomo (*Akira*). When Morrison and Quitely joined forces in *All-Star Superman* (2005–8) they produced what has been widely acclaimed as one of the best Superman stories ever published, and Quitely became one of the most highly regarded comics artists in the world. In 2002 the writer Mark Millar laid the foundation for a more cinematic treatment of superheroes in *Kick-Ass* and *The Ultimates*, helping to develop what became known as 'widescreen' comics, which served as the inspiration for key aspects of the Marvel Cinematic Universe.

Today there is a thriving small press producing innovative comics in Scotland alongside continuing mainstream success. Creators such as the Glasgow-based couple Metaphrog (John Chalmers and Sandra Marrs) blend the comic book aesthetic with the design of children's books in, for example, *Louis: Red Letter Day* (2011) and *The Little Mermaid* (2017). Often inspired by an eclectic and international range of artistic influences, Scottish comics and creators have been hugely influential on comic book design worldwide, and continue to innovate with the medium.
CHRISTOPHER MURRAY

↖ *All-Star Superman*, vol. 1, written by Grant
Morrison, pencilled by Frank Quitely, inked
and coloured by Jamie Grant, lettered by Phil
Balsman, with introduction by Bob Schreck

Published by DC Comics in New York, c.2007–9
Printed book
V&A: NATIONAL ART LIBRARY, 38041009208414

Morrison's Superman is a sun-god, drawn from
mythology, and the twelve-issue series marks a
solar cycle. Quitely's artwork captures the sublime
aspects of this character in a homage to the supposed 'Silver Age' of 1950s and 1960s comics, but
his page design also decompresses the action, using
compositional techniques drawn from Japanese
comics and animation.

↑ *Kick-Ass* graphic novel, written and co-created by Mark Millar,
pencilled and co-created by John Romita Jr, inked by Tom Palmer,
coloured by Dean White, lettered by Chris Eliopoulos and edited by
John Barber

Published by Titan Books Ltd, London, 2010
Printed book
V&A: NATIONAL ART LIBRARY, 38041012074266

The Scottish writer Mark Millar took the central concept of Stan Lee and Steve
Ditko's *Spider-Man* and redesigned it, adding strong elements of parody and
cynicism, which recalls the tone of Frank Miller's revisionist take on Batman,
The Dark Knight Returns (1986). John Romita Jr, whose father was one of the
key *Spider-Man* artists of the 1960s, follows these cues perfectly, with visual
allusions to a range of comics. This comic, originally published as a series by
Icon between 2008 and 2010, offers a satirical commentary on the changing
values of the superhero in the modern world.

The Birth of the Videogames Industry in Dundee

The emergence of videogame development in Dundee in the mid-1980s can be linked to the manufacture of Sir Clive Sinclair's Spectrum home computer in the city and the increasing popularity of hobby programming clubs. The Kingsway Amateur Computing Club, which met at a local college to develop games for the Spectrum, became the meeting place for a group of young game developers who would go on to create the most successful game in history, *Grand Theft Auto*.

The establishment of DMA Design in 1984 marked the birth of the games industry in Dundee. The studio can be credited with pioneering processes and technical innovations based on iterative and collaborative approaches to games design that would become standard industry practice. This way of working involved the whole team in the design of the look, feel and functionality of the game.

In 1993 the success of *Lemmings* established DMA as a world-leading studio and by 1995 it had embarked on the development of a game that would allow the player to freely roam the game world, choosing when and where to embark on missions. Two years later the success of *Grand Theft Auto* established this mode of play, now known as sandbox games, as a new genre and, with it, Dundee as a global hub for games design.

By the late 1990s Scottish studios were leading the world in designing some of the most popular and innovative games by pushing the limits of real-time 3D graphics, dynamic material physics and visual fidelity. Games created in Scotland such as *State of Emergency*, *F1*, *Grand Theft Auto*, *Harry Potter* and *Medal of Honor* consistently topped the games charts.

Meanwhile, a small Dundee studio, established by the ex-DMA audio engineer Colin Anderson, would become a pioneer of 'casual gaming'. The company developed a design process for the creation of small, 2D, cartoon-style games with addictive repeatable gameplay. Through the development of 180 games, this studio, Denki, established many of the conventions and standards for the production of the casual and mobile games that dominate the industry today. GREGOR WHITE

← **Cover of *Lemmings*, by DMA Design, published by Psygnosis**

Dundee, 1991
Videogame
DUNDEE CITY COUNCIL (DUNDEE'S ART GALLERIES AND MUSEUMS): 2017–42–5

Recognized as one of the best games of the early 1990s, *Lemmings* is estimated to have sold more than 15 million copies in multiple versions. Its design and development exemplify ways of working that have become standard design practice in the games industry. As a result of the fundamental interdependencies between technical constraint, functionality and player experience, collaborative design practices were pioneered and refined at this time that bring together visual art, games design and programming.

↑ **Screen shot from *Grand Theft Auto***

Dundee, 1997
Videogame
ROCKSTAR GAMES

Originally entitled *Race 'n' Chase*, *Grand Theft Auto* started life as a 'demolition derby'-style racing game set in cityscapes where everyday traffic, including pedestrians, became obstacles in the race. The iterative design of the game has become an established method in the software development industry. Cycles of design, prototyping and evaluation resulted in the evolution of the racing game into Rockstar Games' genre-defining open world series, which became the fastest-selling media product of all time.

A Tweed Suit

Vivienne Westwood has championed the romantic use of Scottish fabrics and dress forms since her work with Malcolm McLaren in the mid-1970s, when strident tartan plaids were a staple part of the visual repertoire of punk. But it was in the late 1980s that a more explicit connection between Westwood's iconoclastic approach to design and tweed, the most traditional of wool weaves, was formed.

Westwood's 'Harris Tweed' collection of Autumn/Winter 1987/88 brought to the fore her interest in subverting ideas of heritage and monarchy, aristocratic taste and pursuits, and practices of tailoring and construction. Using the cloth of the Outer Hebrides, which shares in the reputation the islands have for rugged wildness and non-conformity, enabled her designs to undermine any stable understanding of national identity while drawing on the long-standing conservative codes of the British gentleman's wardrobe.

By the mid-1990s Westwood's interests extended to the reframing of male and female bodies and their relationship to politics and history, and in collections including 'Anglomania' of 1993 and 'On Liberty' of 1994 she drew heavily on the repertoire of Romanticism, French Revolutionary philosophy and dandyism. The sweeping drama of Walter Scott's novels and the ideas of the Scottish Enlightenment were never far from the provocative public explanations she offered of her work.

Westwood's hardcore followers, drawn to her London outlets, have generally come from a largely London-based media, club and fashion scene. But interestingly it is in Japan, China and South Korea that her work has enjoyed the most significant commercial success. Here her eccentricity and iconoclasm signify an energy and anti-conformist ideal attractive to a generation of consumers frustrated by the pressures of the status quo in society and work. It is perhaps also no coincidence that these are the very markets attracted most passionately to those staples of Scottish tourism: whisky, tartan and sublime wilderness. Through the rugged beauty of tweed Westwood has been able to weave all manner of myths. CHRISTOPHER BREWARD

→ **Suit, designed by Vivienne Westwood**

United Kingdom, c.1995
Harris tweed jacket, wool waistcoat and trousers
Given by Mark Reed
V&A: T.37:1 TO 3–2011

This ensemble is typical of Westwood's eclectic mixing of different styles and periods. The tartan jacket with contrasting collar and pockets draws on the patterns of late 19th- and mid-20th-century formal tailoring, while the waistcoat's wide shawl collar and voluptuous folds are closer to the forms of early 19th-century dandyism. The whole is unified by the vibrant combination of pattern, colour and texture. It evokes the drama of the baronial hall and grouse moor, but is designed with the bars and clubs of the metropolis in mind.

Reinventing Traditions:
Textile Heritage and Design Innovation

Scotland has a long-held reputation for producing some of the world's most luxurious fabrics. Built on a blend of heritage expertise, traditional skills and design innovation, companies such as Barrie Knitwear and MYB Textiles are today considered by many as Scotland's own 'métiers' (specialist crafts). Actively pursuing a sustainable future, they recognize the importance of preserving heritage skills by investing in training and apprentice-ships, teaching highly specialized techniques in-house.

Established in the Scottish Borders in 1903 as a manufacturer of hosiery, Barrie Knitwear later expanded its offer to include cardigans and pullovers. In the 1920s the French fashion designer Gabrielle (Coco) Chanel spent time in Scotland as a companion of the Duke of Westminster and was famously inspired by the colours and textures of Scottish cashmeres and tweeds. This led to the creation of Chanel's famous two-tone cardigan, which would become synonymous with both her own and Barrie's names. Today Barrie Knitwear is renowned for its outstanding expertise in premium cashmere, employing 250 staff to produce approximately 70,000 garments a year. Chanel acquired Barrie Knitwear in 2012, with the mill launching its epony-mous 'Barrie' label in 2014.

In Ayrshire, another area with a long textiles history, MYB Textiles produces highly crafted lace and madras fabrics, predominantly for the luxury interiors market. Founded in 1900, MYB is the sole remaining lace designer and manufacturer in Scotland. Originally, MYB exclusively manufactured the 'Scottish Leno Gauze weave', a semi-sheer muslin with openwork patterns. This became known as 'Scottish Madras' due to the large quantities exported in the early twentieth century to the Indian city (now Chennai), where it was a popular choice for curtains and furnishing fabrics. Combining centuries-old processes and design with new technologies, MYB's contemporary designs are inspired by the 50,000 pieces in its archive. Design innovation, including the development of unique flame-retardant products, has enabled MYB to enter new markets.

Barrie and MYB stand alongside other firms such as Johnstons of Elgin and Begg & Co. of Ayr, as rare survivors of what were once much larger industries. Their success is partly due to modernization and innovation, but also to the appeal of the 'Made in Scotland' brand, rep-resenting Scottish identity, design heritage, and the highest levels of quality and craftsmanship. Responding to international trends, these 'métiers' push the boundaries of machinery and materials to create some of the world's most sought-after products. TARA WAINWRIGHT

← Pullover, designed by Barrie, made by Barrie Knitwear

Hawick, Spring/Summer 2017
Cashmere
BARRIE KNITWEAR

Barrie's Spring/Summer 2017 collection combines an innovative take on traditional notions of Scotland with the high quality of craftsmanship for which it is renowned. Led by Odile Massuger, Barrie's creative director, the collection includes cashmere in a range of weights, featuring complex intarsia patterns and 3D textured motifs, such as an abstracted thistle, created using a fusion of cutting-edge technologies and artisanal hand-finished processes.

→ 'Fractal', designed by Margo Graham, MYB Textiles

Ayrshire, 2014
Cotton and polyester
MYB TEXTILES

MYB Textiles produces lace in various qualities: 8, 10, 12 and 14 point. Higher numbers of vertical threads per inch increase its delicacy and ability to represent detail. 'Fractal' is typical of MYB's most contemporary designs, from the 'Galloway Sheers' collection, which celebrates the beautiful simplicity of minimalist geometric lines.

Reconnecting Waterways: The Falkirk Wheel

The Falkirk Wheel is the world's first rotating boat lift. Designed to reconnect the disused Forth and Clyde and Union canals, it was conceived by the architect Tony Kettle of the practice RMJM as the spine that would once again link the waterways of east and west Scotland. Facing the same challenges as Scotland's eighteenth- and nineteenth-century canal builders, RMJM worked with a team of skilled engineers and contractors to develop a design that is both functional and inspirational.

A short, industrious spell of canal building from the 1760s to 1840s transformed Scotland's communications network, bringing benefits to the military, trade, industry and agriculture. Scotland's first canal, the Forth and Clyde (built 1768–90), enabled naval and trading vessels to avoid the arduous journey around the northern coast of Scotland. It also opened up the country's west coast to trade with the Baltic, and its east coast to trade with the Atlantic. The canal involved building Scotland's first land-lock, its first large-scale aqueduct and, at the time, its largest man-made reservoir. The Union Canal, built in 1817–22 to provide Edinburgh with direct access to sources of cheap coal from the west, also involved major feats of engineering, including an impressive series of aqueducts. From 1822 a flight of 11 locks, stepping down 25 metres (82 feet) over nearly 1 mile (1.6 km), linked the two canals near Falkirk. However, from the 1860s competition from the railways led to declining profits and 100 years later both canals closed.

Seeing renewed interest in Scotland's canals, and their value to the leisure and tourism industries, British Waterways launched the Millennium Link in 1999, a restoration project to reopen and reconnect the canals. The centrepiece would be a lift allowing boats to travel the 25-metre (82 feet) distance within 15 minutes. An initial review and concept design by the Dundee firm Nicoll Russell Architects helped secure Millennium Commission funding, and subsequently RMJM was appointed to realize the project. After much experimentation, RMJM proposed its revolutionary design for the Falkirk Wheel: a rotating beam that transports two boats up in one gondola at the same time as bringing two boats down in another. RMJM's design also involved extending the Union Canal, building a tunnel beneath the Antonine Wall (an ancient Roman fortification) and designing an aqueduct to connect the Wheel to the Forth and Clyde Canal. Achieving a feat of engineering to meet the brief, RMJM also created a structure of great beauty, with sculptural hooked arms that amplify the Wheel's sense of movement. MEREDITH MORE

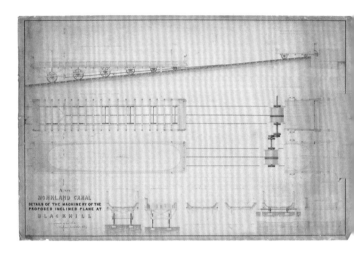

↑ *Details of the Machinery of the Proposed Inclined Plane at Blackhill, Monkland Canal*, by James Leslie

Probably Glasgow, 1839
Ink on paper
SCOTTISH CANALS: 1839. 56

Canal builders have been searching for alternatives to time-consuming lock systems since the 18th century. This tender drawing proposed an inclined plane for the Monkland Canal to reduce the time needed to transport boats up and down the hill at Blackhill by 30 minutes. From 1850 to 1887 boats were floated in iron containers and hauled up the inclined plane, bringing supplies of coal more quickly and reliably from the Monklands coalfields to Glasgow.

→ **The Falkirk Wheel, designed by RMJM**

Near Falkirk, 2002

RMJM took inspiration from a wide variety of sources when designing the Falkirk Wheel. The regular, yet fluid and organic form of the aqueduct references the elegance of Victorian examples, but was also inspired by the spine of a fish and the ribcage of a whale. The shape of the hooked arms recalls a Celtic double-headed axe, and their movement the vast turning propellers of a Clyde-built ship.

Fashion Design in the 21st Century

In the early twenty-first century Scotland is producing impressive fashion design talent. Recognized by the Scottish and British Fashion Awards and internationally, a range of designers born and trained in Scotland are continuing the country's long history of textile design within a fashion context. They are forging a path in Scotland, London and across the world, working with global brands or establishing their own labels, exploring eclectic aesthetics and influencing style.

One of the leading Scottish designers of the 2010s is Lanarkshire-born Christopher Kane, a graduate of Central St Martins, London. Since establishing his own label in 2006 in collaboration with his sister Tammy, who studied at the Scottish College of Textile Design in Galashiels, Kane has won numerous awards and achieved critical acclaim for his innovative and highly creative garments. From the bright neon bandage dresses that dazzled audiences at his graduate collection onwards, Kane has taken eclectic influences ranging from the film *Gone with the Wind* and outsider art to a Scottish Roman Catholic shrine, combined with an imaginative and novel approach to the cut, texture and juxtaposition of different fabrics. These have included Gainsborough silk damasks, metallic lamé, stretch lace and hand-crocheted cashmere. This last was produced in collaboration with Johnstons of Elgin, contributing to the revival of this traditional brand. Kane's success can be judged in part by the fact that in 2013 the luxury group Kering acquired a 51 per cent stake in his label, enabling its further global expansion.

The influence on Kane of his Scottish background and his use of Scottish fabrics (among others) are shared, if explored in very different ways, by a number of other designers. Charles Jeffrey, another Central St Martins graduate, has included cashmere by Begg & Co. of Ayr in his Charles Jeffrey LOVERBOY garments as well as traditional Aran knits, cut up and joined together with electrical tape. Dundee-born and -trained Hayley Scanlan references her Scottish identity in another way, creating studded leather garments that represent a strong, rebellious femininity inspired by heroines including Mary, Queen of Scots.

A continuation of Scotland's long history in textile design can also be seen in the strength of printed textiles created by some of these designers. Holly Fulton, who studied at Newcastle, Edinburgh College of Art and the Royal College of Art, London,

→ **Look 23, designed by Christopher Kane**

Spring/Summer 2017

For his 10th anniversary show in Spring/Summer 2017, Christopher Kane took the theme of wartime austerity and resourcefulness, combined with inspiration from his childhood, particularly the Carfin Grotto, a Roman Catholic shrine near Motherwell. The collection included sweatshirts printed with a St Christopher medallion motif, stone-encrusted Crocs™ footwear, and garments crafted from fragments of fabrics or juxtapositions of archival designs, evoking a make-do-and-mend approach.

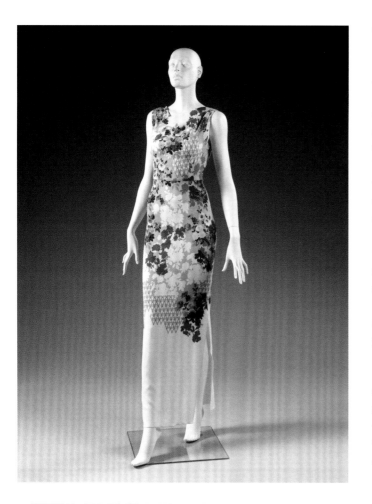

and who is Head of Fashion at Cambridge School of Visual & Performing Arts, is noted particularly for her bold, hand-drawn prints, often inspired by Art Deco architecture or by the 1960s aesthetics of Pop Art and the artist Eduardo Paolozzi. Designing prints at the same time as cutting patterns to ensure the specific way a print falls on the body, Fulton carries her interest in surface decoration into her jewellery, often designed to be worn with her garments to create an overall effect. Also acclaimed in print design is Jonathan Saunders, who studied printed textiles at The Glasgow School of Art before going on to fashion design at Central St Martins. Commissioned within 48 hours of his graduation show in 2002 to design prints for Alexander McQueen, Saunders has since created garments characterized by bold and brightly coloured prints combined with technical craftsmanship, first under his own label and from 2016 to 2017 as Chief Creative Officer for Diane von Furstenberg.

The challenge of achieving commercial success in fashion is universally acknowledged, and various initiatives exist to assist young designers in their early careers, including Scotland Re:Designed, Fashion Foundry, Fashion East and the British Fashion Council's NEWGEN (New Generation) scheme. The achievement of some of Scotland's young designers in winning support from these competitive schemes, and in taking it forwards to commercial success and award-winning acclaim, is testament to their talent and creativity and represents a thriving area of Scottish design. JOANNA NORMAN

↑ **'Celyn' evening dress,
by Jonathan Saunders**

London, Spring/Summer 2011
Printed silk crepe
V&A: T.69–2011

Several garments in Jonathan Saunders' 'Resort' 2011 collection featured a floral print that the designer had found in a Victorian textile archive. Saunders set the floral design alongside a geometric grid inspired by London's Art Deco architecture. He created a similar juxtaposition in the shape of the dress: a simple column but slit almost to the thigh, giving an edge to the elegance and a contemporary take on a traditional floral print.

→ **Dress, by Holly Fulton**

London, Autumn/Winter 2011
Silk and leather
V&A: T.56–2013

For her Autumn/Winter 2011 collection Holly Fulton took inspiration from the love affair between the Duke of Westminster and the French fashion designer Coco Chanel, set against the backdrop of the Duke's Scottish estate. The collection featured garments in Scottish fabrics such as tweeds as well as graphic prints including motifs referencing 1930s architecture. Several pieces featured Fulton's striking lip print, which she characteristically drew by hand, making each pair of lips unique.

Jewellery in Scotland

Scotland has a proud history of jewellery design from antiquity, seen in objects such as the eighth-century Hunterston brooch (now in National Museums Scotland), to the present day. The twentieth and twenty-first centuries have seen periods of strong, independent flowering of a Scottish jewellery culture, rooted in dynamic art schools, an active museum sector, informed patrons and international exchange through exhibitions in both museums and independent galleries.

Early twentieth-century jewellery design in Scotland was dominated by two distinct forces. The first was the linear European style fostered at The Glasgow School of Art under the direction of Francis Newbery, given form in jewellery by Talwin Morris and Jessie M. King's designs for Liberty & Co. of London. The second was a more pictorial style rooted in Arts and Crafts traditions, seen in works by the Edinburgh-based Phoebe Anna Traquair and the Aberdonian James Cromar Watt (see pp. 94–97).

After 1945 the teachings of the silversmith John Leslie Auld again drew the focus to Glasgow. He instilled in students a strong respect for the discipline of fine metalwork, together with a firm commitment to art-school teaching as a route to creative development. Pre-eminent among Auld's students were the silversmith Roger Millar and the jeweller Dorothy Hogg, who began a fruitful line of Scottish talent earning coveted postgraduate places at the Royal College of Art in London. They went on respectively to run and lecture at Duncan of Jordanstone College of Art in Dundee and then to run the jewellery courses at The Glasgow School of Art and Edinburgh College of Art.

Beneficial exchange with London is also visible in other ways. The Edinburgh-trained painter Alan Davie became part of the dynamic flowering of the Central School of Art in London in the 1950s under William Johnstone, who encouraged artists to teach in the Jewellery Department, stimulating cross-fertilization. The London designer Eric Spiller joined Grays School of Art in Aberdeen in the 1980s, overseeing the establishment of one of the earliest computer-aided design (CAD) 3D design facilities in a UK college.

The culture fostered by these educators bore fruit in the following generation's diverse careers. Having studied with Hogg and Millar at Dundee, Jack Cunningham took up the baton in education, running jewellery schools in Glasgow and Birmingham. Judy McCaig, based in Barcelona, also studied

↑ **Brooch from the 'Artery Series', by Dorothy Hogg**

Edinburgh, 2008
Oxidized silver and coral
The Louise Klapisch Collection, given by
Suzanne Selvi
V&A: M.32–2014

Dorothy Hogg first began her 'Artery Series' in 2000, and was still working on it when she undertook a six-month residency at the V&A in 2008. For the series she worked principally in sheet metal (usually silver), formed into tubes, with accents of symbolic red: in this case coral. She notes, 'I am interested in how silver and other metals can be fabricated to create hollow forms that have visual weight without physical density.'

→ Necklace, by Alan Davie

United Kingdom, 1954–55
Silver, copper and twisted silver wire
V&A: CIRC.374–1961

The multidisciplinary approach
fostered at Central School of Art
inspired Davie to create his own
neo-Primitivist works informed by an
interest in jazz improvisation. Davie's
jewellery was exhibited alongside that
of other artists in the International
Exhibition of Modern Jewellery held
at Goldsmiths' Hall in London in 1961.
This groundbreaking exhibition aimed
to 'encourage British designers in this
field' and 'show that creative imagina-
tion shown in one visual art can often
be diverted into another'.

at Dundee. Her miniature narratives in the form of brooches, sculptures and etchings echo the interdisciplinary pattern of working of earlier periods.

Other influential jewellery designers moved to Scotland in the post-war period. The artist and world-class engraver Malcolm Appleby established his first studio in Aberdeenshire in 1969. Peter Chang, a Liverpool- and London-trained sculptor and print-maker, moved to Glasgow in 1987, which catalyzed a new visibility for his avant-garde thermoformed recycled plastic jewellery and objects. The London-trained jeweller Adam Paxon spent a fruitful decade in Glasgow in the 1990s creating a famously sensuous 'creatures to wear' collection in carved, iridescent acrylics.

In the 1990s Edinburgh College of Art began to emerge as an outstanding school in jewellery design under the direction of Hogg and her colleague Susan Cross. Cross joined the college in 1989: her approach to crochet, knitting and binding metal wire introduced new ways of constructing metal form. Edinburgh style was essentially linear, growing from a strong emphasis on drawing, characterized by works such as those by Anna Gordon, who used oxidized silver and gold to construct simple geometric forms. The optically dazzling wirework of Andrew Lamb carried this into a new realm in 2000, winning him a coveted Dewar Arts Award in 2003 (the award established in memory of Donald Dewar in 2002 to support young artists, in all disciplines, at a pivotal point in their career). Lamb and Gordon both teach part-time at Glasgow, bringing their skills to the next generation. A following cohort of designers is exploring the interface between this Scottish educational strength of traditional hand skills and computer coding; they include Jonathan Boyd in Glasgow and the former aerospace engineer Lynne Maclachlan in Dundee.

Jewellery design in Scotland is a dynamic, shifting practice that has benefited from outstanding art schools and a cross-border exchange of ideas and people. Contemporary practitioners enjoy international recognition and the field continues to reveal itself as an experimental force in Scottish culture, with deep roots in traditions of fine metalwork, interdisciplinary working and scholarly knowledge of the global nature of jewellery cultures.

AMANDA GAME

↑ *Dear Green Place* brooch,
by Jack Cunningham

Glasgow, 2005
White metal, wood, ready-mades, carnelian
V&A: M.32–2017

Cunningham is known for creating subtle, coded pictograms in the form of brooches that explore his personal relationships to place and people in Scotland. *Dear Green Place* is the last of a series of four brooches in which he reinterprets Glasgow's coat of arms, combining elements to illustrate the following motto:

Here's the bird that never flew,
Here's the tree that never grew,
Here's the bell that never rang,
Here's the fish that never swam.

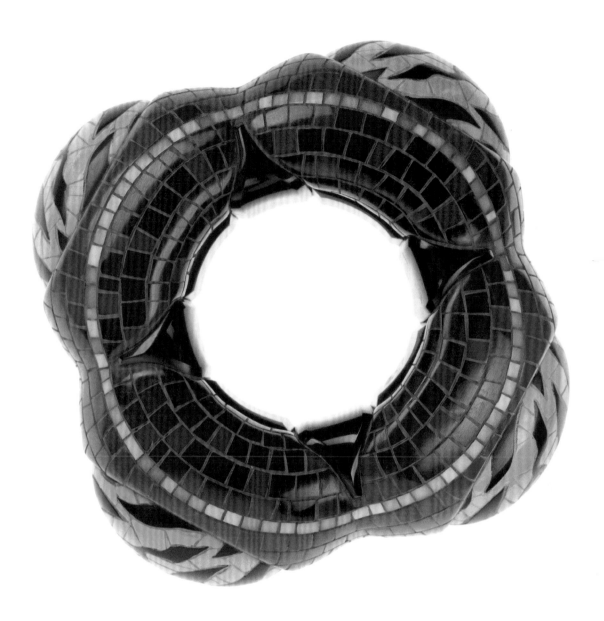

↑ *Bracelet 2*, by Peter Chang

Glasgow, 1987
Polystyrene foam, acrylic and PVC
NATIONAL MUSEUM OF SCOTLAND: A.1991.517

Peter Chang's preferred material for his sculptural jewellery was acrylic. His work sometimes involved found objects and recycled elements, and always used a time-consuming process of handcrafting. His futuristic, organic forms have graced fashion catwalks (for example Rifat Ozbek) and have been the subject of important museum shows (such as at the Museum of Arts and Design, New York; National Museums of Liverpool). He received major awards (Jerwood, 1995; Creative Scotland 2000) for the daring brilliance of works that display intricate depth of surface detail found in traditional crafts such as lacquer or mosaic, yet executed in (and transforming) the low-value material of plastic.

Craftsmanship, Character and Curiosity: Approaches to Contemporary Product Design

A belief shared by many of Scotland's leading designers is that, alongside improving lives, design can make the world more beautiful and more fun. Driven by a curiosity to explore, they create products that enrich our everyday experience and convey the personality of the designer. This is well illustrated in the work of two Scottish designers, Scott Jarvie and Angus Ross. Common to both is an attention to detail, hands-on craftsmanship and a desire to exploit the possibilities of the materials they are passionate about.

Angus Ross creates 'sketches in wood' from his Aberfeldy workshop in Highland Perthshire. He sources timber primarily from his own woodland, just five miles away, which is home only to native species – oak, ash and cherry. Carefully managing the woodland's sustainability, Ross selects a few trees a year to be felled based on his production requirements. This sense of place is vital to his work: Ross describes his creations as being 'rooted in Scotland, with a nod to the tradition of vernacular Scottish furniture'.

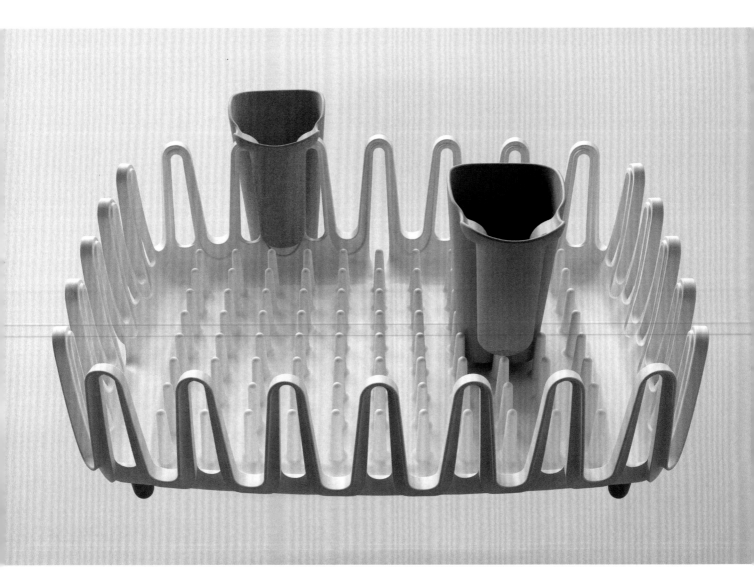

↙ 'Clam Shell' Dish Drainer, by Scott Jarvie for Lakeland

Designed in Scotland, made in China, 2015
Polypropylene

Of the products that Jarvie has designed for the kitchenware company Lakeland, he is most proud of the 'Clam Shell' Dish Drainer. Its key feature is flexibility, achieved through removable cutlery pots and a grid of prongs that allow dishes to be stacked in various configurations. Drainage can be controlled by changing the position of removable silicone feet to make the rack flat (to retain water) or sloping (to drain it): a simple, yet highly functional and adaptable design.

→ *Safe Cabinet*, by Scott Jarvie

Scotland, 2016
Bead-blasted aluminium, grey ash, layered birch

Inspired by bank-vault mechanisms and an interest in the disconnect between popular culture and 'the real world we build to live in', the *Safe Cabinet* is designed to bring an element of theatre to everyday life. Turned via the central hand wheel, the mechanism rotates continuously between the locked and unlocked position, creating the 'theatre' – a mesmerizing visual effect.

Describing himself as 'designer, maker and woodsman', Ross believes that this combination of disciplines is essential, underlining the many processes involved in his practice. Preserving craftsmanship for future generations is important to him: he runs apprenticeships and work-experience placements from his studio, enabling craftsmen from all over the world to spend time there honing their skills.

In contrast to Ross's materials-led approach, Glasgow-based Scott Jarvie designs for products with varying purposes, processes and materials. He describes his work as having – rather than a particular style – 'more of a personality that each piece conveys': playful, entertaining but always underpinned by a beautiful functionality.

The highest quality and craftsmanship is apparent in the work of both Ross and Jarvie, regardless of whether it is a mass-produced piece in injection-moulded plastic (Jarvie's work for the kitchenware company Lakeland) or the 'Unstable Stool' (Ross's most popular piece). Ross steam-bends 'green' (unseasoned) timber, enabling him to utilize a material that would otherwise serve as firewood. He states that 'steam bending is an art rather than a science' and relishes the non-uniformity of the process, as it allows the character of the wood to speak for itself.

Both designers share the view that good design is informed by 'robust thinking', and that Scotland has produced some of the world's greatest creative minds, Ross citing Charles Rennie Mackintosh as a particular inspiration. Jarvie describes how, with a detailed understanding of purpose, a designer can turn their hand to most disciplines – 'if you understand it, you can create it'. This notion allows him to work with ease across mass-produced pieces and also bespoke commissions. Both these designers have worked in or with industry, and are interested in making high-quality design accessible to a wider market: for this reason Ross takes on regular public commissions.

Both Ross and Jarvie love what they do and the freedom that design gives them to experiment with form, function and material. Their work provides an intriguing insight into the process of design, whether in the creation of a table, chair, vase, bean slicer or jelly strainer. Whatever the product, they share a methodology fuelled by curiosity and playfulness, and a desire to respond with an intuitive design that ultimately makes our experience of the world more enjoyable. TARA WAINWRIGHT

Forth Bench, by Angus Ross

Scotland, 2015
Oak

Sourced from Ross's own woodland, a single
length of oak is steam-bent into a spiral form
and transected with a 'love-seat' bench
created from steam-bent oak 'loops'. Ross
prefers to develop his work 'on the bench',
without the aid of drawings or models, allowing the character of the material 'to play
a role in defining its own shape and form'.

Designing for Performance Clothing

With Scotland's northerly latitude, mountainous terrain and heritage of textile manufacturing it is perhaps no surprise that the country's designers and entrepreneurs have developed a number of iconic outerwear and sporting brands. These include traditional brands such as Hunter, as well as the relative newcomer Endura, which makes high-tech cycle clothing. Both businesses have innovation at their heart and use design-led approaches to create high-quality products, responding directly to changing customer needs, fashions and new markets.

The North British Rubber Company (now Hunter Boot Ltd) was founded in Fountainbridge, Edinburgh, in 1856 by the American Henry Lee Norris, who emigrated to Scotland with a patent to produce vulcanized rubber, a revolutionary material created by adding sulphur to natural rubber to increase the material's durability. The company's original products were waterproof boots and 'storm resisting overshoes' but by the mid-twentieth century its output ranged from golf balls to bicycle tyres. In the First World War the firm made boots for over one million soldiers, helping to reduce the number of trench foot cases. Traditionally popular with farming, fishing and hunting communities, Hunter has two Royal Warrants and more recently, under the creative direction of Alasdhair Willis, has increased its fashionable appeal to younger urban customers across the globe.

A company with very different origins, Endura was established by the engineering graduate Jim McFarlane in 1993. Based in Livingston, West Lothian, it is now the UK's largest cycle clothing brand, acclaimed for its road bike-racing kit for Movistar Team and Cervélo-Bigla Pro Cycling, respectively Spanish men's and Swiss women's professional cycling teams. As a mountain biker, disappointed with the cost and quality of available products, McFarlane identified an opportunity to design clothing to cope with mud, abrasion and tear resistance, and recruited skilled machinists from the declining textile industry to produce the garments. The increasing costs of manufacture in China and the technical nature of the clothing justify the cost of employing skilled workers to manufacture the professional kits in Scotland, and has other benefits, as Jim explains: 'Endura's competitors don't manufacture so that strengthens our brand story and our staff feel a sense of pride because it's designed and made in Scotland.' SARAH SAUNDERS

↑ **Alex Dowsett wearing an Endura Movistar aero suit in the Drag2Zero Wind Tunnel**

2015

Endura works with multiple partners to co-design their products, informed by consumer feedback. Designs are digitally printed onto heat-resistant paper, transferred onto fabric using a heat press and then laser-cut, before undergoing ultrasonic bonding and the application of silicone. The garments are then field and lab tested. For professional cyclists such as Alex Dowsett, Endura uses laser scanning to make 3D prints of their bodies, ensuring individual fit and enhanced aerodynamic performance.

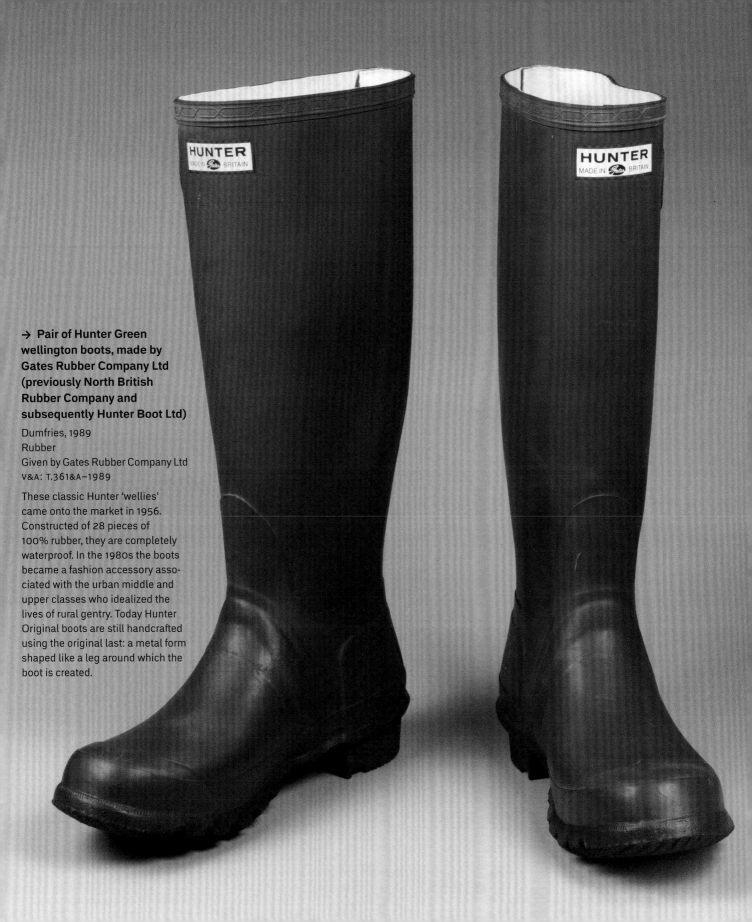

→ **Pair of Hunter Green wellington boots, made by Gates Rubber Company Ltd (previously North British Rubber Company and subsequently Hunter Boot Ltd)**

Dumfries, 1989
Rubber
Given by Gates Rubber Company Ltd
V&A: T.361&A–1989

These classic Hunter 'wellies' came onto the market in 1956. Constructed of 28 pieces of 100% rubber, they are completely waterproof. In the 1980s the boots became a fashion accessory associated with the urban middle and upper classes who idealized the lives of rural gentry. Today Hunter Original boots are still handcrafted using the original last: a metal form shaped like a leg around which the boot is created.

Healthcare by Design

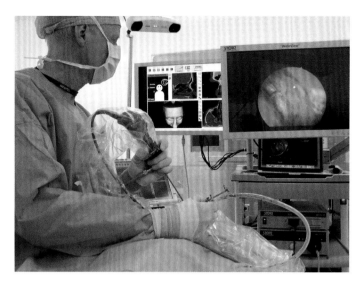

The multifaceted role of design in healthcare is being actively explored in various ways in Scotland. The development of new technologies, skills and techniques has revolutionized healthcare: the design of precision instruments, for example, has facilitated less invasive forms of surgery. However, the applications of design extend beyond instruments to the manner in which healthcare is practised and delivered in a digital era.

Healthcare design is founded on principles of empathy and understanding human interaction within health and social care systems. A design-led mindset introduces a strong focus on the emotional experience of care, not only for patients and carers, but also for healthcare workers and managers. The Maggie's Cancer Caring Centres (see pp. 188–89), which originated in Scotland in the 1990s, are excellent examples of architectural and interior design that create a warm, caring human experience for patients. User-centred design principles have led to advances in product design, with improved human interfaces and ergonomics, new materials, scaled-down sizes and features that allow doctors to see things better through high-definition visualization, augmented reality and radiological guidance. Digital design is a key element to all modern healthcare technology: inbuilt computation and robotic control reduce error, and gaming technologies facilitate the study of medical data, while 'wearable' devices, sensitive to human physiology, usher in continuous and safer patient monitoring. Online platforms enable diabetic patients to monitor their own care at home, empowering them to personalize this and engage easily with their healthcare support teams.

The redesign of health and social care services follows the values of service design methodologies: placing human experience at the very core of problem finding and the co-design of novel solutions. In 2016 the Scottish Chief Medical Officer introduced groundbreaking proposals for a mindset change in the practice of healthcare, which she described as 'Realistic Medicine'. She challenged doctors to be less paternalistic and to move towards more empathic, sustainable, personalized and shared models of caring, which have now become globally recognized. These are now being tackled through new design-led collaborations between the National Health Service and Scottish art and design colleges, uniting science, art and the creative industries to co-design future solutions for local and global healthcare. RODNEY MOUNTAIN

← Endoscopic surgery and associated skills training

Dundee, 1980s–present

From the 1980s a Dundee-based surgeon, Professor Sir Alfred Cuschieri, was part of a European effort to pioneer many of the now-standard techniques used in endoscopic, or 'keyhole', surgery. This involved close collaboration with the company Karl Storz, designers and manufacturers of rod-lens telescopes, high-definition video cameras and multifunctional micro-instruments. A new centre in Dundee was established to train surgical teams to work safely with these new technologies.

↙ McGRATH™ MAC
Enhanced direct laryngoscope (EDL), designed by Matt McGrath

Scotland, 2004
Steel alloy overlaid with medical grade thermoplastics, and medical-grade optical polymers

In 1999 Matt McGrath, a designer born in Benbecula, took up a Royal Society of Arts challenge to revitalize anaesthetic laryngoscopes, the design of which had not changed for years. His Fife-based company, Aircraft Medical, prototyped, developed and manufactured the world's first fully portable video laryngoscopes, which are now used globally. The design of the McGrath laryngoscope has allowed anaesthetists to see areas of the larynx that were previously inaccessible.

→ *Chief Medical Officer's Annual Report 2016: Realistic Medicine*, by Catherine Calderwood, graphic by APS Group Scotland

Scotland, 2016

Catherine Calderwood, Scotland's Chief Medical Officer from 2015, published a revolutionary report in 2016 called *Realistic Medicine*. It challenged healthcare workers to review the style, manner and way in which health and social care is practised and has gained significant global recognition. 'Realistic Medicine' is framed around key principles of shared decision-making, personalized care, collaboration, communication, creativity and culture change: all of which support a design-led approach to modernizing models of health and social care.

← snap40, designed by Christopher McCann and Stewart Whiting

Scotland, 2017
Plastic and electronics
SNAP40 LTD

snap40 is a tech start-up based in Edinburgh and founded by Chris McCann, a Glasgow-born Dundee medical student with a background in computing. snap40 aims to bring physicians quickly to patients at high risk of health deterioration, using artificial intelligence to automatically identify warning signs. A wearable device continuously monitors multiple vital signs, including respiratory rate, heart rate, relative change in systolic blood pressure, oxygen saturations, temperature, posture and movement.

Chief Medical Officer's Annual Report 2014-15
REALISTIC MEDICINE

REALISTIC MEDICINE
CAN WE:

CHANGE OUR STYLE TO **SHARED DECISION-MAKING?**

BUILD A **PERSONALISED** APPROACH TO CARE?

REDUCE HARM AND WASTE?

REDUCE **UNNECESSARY VARIATION** IN PRACTICE AND OUTCOMES?

MANAGE RISK BETTER?

BECOME IMPROVERS AND INNOVATORS?

Maggie's Cancer Caring Centres

'A Maggie's is all about a different kind of care, a care that is dispensed from a domestic scaled building yet it is not a house nor is it a hospital nor is it a church. Virtually all Maggie's plans evolve from the kitchen table; around having somewhere to go to the moment you enter the building. Our plan too develops from the kitchen table outwards to the courtyards, the trees and beyond.'
(Neil Gillespie of Reiach and Hall Architects, 2015)

From the modest idea, conceived in Edinburgh in 1994, of converting a rundown stable in the hospital car park that had been used to store ice into a beautiful space with a view of nature, Maggie's Cancer Caring Centres have become a phenomenon of contemporary architecture. Living with advanced cancer, and wishing to do something to improve the experience for others, Maggie Keswick Jencks, her husband, the cultural theorist, landscape designer and architectural historian Charles Jencks, and her cancer nurse Laura Lee devised a blueprint for a new kind of architecture: a cancer caring centre that would offer patients practical, social and emotional support, but that would also, through its design, inspire and uplift people, and take them beyond feeling like 'just another cancer patient'.

This blueprint forms the basis of the architectural brief for all Maggie's Centres. It challenges architects, practically and conceptually: sites are often awkward, the designs should be imaginative and beautiful, yet built as economically as possible, and should be able to provide a range of functions within a small footprint. Often working pro bono, architects have responded to the demands of this brief in varied and inventive ways, their designs inspired, for example, by minerals (Zaha Hadid, Fife), a pebble (Snøhetta, Aberdeen) or a treehouse (Piers Gough, Nottingham). At the heart of them all is the kitchen: the convivial and domestic hub into which visitors are welcomed.

With an ageing population and more people living longer with cancer, Maggie's Centres are used by an increasing number of people. With new centres opening in Scotland, the rest of the UK and internationally, Maggie's Centres continue their mission to, as the architect Frank Gehry says, 'engender life and optimism' through architecture. JOANNA NORMAN

→ **Maggie's Centre, Dundee, designed by Frank Gehry of Gehry Partners (garden by Arabella Lennox-Boyd)**
Dundee, 2003

Frank Gehry's design for Dundee brought Maggie's Centres to international attention. Its white-harled exterior reflects traditional Scottish building techniques, while its conical tower recalls Iron Age brochs (drystone conical domestic structures found in Scotland), and is set off by a folded metal roof said to be inspired by a Vermeer painting of a woman in a ruff. Inside, curving timber walls and ceilings envelop the visitor, while huge windows offer spectacular views, away from Ninewells Hospital and across the River Tay.

← **Sketch of the Maggie's Centre, Lanarkshire, by Neil Gillespie, Reiach and Hall Architects**
Edinburgh, 2017
Ink on paper
REIACH AND HALL ARCHITECTS

Taking his starting point from mature lime trees on the site, Neil Gillespie designed the Lanarkshire centre as a series of walled gardens, with perforated brick and glass walls creating a fluid relationship between inside and outside.

→ Model for Maggie's Centre, Highlands, by Page\Park Architects and Charles Jencks

c.2005 · Card, paper and wood
MAGGIE'S

The curved building and landscape of the Highlands centre in Inverness are designed as a harmonious, symbolic whole, representing the division of healthy human cells and so affirming life in defiance of cancer. In this collaborative design Page\Park's green patinated copper roof reflects Jencks's grassy landforms, while inside the centre birch-ply walls lean gently outwards, bringing natural light into the building.

Shaping Domestic Life

The way in which we organize our public life and the patterns and habits of our private lives are embodied in housing design. The formal arrangement of our homes – whether open-plan or cellular, detached cottages or tenement blocks – provides a clear expression of how we choose to live at any given moment in time. Architects are charged with giving shape to those aspirations, while at the same time meeting the parameters set by those who fund and build our homes.

The cottage and the tenement are forms of housing that have had a significant impact on the rural and urban landscapes of Scotland. The cottage is a potent reminder of how we have made our homes within the natural and rural landscape, and the tenement provides clues as to how we might live comfortably beside our neighbours in towns and cities.

In the last decades of the twentieth century architects working in Scotland's cities put considerable energy into thinking about the tenement. While tenements had been condemned as slums in the immediate post-war period, many were rehabilitated in the 1970s. By the 1990s tenement features such as the shared stair and the bay window overlooking the street seemed to offer some clues as to how to make good streets and urban spaces. Glaswegian architects, such as the firm of Elder and Cannon, explored how the tenement building form, with its shared gardens, high ceilings and elegant street façades, might evolve to suit the less rigidly structured lifestyles of a new generation.

Since the start of the new millennium political and creative attention has shifted towards the question of rural housing. Flexible working arrangements and digital technology, the need to attract key workers to remote communities, and the romantic impulse to 'escape to the country' mean that Scotland's rural settlements are confronting a complex mix of depopulation and rural growth.

→ House at Colbost, by Dualchas Architects

Waternish, Isle of Skye, 2012

This family house on open croft land overlooking Dunvegan Bay is clad in black timber to mimic the qualities of the agricultural buildings typical of the area. Rather than grouping together all of the rooms into a single volume, Dualchas created three forms around a courtyard: one large, open living space for eating and relaxing; a one and a half-storey element containing four bedrooms; and an outhouse for storing wood and other items.

Historically, planners overseeing developments in the Scottish countryside have set visual constraints on building elements such as the pitch of a roof or the use of a particular material: constraints that have tended to prevent design innovation. However, in 2001 the Scottish Government published *Designing Places*, a policy aimed at raising the quality of rural development, and some architects took up the challenge to develop housing that was innovative and energy-efficient, and that expressed a distinct regional language. Some of the first practices to address this question were those working in remote locations outside of the Central Belt: Dualchas and Rural Design, on the Islands, and Neil Sutherland, who set up MAKAR, his own timber-frame business, near Inverness.

Research into low-energy design has been undertaken in both practice and universities across the country, developing a serious expertise in passive approaches to environmental design. At the same time a number of larger established urban practices have participated in this ongoing discussion by building some very modern but romantic and evocative individual rural homes. Sometimes this design work is inspired by cottage forms, but cottages can be dark and their rooms are small. One response has been to adopt an aesthetic inspired by agricultural buildings such as the barn: providing large, open-plan living spaces which are both light and flexible, and openings that can be extended in summer and closed up in winter.

As this work has developed the forms adopted by architects seem to take their clues from land forms, the history of land use, or even the path of the sun and its casting of shadows. New computer software, digital manufacturing and new efficient structural systems such as cross-laminated timber allow architects to adopt a more playful approach to built form. These new homes, with their split sections and rising eaves and ridges, appear to have a more organic relationship to the landscape. PENNY LEWIS

↓ **Competition proposal for Fasque Castle Estate, by Sutherland Hussey Harris**

Fettercairn, Aberdeenshire, 2016

Fasque Castle sits within a historic landscape dating back to the 18th century. In 2013 the Fasque Castle Estate commissioned a masterplan for 100 housing units in the estate grounds and in 2015 they ran a competition for new housing designs. Sutherland Hussey Harris's proposal was inspired by the estate villages of the area. They imagined an innovative composition of terraces and detached houses organized around a verdant, car-free landscape with a farm shop and a sports hall. The approach provides a radical alternative to standard site layouts produced by many housebuilders.

↑ Turf House, by Rural Design

Kendram, Kilmaluag, Isle of Skye, 2012

This relatively small and affordable house (90 sq m (295 sq ft) in area) sits on the northern tip of Skye and is designed to withstand extreme weather conditions. The unusual form, the turf roof and larch cladding – which will turn silver over time – and the fact that it was built on low land were all design decisions made to minimize the building's visual impact.

→ St Vincent Place, Silvermills, by Reiach and Hall Architects

Edinburgh, 2006

St Stephen's Church (1827) by William Playfair is one of the most elegant churches in the second phase of Edinburgh's New Town. Designing a large tenement housing block on the adjacent site demanded a sensitivity to the enduring qualities of James Craig's design for the New Town. Reiach and Hall designed a new street and a restrained façade in a scheme built by AMA (New Town) Ltd.

Designing for Renewable Energy Production in Scotland

Since the early 2000s, the production of electricity in Scotland has changed considerably. The power sector has become largely decarbonized and, although oil and gas still predominantly meet energy demands for heat and transport, significant gains have been made in transitioning to low carbon in electricity generation. In 2015 renewables represented the largest source of electricity production (60 per cent), serving the majority of Scottish needs, with the remainder produced principally from nuclear plants.

Since the energy crisis of the early 1970s, Scotland has been recognized as a world leader in renewable technology development. Although there is no indigenous Scottish large-scale wind turbine manufacturer, the first multi-megawatt wind turbine was installed on Burgar Hill on Orkney in 1987. Today Scotland boasts some of the largest wind farms in the world, with Whitelee near Glasgow the largest in the UK. Scotland also offers 25 per cent of Europe's offshore wind resource, with the groundbreaking European Offshore Wind Deployment Centre, developed by Aberdeen Offshore Wind Farm Ltd (owned by the Swedish company Vattenfall) to test offshore wind design solutions and their impact on the environment and marine life.

In response to the 1970s' energy crisis Professor Stephen Salter at the University of Edinburgh became one of the modern pioneers of wave energy, designing the 'Salter duck' to generate hydraulic energy from wave power. Salter's research, design and experimentation sowed the seeds for significant developments in renewables from the late 1990s onwards. Every wave tank in the world employs wave-makers developed by the Edinburgh team in the 1980s (now commercialized by Edinburgh Designs Ltd), and hydraulic systems developed for converting the wave energy into electricity have been applied to other uses.

→ Pelamis, by Pelamis Wave Power
Orkney, 2012

The 'sea-snake' Pelamis was developed from 1998 and first tested at the EMEC in 2004. It was designed as a series of several articulated sections floating on the waves, the resulting movement producing energy that drove electrical generators inside the device. Although Pelamis was internationally successful as the first offshore wave device to generate electricity into a national grid, a lack of further funding resulted in the company going into administration in 2014.

Although the Salter duck was never built at full scale, it has influenced subsequent wave energy designs. In the late 1990s Edinburgh-based Ocean Power Delivery placed an interconnected string of 'ducks' perpendicular to the wave front to invent Pelamis, the 'sea-snake'. In parallel, Aquamarine Power, also based in Edinburgh, developed the Oyster Wave marine device in partnership with Queen's University Belfast. An Inverness-based company, Wavegen (originally Applied Research and Technology), developed another Queen's wave device, the Oscillating Water Column (OWC), installing the LIMPET (Land Installed Marine Power Energy Transmitter) device on Islay. Many of these and other devices were tested at the European Marine Energy Centre (EMEC) on Orkney, established in 2004 to provide full-scale grid-connected berths for testing wave and tidal devices. Unfortunately, these world-leading companies were unable to commercialize these technologies. However, the learning gained is being used to develop the next generation of marine technology within the Wave Energy Scotland programme, established by the Scottish government in 2014 to meet the challenge of producing reliable and cost-effective energy generation through wave energy design.

In addition to wave power, Scotland has rich tidal energy resources, with the Pentland Firth, described as the 'Saudi Arabia of tidal energy', having some of the fastest-flowing tides in the world. Since 2010 Atlantis has developed a phased plan for the largest tidal stream project in the world known as MeyGen, located between the northern coast of Scotland and Stroma. Beginning with four, Meygen plans to increase the number of turbines to eventually produce nearly 400 megawatts of energy. The world's first offshore tidal energy array was installed by Nova Innovation in 2016 in collaboration with the Belgian company ELSA, with two Nova M100 turbines in the Bluemull Sound exporting power to the Shetland grid. An alternative design approach has been developed by Scotrenewables, the creators of a floating tidal turbine device.

Although today renewables account for 60 per cent of electricity generated in Scotland, the capacity for increasing this proportion is significant. Scotland's rich natural resources, and the establishment of test facilities at all scales, lab and offshore, have led to Scotland being internationally recognized as a centre for marine research and a hub for leading marine energy technology developers. As the power sector continues to decarbonize, Scotland stands at the forefront of research and testing into design solutions for renewable energy generation.

MARKUS MUELLER

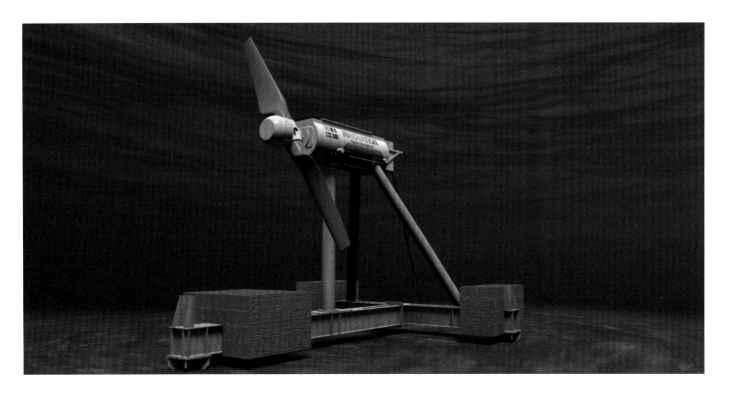

↖ Oyster Wave,
by Aquamarine Power Ltd

Orkney, 2013

Bolted to the seabed, the Oyster Wave was designed as a hinged flap whose movement captured wave power, driving hydraulic pistons to feed water to an onshore hydroelectric turbine. Although a relatively simple design, the Oyster was nonetheless difficult and expensive to produce and install, and its location on the seabed led to concerns about environmental impact. Despite being the only wave technology of its time to operate successfully in all ocean conditions, Oyster was unable to prove commercially viable.

↑ Nova M100 tidal turbine,
by Nova Innovation

Edinburgh, 2015

As tides are more predictable than waves, tidal energy is a much more reliable renewable resource. Nova Innovation is led in its designs by dependability and lowering cost: it uses robust standard parts and modular systems that can be transported and installed around the world using standard containers and vehicles. Its Nova M100 turbine reflects learning taken from the earlier and smaller Nova M30: it is twice as expensive but three times as powerful.

↓ SR2000 2 MW floating tidal turbine,
by Scotrenewables

Orkney, 2017

Scotrenewables Tidal Technology developed the world's first floating tidal turbine. It is designed to harness wave power closest to the surface where it is strongest, to minimize impact on marine life, and to reduce the difficulty and costs of maintenance. Its propellers fold in while being towed to reduce drag, and most of its internal parts sit above the waterline to facilitate access. These design solutions reflect the learning from earlier devices and aim to improve commercial viability.

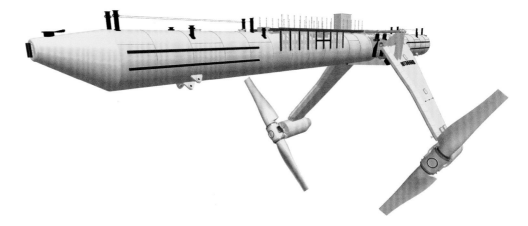

Automated and Electric: The Future of Car Design

The automotive industry is currently undergoing radical changes. Concerns about the safety and environmental impact of cars are leading towards the development of electric vehicles and autonomous driving. Dumfries-born Ian Callum, Director of Design at Jaguar, and his brother Moray, Vice President of Design at Ford, are leading their car companies in different directions to respond to these issues – and to design fundamentally distinct driver experiences.

Since 1999 Ian's design direction has transformed Jaguar back into an energetic, creative marque pushing at the limits of design and engineering. New models including the F-TYPE, a reinvention of the classic E-Type two-seat sports car, helped bridge a period in the 1980s and 1990s when the designs matured along with Jaguar's core audience, causing the company that Ian had loved from childhood to lose its dynamism and excitement.

The company's I-PACE project (2018), Jaguar's first fully electric car, has been designed, like all its others, using a mix of traditional skills and modern technology. 'We still sketch, we still draw, and then we turn that drawing into a 3D model digitally,' Ian explains. Electric motors on both front and rear axles provide instant torque, unlike the acceleration lag of traditional vehicles. Electrification also enables a redesign of the car's interior, as the removal of a combustion engine creates more space and flexibility.

Ford is pushing forwards in a different direction, towards self-driving vehicles for ride-sharing. The company announced plans in 2016 to mass-produce by 2021 an SAE Level 4 autonomous car, at the second-highest level of vehicle automation. The international Society of Automotive Engineers has six levels of automation – from 0 to 5 – with a Level 4 car not requiring a driver to control any part of driving. To achieve this Ford has invested in several technology firms specializing in camera and radar technology, 3D mapping and 'machine learning'.

'Good design is all about problem solving, but the problems change,' says Moray, whose notable designs include the Mazda MX-5 sports car, the new Ford Mustang (2015) and the new Ford GT (2017). He also predicts self-driving cars affecting automotive design in other ways, such as in-car digital screens focusing on passenger entertainment rather than presenting a potential distraction and safety hazard.

'The next ten years in this business is going to be the biggest change and challenge since the turn of the last century when cars took over from horses,' Moray adds. 'To me it's that dramatic.' CHRIS WILSON

→ **Designs for the I-PACE Concept, by Jaguar**
Coventry, 2017
Design sketches
JAGUAR

The fully electric concept car, which has zero vehicle emissions, has been revealed in advance of the production model. Sketches and subsequent 3D digital models form the basis for full-sized models in clay or foam that facilitate the development and testing of the design. The design of the I-PACE Concept combines a spacious, luxurious interior and striking new aerodynamic features – including a scooped-out bonnet – while still being instantly recognizable as a Jaguar.

← **Ford Fusion Hybrid autonomous car**
Dearborn, Michigan, 2016

Self-driving Fords with visible, externally mounted cameras and sensors were first tested in Mcity, the University of Michigan's urban testing environment, before being trialled on roads in Arizona, California and Michigan. The company is now incorporating these cameras and sensors into parts of the car, such as roofracks, in order to create a design that resembles a non-autonomous vehicle as closely as possible.

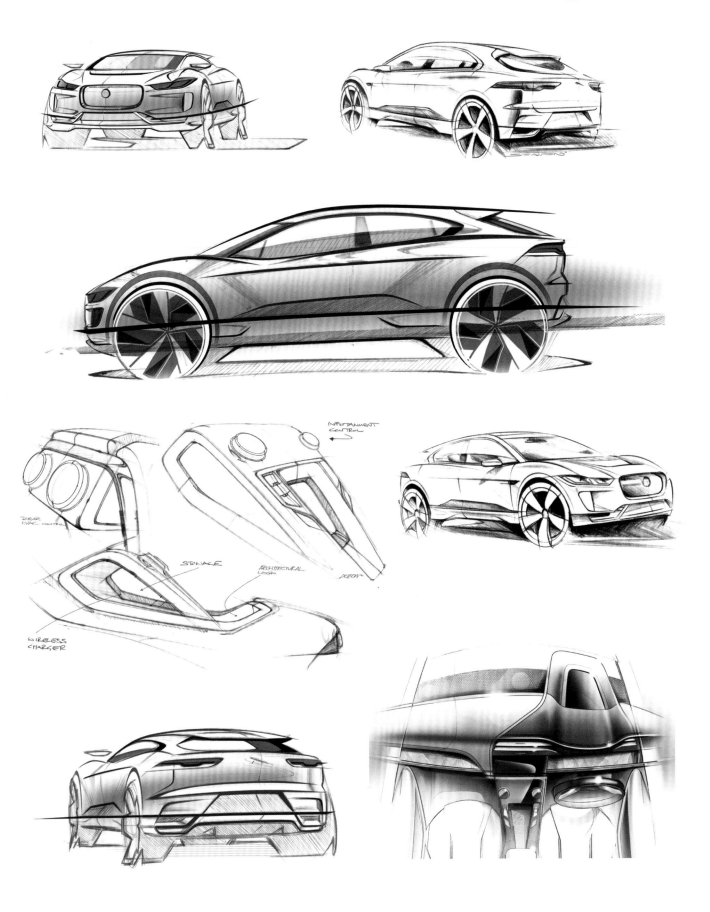

INFOTAINMENT CONTROL

REAR HVAC CONTROL

STORAGE

ARCHITECTURAL LOOP

WIRELESS CHARGER

Videogames Now

In the 2010s the games sector in Scotland is enjoying another transformative period of growth and innovation. Global companies and individual game-makers are leading the way in developing new technologies, approaches and applications to engage games and play in almost infinite game worlds, using games in social and cultural activities, or as tools in science, medicine and industry.

Over more than 30 years commercial games development in Scotland has been through a number of distinct phases characterized by technological and platform innovation, creativity and design ingenuity. Each phase has disrupted the videogames industry and has resulted in cycles of growth, collapse and recovery. Throughout these cycles the industry has learned, matured, diversified and grown.

The surge in popularity of videogames that accompanied the personal computer revolution in the 1980s soon led to the dominance of games consoles and a race to improve visual fidelity, scale and complexity throughout the 1990s. The 2000s brought the mobile computing revolution and the advent of touchscreens, motion controls and tablet computing. Ubiquitous network access and the pervasiveness of interactive digital media have led to the adoption of gamelike experiences and playful interactions in new social and cultural contexts.

Today, games are no longer solely the preserve of teenagers or even the entertainment industry. As games, and the way in which we interact with them, become more sophisticated, the conventions and processes once exclusive to videogames are being used to bring extra dimensions to the way in which we experience other, more traditional cultural forms. They are increasingly used to educate, to interrogate ideas, and to visualize and explore complex information, situations and environments.

Many of the creative practices in games development find their roots in traditional art forms; storytelling, visual design and musical composition are all deployed in games. Recent interactions between games designers and cultural practitioners have proved to be a rich, creative space for the innovation of new engaging experiences and the cross-fertilization of audiences across these distinct traditional and contemporary styles.

In 2013 the Dundee-based games developer Quartic Llama collaborated with the National Theatre of Scotland to create

→ **Screenshots from 'Player One' and 'Player Two' sections of** *Killbox*, **a collaboration between artist Joseph DeLappe and game developers Malath Abbas, Tom De Majo and Albert Elwin of Biome Collective**
Dundee, 2017
Videogame
BIOME COLLECTIVE

Taking its name from a military term for a 3D target space for joint weapons fire, *Killbox* is an online game and interactive installation that enables the player to assume the role of either drone pilot or civilian. The game confronts current manifestations of political and military power and highlights the ways in which virtualization and abstraction have changed contemporary attitudes to war. *Killbox* exposes videogames' fascination with military conflict in the most chilling of experiences.

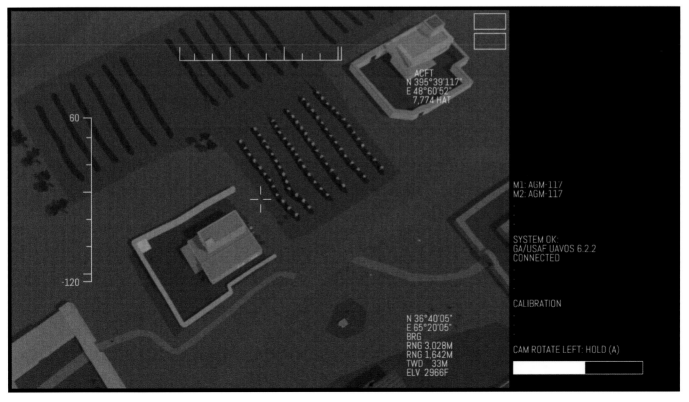

ACFT
N 395°39'117"
E 48°60'52"
7,774 HAT

60

-120

N 36°40'05"
E 65°20'05"
BRG
RNG 3.028M
RNG 1.642M
TWD   33M
ELV 2966F

M1: AGM-117
M2: AGM-117

SYSTEM OK:
GA/USAF UAVOS 6.2.2
CONNECTED

CALIBRATION

CAM ROTATE LEFT: HOLD (A)

Other, an award-winning location-based game that was a companion piece to the Dundee Repertory Theatre's production of *Let the Right One In*. That same year the book publisher Faber & Faber came together with the designer Simon Meek to create a visually rich and deeply interactive adaptation of John Buchan's 1915 novel *The Thirty-Nine Steps*. These pioneering works have inspired games developers to investigate new formats, locations and communities where play can be used to explore and present new expressions of contemporary cultural life.

As games have become increasingly sophisticated, Dundee has become associated with the development of videogames that engage with significant social challenges. Games designers in the city have begun to work with third-sector organizations to create games that offer insight into issues such as transitioning out of care, or sexual consent, through the use of simulated, playable scenarios. Similarly, games that are intended to educate players about environmental sustainability, energy use and healthcare

↑ **'A Meeting at Nijinsky's Bar', screen shot from *Beckett*, by The Secret Experiment**

Glasgow, 2018
Videogame
THE SECRET EXPERIMENT

Simon Meek, The Secret Experiment's Creative Director, describes *Beckett* as an 'ugly' game: not in its visual design but in the emotions, fears and motivations of its characters. Simon sees himself as an anti-establishment game-maker offering an alternative to mainstream games by engaging with human emotions and dramatic themes through the adaptation of literary works. By disaggregating the story components of existing works, these 'digital adaptations' reconfigure characters, locations and events into an interactive playable experience.

↑ 'Quarrel map',
screen shot from *Quarrel*, by Denki

Dundee, 2011
Videogame
DENKI

Winner of 'Best Game' at the BAFTA Scotland
awards in 2011, *Quarrel* is Denki's most
critically successful game. It embodies the
studio's design philosophy, which builds on
a deeply held commitment to the craft of
game-making, honed over the development of
more than 180 games. On these foundations,
the studio built its repertoire of play strategies,
consistently seeking inspiration in other forms
of play, from action figures to board games.

have been developed in partnership with researchers in local
universities.

At the cutting edge of the interface of games and science,
researchers at Abertay University have been using games
development processes and techniques to simulate complex,
data-rich and dynamic experimental environments that support
medical and environmental modelling, planning and prediction.
The future of games design in the city and Scotland remains as
diverse, unpredictable and exciting as ever. GREGOR WHITE

Contributors

FRANK ANDREWS Glass Historian

MARTIN BELLAMY Research and Curatorial Manager, Glasgow Museums

CHRISTOPHER BREWARD Director of Collection and Research, National Galleries of Scotland

ALISON BROWN Curator of European Decorative Art from 1800, Glasgow Museums

SAU FONG CHAN Curator, Asian Department, Victoria and Albert Museum, London

RACHEL CHISHOLM Curator, Highland Folk Museum, Newtonmore

DAN COUGHLAN Curator of Textiles, Paisley Museum

NEIL CURTIS Head of Museums, University of Aberdeen

MAX DONNELLY Senior Curator of 19th-Century Furniture, Department of Furniture, Textiles and Fashion, Victoria and Albert Museum, London

LINDA FAIRLIE AND BRUCE MORGAN Curators, East Ayrshire Leisure Trust

AVALON FOTHERINGHAM Curator, Asian Department, Victoria and Albert Museum, London

FRANCES FOWLE Reader in History of Art and International Director of Edinburgh College of Art, University of Edinburgh; Senior Curator, Scottish National Gallery, Edinburgh

AMANDA GAME Independent Scholar and Curator

ALISON HARLEY Independent Scholar and Practitioner in Design and Textiles

LORENS HOLM Reader in History and Theory of Architecture and Director of the Geddes Institute for Urban Research, University of Dundee

PENNY LEWIS Lecturer, Architecture and Urban Planning, University of Dundee

PHILIP LONG Director, V&A Dundee

MHAIRI MAXWELL Assistant Curator, V&A Dundee

JULIE McCOMBIE Curator of Social History, Dundee Museums and Art Galleries, Leisure and Culture Dundee

MEREDITH MORE Assistant Curator, V&A Dundee

RODNEY MOUNTAIN Surgeon and Lead for Healthcare Design and Innovation at the Academic Health Science Partnership in Tayside

MARKUS MUELLER Professor of Electronics and Electrical Engineering and Head of the Energy Systems Research Institute, University of Edinburgh

CHRISTOPHER MURRAY Professor of Comics Studies, University of Dundee

JOANNA NORMAN Director of the V&A Research Institute, Victoria and Albert Museum, London, and Lead Curator, Scottish Design Galleries, V&A Dundee

ANGUS PATTERSON Senior Curator, Department of Sculpture, Metalwork, Ceramics and Glass, Victoria and Albert Museum, London

JOHNNY RODGER Professor of Urban Literature, The Glasgow School of Art

SARAH SAUNDERS Head of Learning and National Partnerships, British Museum

SIMON SLADEN Senior Curator of Modern and Contemporary Performance, Victoria and Albert Museum, London

TARA WAINWRIGHT Marketing and Audiences Manager, V&A Dundee

GREGOR WHITE Professor of Applied Creativity and Head of School of Design and Informatics, Abertay University, Dundee

CHRIS WILSON Communications Manager, V&A Dundee

'Skara Brae' furnishing fabric designed by William Scott, made by Edinburgh Weavers
See p. 131

Further Reading

Introduction (pages 8–17)

Jenni Calder (ed.), *The Wealth of a Nation* (Edinburgh 1989)

Tom Devine, *To the Ends of the Earth: Scotland's Global Diaspora 1750–2010* (London 2012)

Dictionary of Scottish Architects, www.scottisharchitects.org.uk, accessed 8 November 2017

Miles Glendinning, Ranald MacInnes and Aonghus McKechnie, *A History of Scottish Architecture from the Renaissance to the Present Day* (Edinburgh 1996)

Ian Gow, *The Scottish Interior* (Edinburgh 1992)

Wendy Kaplan (ed.), *Scotland Creates: 5000 Years of Art and Design* (published to accompany an exhibition at the McLellan Galleries, Glasgow; London 1990)

John Keay and Julia Keay (eds), *Collins Encyclopaedia of Scotland* (London 1994)

Peter J.M. McEwan, *Dictionary of Scottish Art and Architecture* (Woodbridge 1994)

Duncan Macmillan, *Scottish Art 1460–1990* (Edinburgh 1996)

Scotland and France: Design and the Auld Alliance (pages 18–21)

French Connections: Scotland and the Arts of France (Edinburgh 1985)

Renaissance Decorative Arts in Scotland 1480–1650 (Edinburgh 1959)

Rowan Watson, *Western Illuminated Manuscripts: a catalogue of works in the National Art Library from the 11th to the early 20th century, with a complete account of the George Reid collection* (London 2011)

East Coast Trade and its Influence on Design (pages 22–23)

Michael Bath, *Renaissance Decorative Painting in Scotland* (Edinburgh 2002)

James Dow, 'Scottish Trade with Sweden, 1580–1622', *The Scottish Historical Review* (October 1969), vol. 48, no. 146, pt 2, pp. 124–50

Julia Lloyd Williams, *Dutch Art and Scotland: A Reflection of Taste* (Edinburgh 1992)

Matthew Price, 'Crowsteps in Fife', *Context: The Institute of Historic Building Conservation* (March 2013), no. 128, pp. 34–37

T.C. Smout, 'Scottish Commercial Factors in the Baltic at the End of the Seventeenth Century', *The Scottish Historical Review* (October 1960), vol. 39, no. 128, pt 2, pp. 122–28

Craftsmanship, Training and Trade Incorporations (pages 24–27)

W. Cunningham, Presidential Address: 'The Guildry and Trade Incorporations in Scottish Towns', *Transactions of the Royal Historical Society* (1913), vol. 7, pp. 1–24

George Dalgleish and Henry Steuart Fothringham, *Silver: Made in Scotland* (Edinburgh 2008)

G.E.P. How, 'Canongate Goldsmiths and Jewellers', *The Burlington Magazine* (June 1939), vol. 74, no. 435, pp. 282–84, 286–88

Stephen Jackson, 'Trade Incorporation Ceremonial Chairs', *Proceedings of the Society of Antiquaries of Scotland* (1997), vol. 127, pp. 945–56

Scottish Pistols (pages 28–29)

Claude Blair, *Pistols of the World* (London 1968)

David Caldwell, 'Scottish Traditional Gunmaking', *Journal of the Antique Metalware Society* (June 2005), vol. 13, pp. 36–39

Fergus Cannan, *Scottish Arms and Armour* (Oxford 2009)

John Hayward, *The Art of the Gunmaker*, vol. 2: *Europe and America 1660–1830* (London 1963)

Jacobitism: Allegiance through Design (pages 30–31)

Michael Darby, 'Jacobite Garters', *Victoria and Albert Museum Bulletin* (1966), vol. II, pp. 157–63

David Forsyth (ed.), *Bonnie Prince Charlie and the Jacobites* (Edinburgh 2017)

Jacqueline Riding, *Jacobites: A New History of the '45 Rebellion* (London 2016)

Margaret Sankey and Daniel Szechi, 'Elite Culture and the Decline of Scottish Jacobitism 1716–1745', *Past & Present* (November 2001), no. 173, pp. 90–128

Geoffrey Seddon, *The Jacobites and their Drinking Glasses* (Woodbridge 1995)

Architecture, Innovation and Dissemination (pages 32–33)

Howard Colvin, 'A Scottish Origin for English Palladianism', *Architectural History* (1974), vol. 17, pp. 5–13, 41–52

Eileen Harris, 'Vitruvius Britannicus before Colen Campbell', *The Burlington Magazine* (May 1986), vol. 128, no. 998, pp. 338–46

Eileen Harris, assisted by Nicholas Savage, *British Architectural Books and Writers, 1556–1785* (Cambridge and New York 1990)

Rebecca di Mambro, 'James Smith at Hamilton: a Study in Scottish Classicism', *Architectural History* (2012), vol. 55, pp. 111–43

Alistair Rowan, 'The Building of Hopetoun, *Architectural History*, vol. 27, Design and Practice in British Architecture: Studies in Architectural History presented to Howard Colvin (1984), pp. 183–209

James Simpson, Introduction to facsimile edition of *Vitruvius Scoticus: Plans, Elevations, and Sections of Public Buildings, Noblemen's and Gentlemen's Houses in Scotland* (London 2013)

Enlightenment Edinburgh (pages 34–37)

Frank A. Kafker, 'The Achievement of Andrew Bell and Colin Macfarquhar as the First Publishers of the *Encyclopaedia Britannica*', *British Journal for Eighteenth-Century Studies* (Autumn 1995), vol. 18, no. 2, pp. 139–52

John Lowrey, 'From Caesarea to Athens: Greek Revival Edinburgh and the Question of Scottish Identity within the Unionist State', *Journal of the Society of Architectural Historians* (June 2001), vol. 60, no. 2, pp. 136–57

M.K. Meade, 'Plans of the New Town of Edinburgh', *Architectural History* (1971), vol. 14, pp. 40–52, 142–48

Alison Morrison-Low and J.R.R. Christie, '*Martyr of Science': Sir David Brewster, 1781–1868* (Edinburgh 1984)

Anuradha S. Naik and Margaret C.H. Stewart, 'The Hellenisation of Edinburgh: Cityscape, Architecture and the Athenian Cast Collection', *Journal of the Society of Architectural Historians* (September 2007), vol. 66, no. 3, pp. 366–89

Stana Nenadic, 'Middle-rank Consumers and Domestic Culture in Edinburgh and Glasgow 1720–1840', *Past & Present* (November 1994), no. 145, pp. 122–56

Robert Adam and the Creation of a Style (pages 38–41)

Adriano Aymonino and Manbolo Guerci, 'The Architectural Transformation of Northumberland House under the 7th Duke of Somerset and the 1st Duke and Duchess of Northumberland, 1748–86', *The Antiquaries Journal* (2016), no. 96, pp. 315–61

Eileen Harris, *The Genius of Robert Adam: His Interiors* (New Haven and London 2001)

David Owsley and William Rieder, *The Glass Drawing Room from Northumberland House* (London 1974)

Alistair J. Rowan, 'After the Adelphi: Forgotten Years in the Adam Brothers' Practice', *Journal of the Royal Society of Arts* (September 1974), vol. 122, no. 5218, pp. 659–710

Margaret H.B. Sanderson, *Robert Adam and Scotland: Portrait of an Architect* (Edinburgh 1992)

The Carron Iron Company (pages 42–43)

R.H. Campbell, *Carron Company* (Edinburgh and London 1961)

John Gay, introduced by Gavin Stamp, *Cast Iron: Architecture and Ornament, Function and Fantasy* (London 1985)

Brian Watters, *Carron: Where Iron Runs like Water* (Falkirk 2010)

Scots and North America: Emigration and Entrepreneurship (pages 44–45)

'Thomas Affleck', in *Philadelphia, Three Centuries of American Art* (Philadelphia 1976), pp. 98–99

Vanessa Habib, Jim Gray and Sheila Forbes (eds), *Making for America: Transatlantic Craftsmanship: Scotland and the Americas in the Eighteenth and Nineteenth Centuries* (Edinburgh 2013)

Clark Hunter, *The Life and Letters of Alexander Wilson*, Memoirs of the American Philosophical Society, vol. 154 (Philadelphia 1983)

Laura Rigal, 'Empire of Birds: Alexander Wilson's American Ornithology', *Huntington Library Quarterly* (1996), vol. 59, no. 2/3, pp. 232–68

Scots in Russia (pages 46–47)

Anthony Cross, *By the Banks of the Neva: Chapters from the Lives and Careers of the British in Eighteenth-century Russia* (Cambridge 1997)

Paul Dukes, *The Caledonian Phalanx: Scots in Russia* (Edinburgh 1987)

Miliza Korshunova and Larissa Haskell, 'William Hastie in Russia', *Architectural History* (1974), vol. 17, pp. 14–21, 53–56

Albert J. Schmidt, 'William Hastie, Scottish Planner of Russian Cities', *Proceedings of the American Philosophical Society* (18 June 1970), vol. 114, no. 3, pp. 226–43

Dimitri Shvidkovsky, *The Empress and the Architect: British Architecture and Gardens at the Court of Catherine the Great* (New Haven and London 1996)

Thomas Telford (pages 48–49)

Anthony Burton, *Thomas Telford: Master Builder of Roads and Canals* (London 2015)

Julian Glover, *Man of Iron: Thomas Telford and the Building of Britain* (London 2017)

Chris Morris, *Thomas Telford's Scotland* (Gloucestershire 2009)

Henry Petroski, 'Engineering: Thomas Telford', *American Scientist* (March–April 2008), vol. 96, no. 2, pp. 99–103

The Paisley Weaving Industry (pages 50–51)

Kimberly Chrisman Campbell, 'Paisley Before the Shawl: The Scottish Silk Gauze Industry', *Textile History* (2002), vol. 33, no. 2, pp. 162–76

Maureen Lochrie, 'The Paisley Shawl Industry', in John Butt and Kenneth Ponting (eds), *Scottish Textile History* (Aberdeen 1987), pp. 95–111

Valerie Reilly, *The Illustrated History of the Paisley Shawl* (Glasgow 1996)

A.M. Stewart, *The History and the Romance of the Paisley Shawl* (Glasgow 1963)

Ayrshire Needlework (pages 52–53)

Agnes F. Bryson, *Ayrshire Needlework* (London 1989)

Margaret H. Swain, *The Flowerers: The Origins and History of Ayrshire Needlework* (London 1955)

Margaret H. Swain, *Ayrshire and Other Whitework* (United Kingdom 1982)

Heather Toomer, *Baby Wore White: Robes for Special Occasions, 1800–1910* (United Kingdom 2005)

Highland and Traveller Crafts (pages 54–55)

Jenny Carter and Janet Rae, *Traditional Crafts of Scotland* (Edinburgh 1988)

I.F. Grant, *Highland Folk Ways* (London 1961)

James A. Mackay, *Rural Crafts in Scotland* (London 1976)

Timothy Neat, *The Summer Walkers* (Edinburgh 1996)

Stanley Robertson, *Scottish Travelling People*, Scottish Life and Society, vol. 9 (Edinburgh 2005)

Highlandism: The Romanticization of Scotland (pages 56–59)

Howard Gaskill (ed.), *The Reception of Ossian in Europe* (London 2008)

Catherine Gordon, 'The Illustration of Sir Walter Scott: Nineteenth-Century Enthusiasm and Adaptation', *Journal of the Warburg and Courtauld Institutes* (1971), vol. 34, pp. 297–317

Ian Gow, 'Mary Queen of Scots meets Charles Rennie Mackintosh: Some Problems in the Historiography of the Scotch Baronial Revival Interior', *Furniture History* (1996), vol. 32, pp. 1–32

John Morrison, '"The whole is quite consonant with the truth": Queen Victoria and the Myth of the Highlands', *Victoria and Albert: Art and Love* (London 2010) [e-published collection of essays from study day]

Coleman O Parsons, 'Sir Walter Scott: Yesterday and Today', *Proceedings of the American Philosophical Society* (21 December 1972), vol. 116, no. 6, pp. 450–57

James Scarlett, 'Tartan: The Highland Cloth and Highland Art Form', in John Butt and Kenneth Ponting (eds), *Scottish Textile History* (Aberdeen 1987), pp. 65–77

Dundee: Trade, Travel and Design (pages 60–63)

Malcolm Archibald, *Ancestors in the Arctic: A Photographic History of Dundee Whaling* (Edinburgh 2013)

Charles Mckean (ed.), *Dundee Renaissance to Enlightenment* (Dundee 2009)

Jim Tomlinson and Christopher A. Whatley (eds), *Jute No More: Transforming Dundee* (Edinburgh 2011)

Christopher A. Whatley, David B. Swinfen and Annette M. Smith (eds), *The Life and Time of Dundee* (Edinburgh 1993)

Unilever Archives online catalogue, http://unilever-archives.com/Record.aspx?src=CalmView.Catalog&id=GB1752.UAC, accessed 4 January 2018

A. & S. Henry & Co, Commercial Overprints of Great Britain, http://commercialoverprints.com/s-henry-co/, accessed 4 January 2018

Shipbuilding and Maritime Trade (pages 64–67)

Martin Bellamy, *The Shipbuilders: An Anthology of Scottish Shipyard Life* (Edinburgh 2001)

John Edwards, *Maritime Aberdeen* (Stroud 2005)

George C. O'Hara, *Ironfighters, Outfitters and Bowler Hatters* (Prestwick 1998)

Nick Robins, *Scotland and the Sea* (Barnsley 2014)

Fred M. Walker, *Song of the Clyde* (Edinburgh 2001)

Scots and India (pages 68–71)

Anne Buddle, with Pauline Rohatgi and Iain Gordon Brown, *The Tiger and the Thistle: Tipu Sultan and the Scots in India, 1760–1800* (Edinburgh 1999)

R.A. Cage (ed.), *The Scots Abroad: Labour, Capital, Enterprise, 1750–1914* (London 1985)

T.M. Devine and Angela McCarthy (eds), *The Scottish Experience in Asia, c.1700 to the Present: Settlers and Sojourners* (Cham 2017)

John M. Mackenzie and T.M. Devine (eds), *Scotland and the British Empire* (Oxford 2010)

Scottish Export Ceramics (pages 72–73)

Graeme Cruickshank, *South-East Asia: A Major Export Destination for British Transferware,* https://www.transcollectorsclub.org/resources/Cruickshank_EDITED_Article.pdf, accessed 4 January 2018

From Scotland to South East Asia and Beyond: The Edwin Robertson Collection of Bell Export Pottery (London 2007) [Christie's South Kensington, sale cat.]

Henry E. Kelly, *Scottish Ceramics* (Atglen 1999)

Henry E. Kelly, *The Glasgow Pottery of John and Matthew Perston Bell: China and Earthenware Manufacturers in Glasgow* (Glasgow 2006)

Floorcloth and Linoleum (pages 74–75)

Gerhard Kaldewei (ed.), *Linoleum, History, Design, Manufacture 1882–2000* (Ostfildern-Ruit 2000)

Augustus Muir, *Nairns of Kirkcaldy: A Short History, 1847–1956* (Kirkcaldy 1956)

Pamela H. Simpson, 'Linoleum and Lincrusta: The Democratic Coverings for Floors and Walls', *Perspectives in Vernacular Architecture*, vol. 7: *Exploring Everyday Landscapes* (1997), pp. 281–92

Pamela H. Simpson, 'Comfortable, Durable and Decorative, Linoleum's Rise and Fall from Grace', *APT Bulletin* (1999), vol. 30, no. 2/3, pp. 17–24

Alexander 'Greek' Thomson (pages 76–77)

Mark Baines, *Alexander 'Greek' Thomson* (London 1984)

Gavin Stamp, *Alexander 'Greek' Thomson* (London 1999)

Gavin Stamp and Sam McKinstry (eds), *'Greek Thomson'* (Edinburgh 1994)

Exhibitions, Aestheticism and Exports: The 'London Brethren' (pages 78–81)

Max Donnelly, 'Daniel Cottier, Pioneer of Aestheticism', *The Journal of the Decorative Arts Society 1850 – the Present,* vol. 23, *Pioneers and Eccentrics* (1999), pp. 32–51

Sally Macdonald, 'Gothic Forms Applied to Furniture: the Early Work of Bruce James Talbert', *Furniture History* (1987), vol. 23, pp. 39–66

Annamarie Stapleton, *John Moyr Smith 1839–1912: A Victorian Designer* (Shepton Beauchamp 2002)

Christopher Dresser: Design Reform and Industry (pages 82–85)

Widar Halén, *Christopher Dresser* (Oxford 1990)

Harry Lyons, *Christopher Dresser: The People's Designer, 1834–1904* (Woodbridge 2005)

Michael Whiteway (ed.), *Shock of the Old: Christopher Dresser's Design Revolution* (London and New York 2004)

Industrialization and Urban Design in Glasgow (pages 86–87)

Thomas Annan, with an introduction by William Young, *The Old Closes and Streets of Glasgow* (Glasgow 1900)

T.C. Smout, *A Century of the Scottish People, 1830–1950* (London 2010), pp. 32–57

Patrick Geddes: Three Drawings Towards a Poetics of the City (pages 88–89)

Patrick Geddes, *Cities in Evolution: An Introduction to the Town Planning Movement and to the Study of Civics* (London 1968 [1915])

Lorens Holm (ed.), *The City is a Thinking Machine: Patrick Geddes and Cities in Evolution*, 4 vols (Dundee 2016)

Frank G Novak (ed.), *Lewis Mumford & Patrick Geddes: The Correspondence* (London and New York 1995)

Alessandra Ponte, 'Building the Stair Spiral of Evolution: The Index Museum of Sir Patrick Geddes', in *Assemblage: A Critical Journal of Architecture and Design Culture*, 10 (1989), pp. 46–64

Volker M Welter, *Biopolis: Patrick Geddes and the City of Life* (Cambridge MA 2002)

Railway and Bridge Design (pages 90–93)

Peter R. Lewis, *Beautiful Railway Bridge of the Silvery Tay: Reinvestigating the Tay Bridge Disaster of 1879* (Stroud 2004)

Charles McKean, *Battle for the North: The Tay and Forth Bridges and the 19th Century Railway Wars* (London 2007)

Michael Meighan, *The Forth Bridges through Time* (Stroud 2014)

The Arts and Crafts Movement in Scotland (pages 94–97)

Nicola Gordon Bowe and Elizabeth Cumming, *The Arts and Crafts Movements in Dublin and Edinburgh, 1885–1925* (Dublin 1998)

Annette Carruthers, *The Arts and Crafts Movement in Scotland: A History* (New Haven and London 2013)

Elizabeth Cumming, *Hand, Heart and Soul: The Arts and Crafts Movement in Scotland* (Edinburgh 2006)

Robert Lorimer: Design and Collaboration (pages 98–101)

Annette Carruthers, *The Arts and Crafts Movement in Scotland: A History* (New Haven and London 2013)

Duncan Macmillan, *Scotland's Shrine: the Scottish National War Memorial* (Farnham 2014)

Peter Savage, *Lorimer and the Edinburgh Crafts Designers* (Edinburgh 1980)

Elizabeth F. Wright, 'Thomas Hadden: Architectural Metalworker', *Proceedings of the Society of Antiquaries of Scotland* (1991), vol. 121, pp. 427–35

Douglas Strachan (pages 102–3)

P. Cormack, 'In Praise of Douglas Strachan (1875–1950)', *The Journal of Stained Glass* (2006), vol. 30, pp. 116–28

N. Haynes, 'A Spiritual Enterprise: Douglas Strachan's Stained Glass in the Memorial Chapel, University of Glasgow', *The Building Conservation Directory Special Report on Historic Churches (Twenty-first Annual Edition)* (2014), p. 205

J. MacDonald, '"Let us now praise the name of famous men": Myth and Meaning in the Stained Glass of the Scottish National War Memorial', *Journal of Design History* (2001), vol. 14, issue 2, pp. 117–28

A.C. Russell, *Stained Glass Windows of Douglas Strachan*, 3rd edition (Balgavies 2002)

The Glasgow Style (pages 104–5)

Jude Burkhauser (ed.), *Glasgow Girls: Women in Art and Design 1880–1920* (Edinburgh 1990)

Hugh Ferguson, *Glasgow School of Art: The History* (Glasgow 1995)

Thomas Howarth, *Charles Rennie Mackintosh and the Modern Movement*, 2nd edition (London 1977)

Perilla Kinchin and Juliet Kinchin, *Glasgow's Great Exhibitions: 1888, 1901, 1911, 1938, 1988* (Wendlebury 1988)

Fiona C. MacFarlane and Elizabeth F. Arthur, *Glasgow School of Art Embroidery, 1894–1920* (Glasgow 1980)

Charles Rennie Mackintosh and the Oak Room (pages 108–11)

Roger Billcliffe, *Charles Rennie Mackintosh: The Complete Furniture, Furniture Drawings and Interior Designs*, 4th edition (Moffat 2009)

Glasgow Museums, *Glasgow's Hidden Treasure: Charles Rennie Mackintosh's Ingram Street Tearooms* (Glasgow 2004)

Thomas Howarth, *Charles Rennie Mackintosh and the Modern Movement*, 2nd edition (London and New York 1977)

Wendy Kaplan (ed.), *Charles Rennie Mackintosh* (New York and London 1996)

Perilla Kinchin, *Tea and Taste: The Glasgow Tea Rooms 1875–1975* (Oxford 1991)

Perilla Kinchin, *Miss Cranston* (Edinburgh 1999)

Scotland's Celtic Revival (pages 112–15)

George Bain, *Celtic Art: The Methods of Construction* (London 1996)

F. Fowle, 'The Celtic Revival in Britain and Ireland: Reconstructing the Past', in Julia Farley and Fraser Hunter (eds), *Celts: Art and Identity* (London 2015), pp. 234–59

F. Fowle and B. Thomson (eds), *Patrick Geddes: The French Connection* (Oxford 2004)

Matthew Jarron (ed.), *The Artist and the Thinker: John Duncan and Patrick Geddes in Dundee* (Dundee 2004)

E. Mairi MacArthur, *Iona Celtic Art: The Work of Alexander and Euphemia Ritchie* (Iona 2008)

The Orkney Chair (pages 116–17)

Annette Carruthers, 'The Social Rise of the Orkney Chair', *Journal of Design History* (March 2009), vol. 22, no. 1, pp. 27–45

Bernard Cotton, *Scottish Vernacular Furniture* (London 2008)

Stephen Jackson, 'Chairs of the Northern Isles', in Louise Butler (ed.) *Scotland's Crafts* (Edinburgh 2000), pp. 49–55

Shetland Knitting: From Local Tradition to High Fashion (pages 118–19)

Helen Bennett, 'The Shetland Handknitting Industry', in John Butt and Kenneth Ponting (eds), *Scottish Textile History* (Aberdeen 1987), pp. 48–64

Hilary Grant, *Knitting from the North: Original Designs Inspired by Nordic and Fair Isle Knitting Traditions* (London 2016)

Sarah Laurenson (ed.), *Shetland Textiles 800 BC to the Present* (Lerwick 2013)

Alice Starmore, *The Fair Isle Knitting Handbook* (London 1988)

Jo Turney, 'A Sweater to Die for: Fair Isle and Fair Play in *The Killing*', *Textile* (February 2014), vol. 12, issue 1, pp. 18–33

The Borders Knitwear Industry (pages 120–21)

Hugh Barty-King, *Pringle of Scotland & the Hawick Knitwear Story* (Norfolk 2006)

David Bremner, *The Industries of Scotland: Their Rise, Progress and Present Condition* (Edinburgh 1869)

Olive Checkland and Sidney Checkland, *Industry and Ethos: Scotland, 1832–1914* (Edinburgh 1989)

C. Gulvin, 'The Origins of Framework Knitting in Scotland', *Textile History* (1983), vol. 14, issue 1, pp. 57–65

Gravenor Henson, *History of the Framework Knitters (1831)* (Newton Abbot, 2nd edition, 1970)

National Library of Scotland, Moving Image Archive, *From Wool to Wearer: The Romance of PESCO, 1913* [promotional film made for the Ghent Exhibition (1913) and the Royal Highland Show, Hawick (1914)]

National Library of Scotland, Moving Image Archive, Kelvinhall, Glasgow, *The World of Cashmere,* sponsored by Pringle of Scotland, directed by Frederick Goode, Associated British Pathe Production, 1966

Speedo (pages 122–23)

'Our History', https://speedo.com.au/page/history, accessed 20 April 2017

Christine Schmidt, *The Swimsuit: From Poolside to Catwalk* (Oxford 2012)

Speedo Catalogue, 1929, Speedo Archive (assembled by Gloria Smythe), Museum of Applied Arts & Sciences, Sydney, 92/17284

The Speedo Story, 1957, booklet, Speedo Archive (assembled by Gloria Smythe), Museum of Applied Arts & Sciences, Sydney, 92/17284

'The Speedo Story', http://www.insidespeedo.com/our-heritage, accessed 20 April 2017

Glass in the 20th Century: The Ysart Family, Innovation and Design (pages 124–25)

Shiona Airlie, Brian J.R. Blench and Frank Andrews (Introduction), *Scotland's Glass: 400 Years of Glassmaking 1610–2010* (Birmingham 2009)

Frank Andrews, *Ysartnews UK: Monart & Vasart Collectors Club*, 1986, http://www.ysartglass.com/Ysartnews/Ysartnews1a.htm, accessed 12 December 2017

Charles R. Hajdamach, *20th Century British Glass* (2009)

Mark Hill, *Caithness Glass: Loch, Heather & Peat* (London 2011)

Ian Turner, Alison J. Clarke, and Frank Andrews, *Ysart Glass* (London, 1990)

Donald Brothers (pages 126–27)

Liz Arthur, *Robert Stewart: Design, 1946–1995* (London and Glasgow c.2003)

Christine Boydell, 'Textiles in the Modern House', *Twentieth Century Architecture* (1996), no. 2, pp. 52–64

Lily Crowther, *Award-winning British Design, 1957–1988* (London 2012)

Helen Douglas, 'Emergence of Donald Brothers as Manufacturers of Decorative Fabrics: (the Feel for Rugged Texture)', unpublished PhD thesis, Edinburgh College of Art, 1997

Margaret Duckett, 'How Donald Brothers Stay Small and Influence People', *Design Journal* (1970), no. 254, pp. 28–31

Valerie Mendes, 'Marion Dorn: Textile Designer', *The Journal of the Decorative Arts Society 1890–1940* (1978), no. 2, pp. 24–35

'Out of an Office Pot Plant, an Exotic Textile Design', newspaper article (unknown source), Wednesday 22 May 1968, p. 155

Paul Reilly, 'Ten Years of Design Council Awards', *Design Journal* (1966), no. 209, pp. 58–71

Edinburgh Weavers (pages 128–31)

Lesley Jackson, *Twentieth-century Pattern Design: Textile & Wallpaper Pioneers* (London and New York 2002)

Lesley Jackson, *Alastair Morton and Edinburgh Weavers: Visionary Textiles and Modern Art* (London 2012)

Jocelyn Morton, *The Mortons: Three Generations of Textile Creation; Alexander Morton & Company, Morton Sundour Fabrics, Edinburgh Weavers* (London 1973)

Bernat Klein (pages 132–33)

Fiona Anderson, 'Bernat Klein: Colouring the Interior', in Christopher Breward, Fiona Fisher and Ghislaine Wood (eds), *British Design: Tradition and Modernity After 1948* (London 2015), pp. 89–100

Bernat Klein, *Eye for Colour* (London 1965)

Bernat Klein and Lesley Jackson, *Bernat Klein: Textile Designer, Artist, Colourist* (Selkirk 2005)

National Library of Scotland, Moving Image Archive, *Weave Me a Rainbow*, National Association of Scottish Woollen Manufacturers, 1962, http://www.nls.uk/collections/moving-image-archive

National Museum of Scotland Resource Centre, Bernat Klein Archive

Penny Sparke, 'At Home with Modernity', in Christopher Breward and Ghislaine Wood (eds), *British Design from 1948: Innovation in the Modern Age* (London 2012), pp. 118–38

The Textile Archive, Heriot-Watt University Borders, Bernat Klein Archive

Basil Spence (pages 134–37)

Louise Campbell, *Basil Spence, Buildings and Projects* (London 2012)

Philip Long and Jane Thomas, *Basil Spence: Architect* (Edinburgh 2007)

Basil Spence, *Phoenix at Coventry, The Building of a Cathedral – By its Architect* (London 1964)

Gillespie, Kidd & Coia: Designing for a New Liturgy (pages 138–41)

Gillespie, Kidd and Coia, *Mac Journal 1* (Glasgow 1984)

Robert Proctor, 'Churches for a Changing Liturgy: Gillespie, Kidd & Coia and the Second Vatican Council', *Architectural History* (2005), vol. 48, pp. 291–322

Johnny Rodger (ed.), *Gillespie, Kidd and Coia: Architecture 1956–1987* (Edinburgh and Glasgow 2007)

Diane Watters, *Cardross Seminary: Gillespie, Kidd and Coia and the Architecture of Post-war Catholicism* (Edinburgh 1997)

Energy and Power in Scotland: The Last 250 Years (pages 142–43)

Stephen Cashmore, *Dounreay: The Illustrated Story* (Wick, Caithness 1998)

Exhibition of Industrial Power, Kelvin Hall, Glasgow: Catalogue and Guide (London 1951)

Alex Kemp, *The Official History of North Sea Oil and Gas* (London 2011)

H.G. Taylor, 'Modern Welding: Three Cantor Lectures', *Journal of the Royal Society of Arts* (3 August 1956), vol. 104, no. 4983, pp. 688–749

Christopher Whatley, *The Industrial Revolution in Scotland* (Cambridge 1997)

Design for Pantomime (pages 144–45)

Joyce Branagh and Keith Orton, *Creating Pantomime* (Ramsbury 2011)

Kate Burnett (ed.), *Make / Believe: UK Design for Performance 2011–2015* (Cardiff 2014)

Vivien Devlin, *Kings, Queens and People's Palaces: An Oral History of the Scottish Variety Theatre 1920–1970* (Edinburgh 1991)

Bruce Frank, *Scottish Showbusiness: Music Hall, Variety and Pantomime* (Totnes 2000)

Millie Taylor, *British Pantomime Performance* (Bristol 2009)

John Byrne and Scottish Theatre in the 1970s (pages 146–47)

Bill Findlay (ed.), *A History of Scottish Theatre* (Edinburgh c.1998)

Robert Hewison, *John Byrne: Art and Life* (Farnham 2011)

Joyce McMillan, *Theatre in Scotland: A Field of Dreams* (London 2016)

Randall Stevenson and Gavin Wallace (eds), *Scottish Theatre Since the Seventies* (Edinburgh c.1996)

Design at the Citizens Theatre (pages 148–49)

Mary Brennan, 'The Glasgow Citizens Theatre', *Theatre Ireland* (December 1983–March 1984), no. 5, pp. 60–64

Giles Havergal, 'Repertory Theatre: The Citizens' Theatre 1969–1993', *RSA Journal* (August–September 1993), vol. 141, no. 5442, pp. 629–37

Robert David MacDonald, Philip Prowse, Giles Havergal and editors, interview: The Citizens Company in Glasgow: 'Four Hundred Miles from Civilisation', *Performing Arts Journal* (1980), vol. 5, no. 1, pp. 50–60

Bill Gibb (pages 150–51)

Bill Gibb: A Tribute to the Fashion Designer of the 70s (Aberdeen 1989)

Iain R. Webb, *Bill Gibb: Fashion & Fantasy* (London 2008)

James Stirling (pages 152–53)

Geoffrey H. Baker, *The Architecture of James Stirling and his Partners James Gowan and Michael Wilford* (London 2016)

Marco Iuliano, *James Stirling: Inspiration and Process in Architecture* (Milan 2015)

Amanda Lawrence, *James Stirling: Revisionary Modernist* (London and New Haven 2013)

Eduardo Paolozzi (pages 154–57)

Judith Collins, *Eduardo Paolozzi* (Farnham 2014)

Hal Foster and Jon Wood, *Eduardo Paolozzi* (London 2017)

Robin Spencer (ed.), *Eduardo Paolozzi: Writings and Interviews* (Oxford 2000)

Buffalo Style: Designing Identity
(pages 158–59)

Paul Gorman, *The Story of The Face: The Magazine That Changed Culture* (London 2017)

Paul Jobling, *Fashion Spreads: Word and Image in Fashion Photography Since 1980* (London 1999)

Terry Jones (ed.), *Smile ID: Fashion and Style: The Best From 20 Years of i-D* (London 2008)

Mitzi Lorenz (ed.), *Buffalo Ray Petri* (London 2000)

Eugenie Shinkle (ed.), *Fashion as Photograph: Viewing and Reviewing Images of Fashion* (London 2012)

Sonnet Stanfill (ed.), *80s Fashion: From Club to Catwalk* (London 2013)

Comic Book Design (pages 160–63)

Jan Baetens and Hugo Frey, *The Graphic Novel: An Introduction* (New York 2015)

James Chapman, *British Comics: A Cultural History* (London 2011)

Paul Gravett and Peter Stansbury, *Great British Comics* (London 2016)

Christopher Murray, *The British Superhero* (Jackson 2017)

Roger Sabin, *Adult Comics: An Introduction* (London and New York 1993)

The Birth of the Videogames Industry in Dundee (pages 164–65)

Jonny Davis, 'Trigger Happy', Monocle (March 2007), vol. 1, issue 1, pp. 147–48

Peter Day, 'How Dundee Became a Computer Games Centre', www.bbc.co.uk, 10 September 2014

Cara Ellison, 'The Story of Rockstar North, Grand Theft Auto and Manhunt', www.list.co.uk, 8 November 2012

Gary Penn and Sean Taylor, 'The Long Way Round: The Story of One of the UK's Longest Lasting Studios', www.eurogamer.net, 10 April 2012

Alex Wade, *Playback – A Genealogy of 1980s British Videogames* (London 2016)

A Tweed Suit (pages 166–67)

Fiona Anderson, *Tweed* (London and New York 2017)

Christopher Breward, *The Suit: Form, Function and Style* (London 2016)

Claire Wilcox, *Vivienne Westwood* (London 2004)

Reinventing Traditions: Textile Heritage and Design Innovation (pages 168–69)

Sandy Black (ed.), *Knitting: Fashion, Industry, Craft* (London 2012)

Amanda Briggs-Goode and Deborah Dean, *Lace: Here: Now* (London 2013)

Horst Friedrichs, *Best of British: The Stories Behind Britain's Iconic Brands* (Munich 2015)

Lynne McCrossan, *Cashmere: A Guide to Scottish Luxury* (Edinburgh 2016)

Rob Thompson, *Manufacturing Processes for Textile and Fashion Design Professionals* (New York 2014)

Claire Wilcox and Valerie D. Mendes, *Twentieth-Century Fashion in Detail* (London 2009)

Reconnecting Waterways: The Falkirk Wheel
(pages 170–71)

Charles Hadfield and Jean Lindsay, *The Canals of Scotland* (Newton Abbot 1968)

Nick Haynes, *Scotland's Canals* (Edinburgh 2015)

James Leslie, *Description of an inclined plane for conveying boats from one level to another on the Monkland Canal, at Blackhill … With … plates. From the Transactions of the Royal Scottish Society of Arts, etc.* (Edinburgh 1852)

RMJM, *The Falkirk Wheel: Art and Engineering* (2002)

Fashion Design in the 21st Century
(pages 172–73)

Jessica Bumpus, 'Where London's print designers went next', *Vogue* (22 September 2015)

Scarlett Conlon, 'Jonathan Saunders steps down from Diane von Furstenberg role', *The Guardian* (15 December 2017)

Imogen Fox, 'Jonathan Saunders to become creative director of Diane von Furstenberg', *The Guardian* (16 May 2016)

Suzy Menkes, '#Suzy LFW Christopher Kane: Make Do and Mend', *Vogue* (19 September 2016)

Sarah Mower, 'Charles Jeffrey Loverboy, Spring 2018 Menswear', *Vogue* (10 June 2017)

Ellie Pithers, 'The world of fashion designer Holly Fulton', *The Telegraph* (15 February 2014)

Doria Santlofer, *50 Contemporary Fashion Designers You Should Know* (Munich, London and New York 2012)

Jewellery in Scotland (pages 176–79)

Jude Burkhauser, *Glasgow Girls: Women in Art and Design, 1880–1920* (Edinburgh 2001)

Elizabeth Cumming, *Hand, Heart and Soul: the Arts and Crafts Movement in Scotland* (Edinburgh 2013)

Jack Cunningham, *Maker, Wearer, Viewer: Contemporary European Narrative Jewellery* (Scotland 2005)

George Dalgleish (ed.), *Silver: Made in Scotland* (Edinburgh 2008)

Amanda Game and Elizabeth Goring, *Jewellery Moves: Ornament for the 21st Century* (Edinburgh 1998)

Amanda Game and Dorothy Hogg, *A Sense of Jewellery: Rediscovering British Jewellery Design* (London, Goldsmiths' Centre, exhib. cat., 2015)

E. Goring and D. Hogg, *Dorothy Hogg: Retrospective* (Edinburgh 2014)

Hogg, Dorothy Hogg, *100% Proof: Contemporary Scottish Jewellery and Silver* (Scotland 2001/2006) [two touring exhib. cats]

Cornelie Holzach, *Peter Chang: Its Only Plastic* (Germany 2007)

Clare Phillips, *Jewels and Jewellery* (London 2006)

Alyson Pollard, *Unnatural Selection: Jewellery, Objects and Sculpture by Peter Chang* (Liverpool 2007)

Craftsmanship, Character and Curiosity: Approaches to Contemporary Product Design (pages 180–83)

Christopher Breward and Ghislaine Wood (eds), *British Design from 1948: Innovation in the Modern Age* (London 2012)

Andrew H. Dent and Leslie Sherr, *Material Innovation: Product Design* (New York 2014)

Lesley Jackson, *Modern British Furniture: Design Since 1945* (London 2013)

Lucy Johnston, *Digital Handmade: Craftsmanship and the New Industrial Revolution* (London 2017)

Judith Miller, *Chairs* (London 2009)

Rob Thompson, *Prototyping and Low-Volume Production* (London 2011)

Designing for Performance Clothing (pages 184–85)

Simon Bain, 'Endura Boss: Manufacturing in Scotland can be Profitable', *The Sunday Herald* (November 2014)

Matilda McQuaid and Phillip Beasley, *Extreme Textiles: Designing for High Performance* (London 2005)

Susan Swarbrick, 'Inside the Endura Factory Leading the Cycle Clothing Revolution', *The Sunday Herald* (March 2014)

Hunter Boot Ltd website, http://www.hunterboots.com

https://www.endurasport.com, April 2017

Healthcare by Design (pages 186–87)

Alfred Cuschieri and George Hanna, *Essential Surgical Practice: Higher Surgical Training in General Surgery*, 5th edition (Abingdon 2015)

Marc Kriege et al., 'Evaluation of the McGrath MAC and Macintosh laryngoscope for tracheal intubation in 2000 patients undergoing general anaesthesia: the randomised multicentre EMMA trial study protocol', *BMJ Open*, http://bmjopen.bmj.com/content/7/8/e016907, accessed 4 January 2018

Maggie's Centres website https://www.maggiescentres.org, accessed 9 June 2017

NHS Scotland, *Realistic Medicine: Chief Medical Officer's Annual Report 2014–15* (Edinburgh 2016), http://www.gov.scot/Resource/0049/00492520.pdf, accessed 4 January 2018

'Christopher McCann – Saving lives with data', V&A Dundee blog, https://www.vandadundee.org/news-and-blog/blog/christopher-mccann--saving-lives-with-data

Maggie's Cancer Caring Centres (pages 188–89)

Edwin Heathcote, 'Maggie's Centres', *British Medical Journal* (23–30 December 2006), vol. 333, no. 7582, pp.1304–5

Charles Jencks, *The Architecture of Hope: Maggie's Cancer Caring Centres*, 2nd edition (London 2015)

Maggie's Architecture and Landscape Brief, https://www.maggiescentres.org/media/uploads/file_upload_plugin/maggies-architectural-brief/architectural_brief_maggies.pdf, accessed 12 December 2017

Shaping Domestic Life (pages 190–93)

N. Burford et al., 'Macro Micro Studio: A Prototype Energy Autonomous Laboratory', *Sustainability* (May 2016), discovery.dundee.ac.uk/portal/files/9002232/sustainability_08_00500.pdf, accessed 4 January 2018

R. Kemsley and C. Platt, *Dwelling with Architecture* (London 2012)

R.J. Naismith, *Buildings of the Scottish Countryside* (London 1985)

S. Penn, *Island: Eight Houses for the Isle of Harris, Outer Hebrides* (Dundee 2014)

Designing for Renewable Energy Production in Scotland (pages 194–97)

R.H. Charlier and J.R. Justus, *Ocean Energies Volume 56: Environmental, Economic and Technological Aspects of Alternative Power Sources* (Amsterdam 1993)

R.H. Charlier and C.W. Finkl, *Ocean Energy: Tide and Tidal Power* (New York 2010)

The Crown Estate, *UK Wave and Tidal Key Resource Areas Project Summary Report* (October 2012)

The Crown Estate, *Wave and Tidal Energy in the Pentland Firth and Orkney Waters: Delivering the First Phases of Projects* (September 2013)

Scottish Executive, *Choosing Our Future: Scotland's Sustainable Development Strategy* (Edinburgh 2005)

The Scottish Government, *2020 Routemap for Renewable Energy in Scotland* (Edinburgh 2011)

The Scottish Government, *Scottish Energy Strategy: The Future of Energy in Scotland* (2017) [draft]

Scottish Renewables, *Industrial Impact: the Power of Scotland's Renewables Sector* (2017)

Automated and Electric: The Future of Car Design (pages 198–99)

Interview conducted with Ian Callum at Jaguar Coventry headquarters, July 2016

Alisa Priddle, 'Go inside secret lair where Ford developed the GT super car', *Detroit Free Press* (12 May 2015)

Elizabeth Stinson, 'The secret sauce to a Mustang's design is still clay and tape', *Wired* (17 April 2014)

I-PACE concept design, Jaguar website, https://www.jaguar.co.uk/jaguar-range/i-pace-concept-car/design.html, accessed 4 January 2018

'Ford Targets Fully Autonomous Vehicle For Ride Sharing In 2021; Invests In New Tech Companies, Doubles Silicon Valley Team', Ford press release (16 August 2016), https://media.ford.com/content/fordmedia/fna/us/en/news/2016/08/16/ford-targets-fully-autonomous-vehicle-for-ride-sharing-in-2021.html, accessed 4 January 2018

'Looking Further', Ford website, https://corporate.ford.com/innovation/autonomous-2021.html, accessed 4 January 2018

Videogames Now (pages 200–4)

Ian Bogost, *Persuasive Games: The Expressive Power of Videogames* (Cambridge MA 2007)

Keith Bruce, 'Theatre that takes video gaming to new levels', www.heraldscotland.co.uk, 10 October 2014

Mure Dickie, 'Dundee, Scotland – Serious About Games', www.ft.com, 14 June 2016

May Flanagan, *Critical Play: Radical Game Design* (Cambridge MA 2013)

Ute Ritterfeld, Michael Cody and Peter Vorderer (eds), *Serious Games: Mechanisms and Effects* (New York 2009)

Acknowledgments

This book and the associated Scottish Design Galleries would not have been possible without a great many people from the V&A, V&A Dundee, the project's founding partners and funders, lenders to the galleries, and a host of academics, experts and design practitioners.

The Scottish Design Galleries have been created as part of the overall development of V&A Dundee, under the chairmanship of Lesley Knox. At the V&A the project has been led by three directors: it was spearheaded by Sir Mark Jones, continued by the late Dr Martin Roth and came to completion under Dr Tristram Hunt. At Dundee City Council, David Dorward and David Martin (successive chief executives) and their colleagues have supported the vision to develop galleries devoted to Scotland's design throughout the responsibility they have taken for the construction of the new museum. We would also like to thank the core team responsible for delivering the galleries working across the V&A and V&A Dundee: Sarah Davies, Jane Ferguson, Jamie Gray, Mhairi Maxwell, Sophie McKinlay, Pamela Roberts, Sarah Saunders, Tara Wainwright and Chris Wilson, and the project manager John Tavendale. We are immensely grateful to Meredith More, Assistant Curator, for her invaluable contribution across all curatorial aspects of delivering the galleries and this book.

We are deeply indebted to the authors who have contributed to *The Story of Scottish Design*. They have all generously shared their expertise for the benefit of the project, and in many cases have helped to select objects for display in the Scottish Design Galleries. A host of scholars, curators and collectors have also contributed to the project over the years. We would particularly like to thank Ghislaine Wood, now Deputy Director at the Sainsbury Centre, formerly lead curator at the V&A for the Scottish Design Galleries, whose initial development of the galleries, assisted by Katherine Elliott, identified over 12,000 Scottish objects in the V&A's collections, and whose early research defined some of the galleries' overarching themes. Many V&A curators have generously contributed their knowledge and expertise to the development of themes and selection of objects. In addition to those represented in this book we would also like to thank Clare Browne, Oriole Cullen, Edwina Ehrman, Hanne Faurby, Marie Foulston, Kirsty Hassard, Ruth Hibbard, Jenny Lister, Leela Meinertas, Liz Miller, Sonnet Stanfill, Olivia Horsfall-Turner and Becky Wallis. We would particularly like to thank Beth McKillop, former Deputy Director of the V&A, for her advice and support of the project over several years. We are also grateful to the volunteers who have assisted with research over the course of the project: Stephanie Blythman, Erin Kirk and Meghan Lynch. In addition we have been grateful for the advice of a number of external experts, including Jo Bletcher, Christopher Breward, Alison Brown, Annette Carruthers, Peter Cormack, Elizabeth Cumming, George Dalgleish, Amanda Game, Miles Glendinning, James Gunn, Sally-Anne Huxtable, Stephen Jackson, David Jones, Murdo Macdonald, Jennifer Melville, Jon Rogers, James Robinson, Sarah Rothwell, Jane Thomas, Sally Tuckett, Jill Turnbull and to the members of the V&A Dundee Advisory Council: chair Andrea Nixon, Jan Boelen, Mark Brearley, Sir Mark Jones, Patricia Lankester, Dr Brian Lang, Juliet Kinchin, Janice Kirkpatrick, Stewart Murdoch, Victoria Pomery, Vicky Richardson, Bill Sherman and Sir John Tusa.

For this book, special thanks to Tom Windross and Kirstin Beattie from V&A Publishing, Julian Honer, Susannah Lawson and Sarah Yates from Thames & Hudson, and to Sarah Tucker for the picture research. Thank you also to the V&A Photo Studio for providing new photography of the objects and to colleagues in Conservation for conserving objects for the galleries, especially Zoe Allen, Nigel Bamforth, Victoria Button, Nicola Costaras, Elizabeth-Anne Haldane, Charlotte Hubbard, Fiona Jordan, Victoria Oakley, Keira Miller and Donna Stevens.

We are immensely grateful to all the institutions and individuals who generously welcomed and assisted us during the research process for this book and the Scottish Design Galleries. Many of their objects are illustrated in this book, and their support, expertise and generosity have been greatly appreciated. Our special thanks to the staff at Aberdeen Art Gallery and Museums, Aberdeen University Museum, Blair Castle and Gardens, British Golf Museum, Caithness Horizons, the Crafts Council, DC Thomson, Dumfries House, Dunfermline Carnegie Library & Galleries, Dundee Heritage Trust, East Ayrshire Museums, Edinburgh Museums, Glasgow Museums & Collections on behalf of Glasgow City Council, Glasgow School of Art and Glasgow School of Art Archive, Groam House Museum, Hawick Museum, Heriot-Watt School of Textiles and Design, Highland Folk Museum, Historic Environment Scotland, Inverness Art Gallery and Museum, Jaguar, Kirkcaldy Galleries, Leicestershire Museums, the Lucas Museum of Narrative Art, Maggie's Cancer Caring Centres, The McManus Museum and Art Gallery, Mount Stuart, the Museum of the University of St Andrews, Network Rail Archive, National Galleries Scotland, National Library of Scotland, National Museums Scotland, National Records Scotland, National Trust for Scotland, Natural History Museum, Paisley Museum and Art Gallery, Perth Museum and Art Gallery, Philadelphia Museum of Art, The Royal Collection, Royal Bank of Scotland, Royal Incorporation of Architects in Scotland, Royal Scottish Academy, The Science Museum, Scone Palace, Scottish Ballet, Scottish Canals, Scottish Maritime Museum, Scottish Opera, Sotheby's, The Stirling Smith Art Gallery and Museum, Stirling University, Strathclyde University Archive and Tain & District Museum, as well as to Jane Lorimer, William Lorimer, Mairi MacArthur and the Mary Roxburghe Trust. In addition, a great many contemporary designers and design firms also kindly contributed advice and images for this publication. Special thanks are due to John Byrne, Barrie Knitwear, Biome Collective, the late Peter Chang, Barbara Santos Shaw, Denki, Dualchas, Endura, Scott Jarvie, Simon Meek, Medtronic, MYB Textiles, Reiach and Hall, Rockstar Games, Angus Ross, Rural Design and snap40.

The Scottish Design Galleries, this book and indeed V&A Dundee would not exist without the support of the five founding partners – V&A, Dundee City Council, the University of Dundee, Abertay University and Scottish Enterprise – nor without the support of our founding public funders – Scottish Government, Heritage Lottery Fund, UK Government and Creative Scotland. We are also very grateful indeed for the outstanding generosity of the many trusts, foundations, companies and private individuals who have supported the development of V&A Dundee, in particular Richard and Catherine Burns for their support of the Scottish Design Galleries. The conservation and restoration of Charles Rennie Mackintosh's Oak Room is a collaboration between Glasgow Museums, the V&A Dundee and Dundee City Council. The project is made possible by a long-term loan from the collections of Glasgow City Council and grant funding from the Heritage Lottery Fund, Art Fund, Scottish Government, Dr Mortimer and Theresa Sackler Foundation, Dunard Fund and Tim and Kim Allan.

Finally, Moira Gemmill was a great champion of the V&A Dundee project at the V&A and it would not have happened without her support and advocacy. For this and for her incisiveness, her clarity of vision and her championing of good design, she is much missed and we would like to acknowledge her important contribution to the Scottish Design Galleries and this book.

PHILIP LONG AND JOANNA NORMAN

Picture Credits

Index

Cover, top: Elevation and section of the Forth Bridge, coloured to show dates of construction (1888). Network Rail Corporate Archive: NRCA110040

Cover, bottom: 'Fractal', designed by Margo Graham, MYB Textiles (2014)

First published in the United Kingdom in 2018 by Thames & Hudson in association with the Victoria and Albert Museum, London, and V&A Dundee.

The Story of Scottish Design
© 2018 Victoria and Albert Museum / Thames & Hudson

British Library Cataloguing-in-Publication Data
A catalogue record for this book is available from the British Library

ISBN 978-0-500-48033-5

Printed and bound in China by C&C Offset Printing Co. Ltd

To find out about all our publications, please visit
www.thamesandhudson.com. There you can subscribe to
our e-newsletter, browse or download our current catalogue,
and buy any titles that are in print.

V&A Publishing

Supporting the world's leading
museum of art and design,
the Victoria and Albert
Museum, London